More Praise for
The Year Without Summer

"A great book about one of the least known and most devastating natural disasters in history."

—THEODORE STEINBERG, author of *Acts of God* and *Down to Earth*

"A thought-provoking account describing the far-reaching and long-lasting effects on Europe and America of a single volcanic eruption in the tropics. Tambora's 1815 outburst caused changes in weather patterns with negative impact on agriculture, resulting in famine and disease. Riots and political discord followed and worsened the socio-economic consequences of the Napoleonic wars in Europe. Such an aftermath provides a warning for what our living earth may have in store for the future."

—DR. JELLE ZEILINGA DE BOER, author of
Volcanoes in Human History and *Earthquakes in Human History*

"*The Year Without Summer* puts *Krakatoa* in the shade. This is an erudite, vivid, and fast-paced narrative of the extraordinary consequences of the largest and deadliest known volcanic eruption in history. Linking the stories of a cast of royal, political, and literary characters—Louis XVIII, Madison, Napoléon, and Byron among them—as well as laborers, seafarers, and rabble-rousers, William and Nicholas Klingaman help us visualize and understand how a remote Indonesian volcano helped to foment social, economic, and political turmoil on both sides of the Atlantic."

—CLIVE OPPENHEIMER, author of
Eruptions That Shook the World and *Volcanoes*

"*The Year Without Summer* shows how a volcanic eruption in Indonesia transformed life in the United States and Europe. William and Nicholas Klingaman have placed 1816 on the list of pivotal years in history and have provided a compelling account of the mushrooming effects of a natural disaster. This is environmental and world history at its finest."

—LOUIS P. MASUR, author of
The Civil War, 1831, and *The Soiling of Old Glory*

"Intrigued by the weather? You will be after reading *The Year Without Summer*. Writing with verve and flair, authors William and Nicholas Klingaman show how in 1816 an event in the Far East dramatically influenced weather patterns in Europe and the United States, causing summer blizzards, flooding, and deadly famines. This is a disquieting but important story that throws light on global weather patterns and our precarious hold on life."

—JOHN FERLING, author of
Independence, Almost a Miracle, and *Setting the World Ablaze*

"When a volcanic eruption on a Pacific island swathed the earth with droplets, producing freakish weather that ruined harvests all over the world, how did people react? William and Nicholas Klingaman tell us how the year without summer affected an astonishing variety of people on different continents, including rulers and peasants, working families, Jane Austen, and Mary Shelley."

—DANIEL WALKER HOWE, Pulitzer Prize–winning author of
What Hath God Wrought: The Transformation of America

The
Year Without
Summer

ALSO BY WILLIAM K. KLINGAMAN

1919: The Year Our World Began

1929: The Year of the Great Crash

1941: Our Lives in a World on the Edge

Abraham Lincoln and the Road to Emancipation

Encyclopedia of the McCarthy Era

The First Century: Emperors, Gods, and Everyman

The
Year Without
Summer

1816 AND THE VOLCANO

THAT DARKENED THE WORLD

AND CHANGED HISTORY

William K. Klingaman

AND

Nicholas P. Klingaman

ST. MARTIN'S PRESS ✸ NEW YORK

www.stmartins.com

Design by Meryl Sussman Levavi

ISBN 978-0-312-67645-2 (hardcover)
ISBN 978-1-250-01206-7 (e-book)

First Edition: February 2013

10 9 8 7 6 5 4 3 2 1

To Janet and Emma

CONTENTS

The
Year Without
Summer

1.

THE VOLCANO

JUST BEFORE SUNSET on April 5, 1815, a massive explosion shook the volcanic island of Sumbawa in the Indonesian archipelago. For two hours, a stream of lava erupted from Mount Tambora, the highest peak in the region, sending a plume of ash eighteen miles into the sky.

More than eight hundred miles away, Thomas Stamford Raffles, the lieutenant-governor of Java, heard the blast at his residence and assumed it came from cannon firing in the distance. Other British authorities on the island made the same mistake. Fearing a neighboring village was under attack, the commander of the city of Djogjokarta, in central Java, dispatched troops to repel the invaders. Officials along the coast interpreted the sounds as signals from a ship in distress, and launched rescue boats to look for survivors.

At Makassar on the southwestern tip of Sulawesi, 240 miles northeast of Tambora, the commander of the *Benares*, a cruiser of the British East India Company, reported "a firing of cannon" on April 5. The explosions appeared to come from the south; as they continued, "the reports seemed to approach much nearer, and sounded like heavy guns occasionally, with slighter reports between." Assuming that pirates were in the area, the *Benares* put to sea and spent the next three days scouring nearby islands for any signs of trouble, but found nothing. Nearly five hundred miles farther to the east, the British resident on the island of Ternate heard "several very distinct reports like heavy cannon," and sent another cruiser, the *Teignmouth*, to investigate. It, too, returned empty-handed.

British authorities might have been excused for assuming that the threatening sounds came from potential enemies rather than the earth itself. They were not yet accustomed to the frequent volcanic eruptions that plagued the Indonesian islands. Britain had gained control of Java and the surrounding islands less than four years earlier, when British troops overwhelmed a vastly outnumbered band of French defenders who themselves had held Java for only a short time, having taken it from the Dutch when France conquered the Netherlands in 1794. By the spring of 1815, neither the government in London nor the British East India Company was entirely certain that they wanted to keep the island, since the expense of administering and defending it had outweighed the commercial benefits thus far.

Responsibility for British policy on the scene lay squarely with Raffles himself. The son of a ship's captain, Raffles—who actually was born at sea, off the coast of Jamaica—dreamt of a British maritime empire throughout South Asia, an "Eastern insular Empire" that would provide new markets for English cotton and woolen textiles, and a profitable supply of coffee and sugar for Europe. It was Raffles who had persuaded the governor general of India, Lord Minto, to seize Java in the first place. Raffles also hoped to use Java as an avenue to improve relations with Japan, which he viewed as a rising Asiatic power. Meanwhile, heeding Minto's advice to "do as much good as we can" while governing Java, Raffles reformed the colonial administration of the island, limiting the powers of the great landowners over their tenants and ameliorating the worst abuses of slavery while banning the importation of slaves under fourteen years of age.

But Raffles' interests in the region extended beyond politics and commerce. After years of study, he was sufficiently fluent in the Malay language to conduct discussions directly with local chieftains. He regularly employed botanists and zoologists to obtain— at his own expense—specimens of local flora and wildlife, some of which he had preserved in spirit and shipped back to Britain. In his capacity as president of the Batavian Society, dedicated to the study of Java's natural history, Raffles frequently toured the island and recorded his observations of geological phenomena. Several weeks before Mount Tambora erupted, Raffles became the first European to ascend a nearby mountain known as Gunong Gede; by using thermometers to measure the difference in temperature between the base and the peak, Raffles and his companions determined that they had climbed at least seven thousand feet. "We had a most extensive prospect from the summit," he subsequently wrote to a friend. "The islands all round were quite distinct and we traced the sea beyond the southernmost point of Sumatra; the surf on the south coast was visible to the naked eye."

So Raffles' scientific curiosity was piqued when the cannonlike explosions from the southeast continued throughout the night of April 5 and into the morning hours. Shortly after dawn, a light rain of ash provided evidence that a volcano somewhere in the region had erupted. Few suspected Mount Tambora. It was generally believed that Tambora was extinct, although natives living in the nearest village had reported rumblings from deep inside the mountain during the past year. Besides, few on Java believed that such powerful sounds could have come from a volcano several hundred miles away. As Raffles subsequently noted, "the sound appeared to be so close, that in each district it seemed near at hand, and was generally attributed to an eruption either from the mountains Merapi, Klut, or Bromo."

As a fog of ash drifted across Java, the sun faded; the warm, humid air grew stifling, and everything seemed unnaturally still. The oppressive pressure, Raffles noted, "seemed to forbode an earthquake." Over the next several days, however, the explosions gradually subsided. Volcanic ash continued to fall, but in diminishing quantities. Relieved, Raffles returned to his routine administrative duties.

FAR from Tambora and the island of Java, a different sort of shock greeted the rulers and citizens of Europe in April 1815: Napoléon had returned to Paris.

The Emperor had spent the past year ruling the island of Elba, a rocky, desolate piece of real estate of no discernible strategic importance off the coast of Italy. Sixteen miles long and only seven miles across at its widest point, Elba in the early nineteenth century was home mainly to goats, deserted ruins, a variety of vines and scraggly shrubs on arid hillsides, and approximately twelve thousand impoverished peasants with a well-deserved reputation for being "extremely irritable" and "almost universally ignorant." Its primary natural resource was rocks. One French observer who visited Elba shortly before Napoléon's arrival warned that the island's unremittingly inhospitable topography was likely to "fatigue the senses and impart sensations of sorrow to the soul."

Napoléon had been consigned to Elba by the victorious allied coalition of Britain, Prussia, Austria, and Russia shortly after abdicating the French throne on April 6, 1814. (Perhaps as an ironic jest, they allowed him to retain the title of "Emperor.") But the Allied statesmen who gathered at Vienna to sort out the consequences of nearly two decades of war neglected to provide a jailer, or even an effective network of informants to keep them apprised of Napoléon's movements. Encouraged by press reports of widespread popular disaffection with the restored Bourbon monarchy in Paris, Napoléon decided that his former subjects would welcome him back. And so on February 25, 1815, accompanied by slightly more than a thousand troops, forty horses, and four cannon, Napoléon sailed away from Elba unopposed.

Six days later he landed at Golfe Juan, about a mile west of Cannes. "Frenchmen! In my exile I have heard your complaints and your wishes," he exclaimed. "I have arrived in spite of every obstacle, and every danger." Napoléon marched north rapidly, opposition crumbling as his entourage expanded at every town. "Taking towns at his liking and crowns at his leisure / From Elba to Lyons and Paris he goes," crowed Lord Byron, who admired Napoléon and fancied himself an English counterpart of the Eagle. Although many of Napoléon's former subjects—particularly his troops—greeted him enthusiastically, others responded more warily. Their caution reflected the heavy costs of Napoléon's previous quest for glory: more than 900,000 French soldiers dead, and a depleted national treasury now saddled with millions of francs of reparations due the Allies. Napoléon attempted to allay their anxieties by publicly disavowing any new imperial ambitions. "I want less to be sovereign of France," he told the people of Grenoble, "than the first of her citizens."

News of Napoléon's flight reached Vienna on March 7. Stunned, the Allied representatives decided within hours to send troops to oppose Napoléon, but they also embargoed the news from France for several days until they were prepared to make a public statement. Several days later, they jointly declared that by reappearing in France, Napoléon had proved himself "an enemy and disturber of the peace of the world," and that together, "the sovereigns of Europe would be ready to give the King of France and the French nation the assistance necessary to restore peace."

King Louis XVIII would need all the help he could get. Twenty-two years after the execution of his brother, Louis XVI, few Frenchmen outside of a die-hard circle of royalists desired to return to the days of a pre-Revolutionary monarchy. Too much land belonging to the king, the aristocracy, and the church had been dispensed to too many members of the Third Estate to turn back the clock. Nor had a year of life under the restored Bourbon dynasty endeared King Louis to his subjects. Facing an immense national debt which he inherited from Napoléon, Louis' ministers found it necessary to slash the army budget, cancelling contracts for military supplies and throwing nearly three hundred thousand soldiers out of work. The government also reduced spending on public construction projects while maintaining an oppressive array of taxes. As unemployment rose along with the price of bread, hungry citizens in Channel ports rioted against the shipment of grain to Britain. "We are really going on very badly," wrote one government official, "and we must do better if we do not wish to perish completely."

Louis himself engendered little personal loyalty, or even respect; a British bishop once said that the French king was "a man fit only to cook his own capons." Fifty-eight years old and so grossly overweight that he could not sit on a horse, Louis abhorred hard work and delegated authority with alacrity. Despite a modest measure of charm in private conversations, Louis never developed a compelling public presence. Certainly he paled in comparison with the charismatic former emperor. As Napoléon hastened towards the capital in March, covering two hundred miles in six days, Louis grew increasingly anxious. Ominous strains of the incendiary *Marseillaise* rang through Paris streets; royal troops deserted en masse and went over to Napoléon; and newspaper editorials likened the situation to the eve of the Terror, when nobles and monarchists were slaughtered. Recognizing that, as one writer put it, "the Parisians love for their King has so died down that barely a spark remains," Louis decided on the evening of March 18 to flee Paris.

Three days later, Napoléon entered the city without a shot being fired. By the first week of April, however, it was clear that the weary and impoverished French public lacked any appetite for ambitious schemes to restore the glory of the empire. Napoléon's proposals for new taxes to fund a revitalized army met with widespread opposition. Visible signs of disaffection appeared; rallies in support of the emperor's return clashed with demonstrations demanding his ouster. To bolster his defenses against the Allied assault he knew was coming, Napoléon issued orders on April 8 for a general mobilization of the French nation. Meanwhile, he assured the sovereigns of Europe (whom he formally referred to as "my brothers") that he wanted nothing more than "the maintenance of an honourable peace."

But more than anything else, France—and the rest of Europe—desperately needed a breathing space. A year earlier, the Marquis de Caulaincourt had written that "the need for rest was so universally felt through every class of society, and in the army, that peace at any price had become the ruling passion of the day." Napoléon's return from Elba only deepened the prevailing exhaustion. "Our objective is to make sure that our children have years of peace," noted the Austrian general Karl Schwarzenberg, "and that the world has some repose. The Emperor Napoléon had shown all too plainly of late that he desires neither of these things."

AROUND seven o'clock on the evening of April 10, Mount Tambora erupted once again, this time far more violently. Three columns of flaming lava shot into the air, meeting briefly at their peak in what one eyewitness termed "a troubled confused manner." Almost immediately the entire mountain appeared to be consumed by liquid fire, a fountain of ash, water, and molten rock shooting in every direction. Pumice stones—some walnut-sized but others twice the size of a man's fist—rained down upon the village of Sanggar, nineteen miles away. After an hour, so much ash and dust had been hurled into the atmosphere that darkness hid the fiery mountaintop from view.

As the ash clouds thickened, hot lava racing down the mountain slope heated the air above it to thousands of degrees. The air quickly rose, leaving behind a vacuum into which cooler air rushed from all directions. The resulting whirlwind tore up trees by the roots and swept up men, cattle, and horses. Virtually every house in Sanggar was flattened. The village of Tambora, closer to the volcano, vanished under a flood of pumice. Cascading lava slammed into the ocean, destroying all aquatic life in its path, and creating tsunamis nearly fifteen feet high which swept away everything within their reach. Violent explosions from the reaction of lava with cold seawater threw even greater quantities of ash into the atmosphere, and created vast fields of pumice stones along the shoreline. These fields, some of which were three miles wide, were light enough to float; they drifted out to sea where they were driven west by the prevailing winds and ocean currents. Like giant icebergs, the pumice fields remained a hazard to ships for years after the eruption. The British ship *Fairlie* encountered one in the South Indian Ocean in October 1815, more than 2,000 miles west-southwest of Tambora. The crew initially mistook the ash for seaweed, but when they approached they were shocked "to find it [composed of] burnt cinders, evidently volcanic. The sea was covered with it during the next two days." As there was no land for hundreds of miles (and evidently being unable to believe that the pumice could have traveled that far) the crew attributed the field to an underwater eruption of unknown location.

At ten o'clock the magma columns—which now consisted almost entirely of molten rock and ash, most of the water having boiled away and evaporated—collapsed under their own weight. The eruption destroyed the top three thousand feet of the volcano, blasting it into the air in pieces, leaving behind only a large crater three miles wide and half a mile deep, as though the mountain had been struck by a meteor. Propelled by the force of the eruption, gray and black particles of ash, dust, and soot rose high into the atmosphere, some as high as twenty-five miles above the crumbling peak of the mountain, where the winds began to spread them in all directions. As they moved away from the eruption, the largest, heaviest particles lost their momentum first and began to fall back towards the ground. This gave the ash cloud the shape of a mushroom or an umbrella, with the still-erupting Tambora as the fiery shaft. The lightest particles in the cloud, however, retained their momentum and remained high in the air; some even continued to rise.

By eleven o'clock, the whirlwind had subsided. Only then did the explosions commence. At Bima, on the northeast coast of Sumbawa about forty miles east of Tambora, the British resident reported that the blasts sounded like "a heavy mortar fired close to his ear." A rain of ash poured down upon the villages, heavy enough to crush the roofs of houses, including the resident's, rendering them uninhabitable. Waves surged in from the sea, flooding houses a foot deep and ripping fishing boats from their moorings in the harbor, tossing them high up onto the shore. In place of dawn, there was only darkness.

On board the *Benares*, still moored at Makassar, sailors heard the explosions—far louder than those of the previous eruption—throughout the night. "Towards morning the reports were in quick succession," noted the ship's commander, "and sometimes like three or four guns fired together, and so heavy, that they shook the ship, as they did the houses in the fort." As soon as a semblance of dawn broke, the cruiser again set sail southward, to determine the cause of the blasts.

But the sky troubled the *Benares*'s captain. "By this time," he noted, "which was about eight A.M., it was very apparent that some extraordinary occurrence had taken place. The face of the heavens to the southward and westward had assumed the most dismal and lowering aspect, and it was much darker than when the sun rose." What appeared to be a heavy squall on the horizon quickly took on a dark red glow, spreading across the sky. "By ten it was so dark that I could scarcely discern the ship from the shore, though not a mile distant." Ash began to fall on the decks of the *Benares*. An hour later, nearly the entire sky was blotted out.

By this time, Tambora's umbrella ash cloud extended for more than three hundred miles at its widest point. As the cloud spread, the heavier clumps of ash within it drifted to the ground, but the rest remained aloft. "The ashes now began to fall in showers," the ship's captain wrote, "and the appearance altogether was truly awful and alarming." By noon, the darkness was complete, and the rain of ash—which one sailor described as a tasteless "perfect impalpable powder or dust" that gave off a vaguely burnt odor—covered every surface on the ship. "The darkness was so profound throughout the remainder of the day," continued the commander, "that I never saw any thing equal to it in the darkest night; it was impossible to see your hand when held up close to the eye." Ash continued to fall throughout the evening; despite the captain's efforts to cover the deck with awnings, the particles piled as much as a foot high on many surfaces. At six o'clock the following morning, there was still no sign of the sun, but the accumulated weight of the ash—which one officer estimated at several tons—forced the crew to begin tossing the powder overboard. Finally by noon on April 12, a faint light broke through, and the captain was struck by the thought that the *Benares* resembled nothing more than a giant calcified pumice stone. For the next three days, however, he noted that "the atmosphere still continued very thick and dusky from the ashes that remained suspended, the rays of the sun scarce able to penetrate through it, with little or no wind the whole time."

A Malaysian ship from Timor sailing through the region also found itself in "utter darkness" on April 11. As it passed by Tambora, the commander saw that the lower part of the mountain was still in flames. Landing farther down the coast to search for fresh water, he found the ground "covered with ashes to the depth of three feet," and many of the inhabitants dead. When the ship departed on a strong westward current, it had to zigzag through a mass of cinders floating on the sea, more than a foot thick and several miles across.

On the island of Sumatra, over a thousand miles west of Tambora, local chieftains heard the explosions on the morning of April 11. Fearing a conflict had broken out between rival villages, they hurried down to Fort Marlborough, the British encampment in Bengkulu. Other tribal chieftains on Sumatra and the neighboring islands also assumed the sounds presaged some sort of invasion, but once they received reassurance on that score, they ascribed the explosions to supernatural causes. "Our chiefs here," reported an official at Fort Marlborough, "decided that it was only a contest between Jin (the very devil), with some of his awkward squad, and the manes of their departed ancestors, who had passed their period of probation in the mountains, and were in progress towards paradise."

At Gresik on eastern Java, natives decided that the blasts were the "supernatural artillery" of the venerated South Java Sea spirit queen Nyai Loroh Kidul, fired to celebrate the marriage of one of her children; the ash was "the dregs of her ammunition." If so, her ammunition made most of April 12 utterly dark in the village. When the British resident in Gresik awoke that morning, he had the impression that he had slept through a very long night. Reading his watch by lamplight, he discovered that it was 8:30 A.M., and pitch-black outside from the cloud of ashes descending. He breakfasted by candlelight at 11:00 and thought he could see a faint glimmering of light, but at 5 P.M. he still could "neither read nor write without candle." In the nearby village of Sumenep, ash fell about two inches thick, and "the trees also were loaded with it."

A tsunami reached eastern Java around midnight on April 10–11, and tremors struck the central region of the island eighteen hours after the eruption. Between two and three in the afternoon of April 11, a European observer in the village of Surakarta (Solo) noticed "a tremulous motion of the earth, distinctly indicated by the tremor of large window frames; another comparatively violent explosion occurred late in the afternoon. . . . The atmosphere appeared to be loaded with a thick vapour: the Sun was rarely visible, and only at short intervals appearing very obscurely behind a semitransparent substance." Surakarta remained in darkness for much of the following day, as well. Raffles, too, reported that even at a distance of eight hundred miles, "showers of ashes covered the houses, the streets, and the fields, to the depth of several inches; and amid this darkness explosions were heard at intervals, like the report of artillery or the noise of distant thunder."

Twenty-four hours after Tambora erupted, the ash cloud had expanded to cover an area approximately the size of Australia. Air temperatures in the region plunged dramatically, perhaps as much as twenty degrees Fahrenheit. Then a light southeasterly breeze sprang up, and over the next several days most of the ash cloud drifted over the islands west and northwest of Tambora. By the time the cloud finally departed, villages within twenty miles of the volcano were covered with ash nearly forty inches thick; those a hundred miles away found eight to ten inches of ash on the ground.

Even a small quantity of ash could devastate plants and wild-life. One district that received about one-and-a-quarter inch of ash discovered that its crops were "completely beaten down and cov-ered by it." Dead fish floated on the surfaces of ponds, and scores of small birds lay dead on the ground.

By the time the volcano finally subsided, Tambora had released an estimated one hundred cubic kilometers of molten rock as ash and pumice—enough to cover a square area one hundred miles on each side to a depth of almost twelve feet—making it the largest known volcanic eruption in the past 2,000 years. Geologists mea-sure eruptions by the Volcanic Explosivity Index, which uses whole numbers from 0 to 8 to rate the relative amount of ash, dust, and sulphur a volcano throws into the atmosphere. Like the Richter Scale for earthquakes, each step along the Explosivity Index is equal to a tenfold increase in the magnitude of the eruption. Tambora merits an Index score of 7, making the eruption approxi-mately one thousand times more powerful than the Icelandic vol-cano Eyjafjallajökull, which disrupted trans-Atlantic air travel in 2010 but rated only a 4; one hundred times stronger than Mount St. Helens (a 5); and ten times more powerful than Krakatoa (a 6). Only four other eruptions in the last hundred centuries have reached a score of 7. Modern scientists identify and measure past eruptions using layers of volcanic debris found in ice cores, lake sediments, and other undisturbed soils. Each eruption has a distinct chemical signature that, along with conventional methods of carbon dating, can be used to associate each layer of volcanic material with a particular eruption.

VOLCANO	LOCATION	YEAR OF ERUPTION	VOLCANIC EXPLOSIVITY INDEX
VESUVIUS	ITALY	79	5
HUAYNAPUTINA	PERU	1600	6
TAMBORA	INDONESIA	1815	7
KRAKATOA	INDONESIA	1883	6
SANTA MARIA	GUATEMALA	1902	6
MOUNT ST. HELENS	WASHINGTON, USA	1980	5
PINATUBO	PHILIPPINES	1991	6
EYJAFJALLAJÖKULL	ICELAND	2010	4

(SOURCE FOR TABLE: SMITHSONIAN MUSEUM OF NATURAL HISTORY; HTTP://WWW.VOLCANO.SI.EDU/WORLD/ LARGEERUPTIONS.CFM)

It was also by far the deadliest eruption in recorded history. As soon as the volcano quieted, Raffles ordered the British residents to make a survey of their districts to ascertain the extent of the damage. The reports that reached him detailed a horrific picture.

Before the eruption, more than twelve thousand natives lived in the immediate vicinity of Tambora. They never had a chance to escape. Nearly all of them died within the first twenty-four hours, mostly from ash falls and pyroclastic flows—rapidly moving streams of partially liquefied rock and superheated gas at temperatures up to 1,000 degrees, hot enough to melt glass. Carbonized remains of villagers caught unaware were buried beneath the lava; fewer than one hundred people survived. "The trees and herbage of every description, along the whole of the north and west sides of the peninsula," reported one British official, "have been completely destroyed." Another found that in the area surrounding Mount Tambora, "the cattle and inhabitants were nearly all of them

destroyed . . . and those who survived were in such a state of deplorable starvation, that they would unavoidably share the same
fate." One village had sunk entirely, its former site now covered by
more than three fathoms (eighteen feet) of water. And the Raja of
Sanggar confirmed that "the whole of his country was entirely
desolate, and the crops destroyed." The survivors of his village were
living on coconuts, but even the supply of that food was nearly exhausted.

On April 19, the *Benares* reached Bima. The coastline was
barely recognizable; what had been one of the most beautiful and
regular harbors in Asia now was an obstacle course, littered with
masses of black pumice stone, tree trunks burnt and splintered as
if by lightning, and the prows of previously sunken ships which
the ocean had thrown onto land. The village had only a small supply of rice to stave off starvation. When the *Benares* departed
several days later, it sailed past Mount Tambora, which had been
one of the highest peaks in the archipelago, often used by sailors
as a landmark. Clouds of smoke and ash still obscured the volcano's
peak. Even at a distance of six miles, sailors could see patches of
lava steaming along the mountainside.

A heavy rainstorm on April 17 had left the air cleaner and
cooler, and probably saved a substantial number of lives on the
more distant islands as the rain washed the ash off crops and provided fresh drinking water to help stem an incipient epidemic of
fever. But nothing could save those closer to Tambora. Over the
following month, thousands more perished—some from severe
respiratory infections from the ash that remained in the atmosphere in the aftermath of the eruption, others from violent diar-
rhoeal disease, the result of drinking water contaminated with
acidic ash. The same deadly ash poisoned crops, especially the vital
rice fields, raising the death toll higher. Horses and cattle perished
by the hundreds, mainly from a lack of forage. Lieutenant Owen
Phillips, dispatched by Raffles to investigate conditions and provide
an emergency supply of rice to the inhabitants, arrived in Bima

several weeks after the eruption and reported that "the extreme misery to which the inhabitants have been reduced is shocking to behold. There were still on the road side the remains of several corpses, and the marks of where many others had been interred: the villages almost entirely deserted and the houses fallen down, the surviving inhabitants having dispersed in search of food." In the nearby village of Dompo, residents were reduced to eating stalks of papaya and plantain, and the heads of palm. Even the Raja of Sanggar lost a daughter to hunger.

In the end, perhaps another seventy to eighty thousand people died from starvation or disease caused by the eruption, bringing the death toll to nearly ninety thousand in Indonesia alone. No other volcanic explosion in history has come close to wreaking disaster of that magnitude.

And yet there would be more casualties from Tambora. In addition to millions of tons of ash, the force of the eruption threw 55 million tons of sulfur-dioxide gas more than twenty miles into the air, into the stratosphere. There, the sulfur dioxide rapidly combined with readily available hydroxide gas—which, in liquid form, is commonly known as hydrogen peroxide—to form more than 100 million tons of sulfuric acid. The sulfuric acid condensed into minute droplets—each two hundred times finer than the width of a human hair—that could easily remain suspended in the air as an aerosol cloud. The strong stratospheric jet streams quickly accelerated the particles to a velocity of about sixty miles per hour, blowing primarily in an east-to-west direction. The sheer power of the jet stream allowed the aerosol cloud to circumnavigate Earth in two weeks; but the cloud did not remain coherent.

Variations in the wind speed and the weight of the particles caused some parts of the cloud to travel faster or slower than others, and so the cloud spread as it moved around Earth, until it covered the equator with an almost imperceptible veil of dust and sulfurous particles. It also began to spread north and south, albeit far more slowly. While it took only two weeks for the aerosol cloud to cover the globe at the equator, it was likely more than two months before it reached the North and South Poles.

Rather than a slow, steady broadening of the equatorial cloud into the Northern and Southern Hemispheres, the cloud expanded in fits and starts. As some pieces of the cloud were blown away from the equator, they were quickly caught up in the dominant stratospheric jet streams—which in May blow east to west in the Northern Hemisphere, and west to east in the Southern Hemisphere. The cloud soon began to resemble streamers or filaments, with small portions regularly pushed off the equator and into the middle latitudes in each hemisphere. Eventually, these filaments coalesced into a single, coherent cloud that covered Earth.

And there they remained. Had the aerosol cloud ascended only into the lowest part of the atmosphere, the troposphere, where clouds form, rain would soon have cleansed the ash from the air. But in the more stable stratosphere, conditions mitigate against the formation of clouds of water droplets. The coldest air already is at the bottom of the stratosphere, with warmer air above it, so air rarely rises from the troposphere into the stratosphere. With no rising plumes of warm air to carry moisture into the stratosphere, clouds almost never form; the stratosphere is drier than most deserts. With no clouds, there could be no rain to wash away the stratospheric aerosol veil. Only the slow action of gravity and the occasional circulation of air between the stratosphere and the troposphere could drag the droplets back to the earth. And so the extraordinarily fine sulfur particles from Tambora that reached the stratosphere remained suspended in the air for years, freely transported around the globe by the winds. By the winter of 1815–16, the nearly invisible veil of ash covered the globe, reflecting sunlight, cooling temperatures, and wreaking havoc on weather patterns.

2.

PORTENTS

"The country has all the appearance of the middle of winter . . . "

FROM TERAMO IN central Italy, near the Adriatic coast, came reports in late December 1815 of "the heaviest snow ever known in that country." According to one account, over a six-hour period "a greater quantity of snow [fell] than has been known in the memory of man." More astonishing was the nature of the precipitation. The snow "was of a red and yellow color . . . [which] excited great fear and apprehension in the people." Believing that "something extraordinary has taken place in the air," the local residents organized religious processions to placate God; in the meantime, provincial authorities summoned a professor of physical science from Parma (who was also a Jesuit priest) to study the phenomenon. For the rest of the winter, the Abruzzo region remained cold, with significantly more snow and freezing rain than usual.

Several weeks later, an intense blizzard raged across northeastern Hungary for two days. The snow reportedly covered houses to the rooftops, and killed more than ten thousand sheep and hundreds of oxen. Despite the magnitude of the storm, news accounts focused primarily on the fact that "the snow was not white, but brown or flesh colored." April brought reports of another colored snowfall in Italy, this time around the Tonale Pass, in the Italian Alps: "It was brick red and left an earthy powder, very light and impalpable, unctuous to the touch . . . [with an] astringent taste." The colored snow almost certainly was the result of ice droplets forming with ash particles from Tambora as their nuclei. The deepest clouds associated with severe storms occasionally are able to reach into the stratosphere, which is consistent with the colored snow falling in particularly extreme weather events. Over the course of months—and, in this case, years— gravity also slowly dragged the stratospheric sulfur particles into the upper reaches of the troposphere, where the particles could more easily form the centers of ice crystals.

No contemporary accounts appear to have made the connection between the phenomenon of colored snow in Italy and Hungary and the eruption of Mount Tambora nearly halfway around the world, although reports of Tambora had reached London by the end of 1815, and a few amateur scientists—most famously Benjamin Franklin—had previously essayed a connection between volcanic eruptions and unusual atmospheric conditions. Following the eight-month-long eruption of Laki in southern Iceland in June 1783, Europe and North America experienced highly unusual weather, including a persistent dry haze during the summer and an extremely cold and snowy winter that killed thousands of people across Europe. Although Franklin, who was living in Europe at the time, acknowledged in a 1784 lecture to the Manchester Literary and Philosophical Association that "the cause of this universal fog is not yet ascertained," he suggested that it may have been "the vast quantity of smoke, long continuing, to issue during the summer [from Laki] . . . which smoke might be spread by various winds, over the northern part of the world." And the frigid temperatures, he proposed, probably resulted from this fog blocking the rays of the sun, thereby reducing the amount of solar energy that reached Earth.

Throughout the winter of 1815–16, the spreading aerosol cloud from Mount Tambora had been doing precisely that: cooling global temperatures by reflecting and scattering sunlight. Although the cloud reflected only one half to one percent of the incoming energy, it reduced the Northern Hemisphere average temperature in 1816 by about three degrees Fahrenheit. This seemingly small cooling had a considerable impact on global weather patterns, with devastating consequences for agriculture on both sides of the Atlantic. Ironically, however, the effects of Tambora's aerosol cloud could have been far worse if the eruption had been slightly weaker. While immense in size and scope, Tambora's aerosol cloud was not particularly efficient at reflecting sunlight. Stronger volcanic eruptions tend to eject more sulfur dioxide into the stratosphere than weaker eruptions, which leads to more sulfuric acid droplets within the same volume of atmospheric gases. A greater number of droplets increases the chance that droplets will meet and collide, forming larger droplets that will be removed more quickly from the stratosphere by gravity. A single, larger droplet also has less total surface area than two smaller droplets, and so is less effective at scattering sunlight. There is therefore a balance to be struck between eruptions that are too weak to penetrate into the stratosphere—and so produce small, short-lived cooling—and eruptions that produce large, less effective sulfuric acid droplets. By measuring the remnants of Tambora's aerosol cloud in ice cores and lake sediments, modern scientists have determined that the climatic consequences—while undoubtedly devastating—could have been far worse if the particles had been roughly half their size.

Unlike the sudden drop in temperatures in the Indonesian archipelago that occurred immediately after the eruption of Mount Tambora, the planet-wide cooling was a gradual process that took up to a year to be fully realized. While air temperatures can, and frequently do, change rapidly in response to variations in solar energy, soil and ocean temperatures adjust much more slowly. The land and sea possess considerable capacity to store heat, while the atmosphere has practically no storage. When the atmosphere is cooler than the land and sea, heat will flow from these reservoirs back into the air; but since the air cannot store heat for long, much of this is soon lost to space. If, on the other hand, the atmosphere is warmer, some of that excess heat will be stored in soil and water until a balance is reached. This process may be seen clearly in summer: The warmest weather often occurs not in June, when the sun is strongest, but in August, when the ocean and land have warmed.

As Tambora's stratospheric aerosol cloud began to cool temperatures by subtly reducing the amount of solar energy reaching the earth, the land and oceans would have resisted this cooling by transferring stored heat into the atmosphere, and cooling themselves as a result. By early 1816, the land, ocean, and atmosphere were shifting toward a new balance of energies, largely as a result of the solar-dimming effect of the aerosol cloud. The adjustment cooled first air, then land, and finally ocean temperatures across the globe. Using information from tree rings—the width of each ring is related to the growing conditions (mostly temperature and precipitation) that year—climatologists have determined that 1816 was the second-coldest year in the Northern Hemisphere since 1400, surpassed only by 1601, following the eruption of Huaynaputina in Peru. Even as the aerosol began to settle out of the atmosphere through gravity, it would take years for land and ocean temperatures to return to normal. And so 1817 was the fifth coldest, 1818 the twenty-second coldest, and 1819 the twenty-ninth coldest year in the Northern Hemisphere since 1400.

In the meantime, the aerosol cloud had produced other noticeable optical phenomena, most notably a series of spectacular red, purple, and orange sunsets in London in the summer and autumn of 1815. Observers noted repeatedly that "the sky exhibited in places a fire," with "crimson cirri" [high-altitude cirrus clouds,

composed of fine ice particles] and "much redness in the twilight."
"The evening twilight has been generally coloured of late," wrote
one contemporary, "and at times streaked with converging shad-
ows, the origin of which could not be traced to clouds intercepting
the light." On several particularly unsettled September nights, the
storm clouds continued to glow various shades of red for half an
hour after sunset.

Sunsets typically appear yellow, orange, or red because atmospheric gases scatter blue light more effectively than other colors,
skewing the visible-light spectrum toward red. The effect is even
more pronounced when the sun is low on the horizon, since its light
must pass through a thicker layer of the atmosphere to reach the
ground, resulting in less blue and more red light.

Stratospheric ash, dust, and soot particles from volcanic
eruptions—or from pollution or fires—enhance this atmospheric
scattering effect, leading to brilliant red sunsets. After the sun
passes below the horizon and light no longer reaches the surface,
some sunlight still passes through the upper portions of the atmosphere. Aerosol veils reflect this sunlight toward Earth, giving the
colorful postsunset glows reported in London. So exceptional were
these sunsets that Londoners commented on them repeatedly in
letters, journals, and newspaper articles, which suggests that they
likely were caused by the Tambora aerosol cloud rather than the
heavy industrial pollution that habitually afflicted the city during
that era. In fact, scientists have taken advantage of this effect by
using the amount of red in contemporary paintings of sunsets to
estimate the intensity of volcanic eruptions. Several Greek scientists, led by C. S. Zerefos, digitally measured the amount of red—
relative to other primary colors—in more than 550 samples of
landscape art by 181 artists from the sixteenth through the nineteenth centuries to produce estimates of the amount of volcanic
ash in the air at various times. Paintings from the years following
the Tambora eruption used the most red paint; those after Krakatoa came a close second.

* * *

AMERICANS greeted the year 1816 with confidence and optimism. They had recently concluded two and a half years of war with Great Britain, arguably the strongest and certainly the wealthiest nation in the world, and the conflict had ended essentially in a draw. Admittedly the British had captured and partially burned the nation's capital, forcing President Madison and his wife, Dolley, to flee for their lives, accompanied by several wagons full of White House valuables and Cabinet papers stuffed into trunks. But American troops led by General Andrew Jackson had ended the fighting on such a positive note with their overwhelming victory over a numerically superior force of British regulars at New Orleans in January 1815, that many Americans believed they had actually won the War of 1812.

European events since that time offered hope that the United States could look forward to a long period of peace, undisturbed by events abroad. On June 18, 1815, British and Prussian troops commanded by the Duke of Wellington and Marshal Blucher dealt a crushing defeat to Napoléon's army outside the Belgian town of Waterloo. The outcome had hung in the balance for most of the day; Wellington later acknowledged that the battle had been "the nearest run thing you ever saw in your life." It had been exactly a hundred days since Napoléon had entered Paris in triumph. This time, the Allied statesmen at Vienna gave the British government sole authority to choose the site of the Eagle's exile—it selected the remote island of Saint Helena, in the South Atlantic—and sole responsibility for keeping him there. With Napoléon removed from the scene, it seemed unlikely that the United States would be drawn into European affairs anytime in the near future. "We are, happily, at peace with all the world," exulted one Massachusetts congressman, "and there are no indications which threaten soon to disturb this tranquility."

Everything in the United States appeared to be expanding.

Since 1789, the nation had added five new states and five territories. By European standards, the United States's population was growing at an astonishing rate. In 1815, there were nearly 8.5 million Americans, twice as many as there had been only twenty-five years earlier. Immigration—primarily from northern and western Europe—contributed to this prolific growth, but most of the increase came from Americans who married young and had large families; on average, American women in the early nineteenth century had between seven and eight live births. It was also a very young population: 85 percent of the population was under the age of forty, including nearly all of the leaders of Congress.

Slightly more than 80 percent of Americans were white, and in a nation where land was cheap but labor scarce, the vast majority of white adults—more than 80 percent—made their living as subsistence farmers. Most American farmers spent only a portion of their working hours tending their crops, however, doubling as coopers, or tanners, or blacksmiths, or shoemakers. Wives and children frequently carded wool or spun linen in the evenings after spending their days in the fields. Farm families produced enough goods for their own needs, and sold the rest. "Go into the interior of the country," wrote Albert Gallatin, former secretary of the treasury, "and you will scarcely find a farmer who is not, in some degree, a trader. In a grazing part of the country, you will find them buying and selling cattle; in other parts you will find them distillers, tanners, or brick-makers."

Fewer than seven percent of Americans lived in cities, the largest of which were New York and Philadelphia, but neither even remotely approached the size of London or Manchester. Nearly all of the nation's towns were located on the East Coast, relying on commerce for their prosperity. Most municipalities lacked any public sewer or water system, which meant that garbage, dead animals, and human waste routinely accumulated in the streets.

Manufacturing remained relatively primitive. Beyond the products of farm families, most of the goods offered for sale were fashioned by mechanics working by hand, either in a small shop or at home. Transportation was even less advanced. Goods and passengers rarely traveled very far over land; American roads were notoriously poor, many no more than narrow, bumpy, overgrown trails that turned into quagmires when it rained. (Travelers told stories of horses actually drowning in the pits, and wagons sinking slowly out of sight.) It cost as much to send a ton of goods thirty miles from an ocean port inland as it did to ship it three thousand miles across the Atlantic. And progress was slow; a traveler who set out by carriage from Boston in April would not arrive in Charleston, South Carolina, until July. In 1802, Congress had authorized the construction of the National Road across the Appalachians, but fourteen years later the road had not yet crossed the Ohio River. Hence merchants and farmers continued to rely on river systems to move goods in the interior.

Yet significant improvements lay close at hand. Steamboats, dismissed as "floating smokestacks" by skeptical observers when Samuel Fulton's prototype made its debut on the Hudson River in 1807, were slowly gaining popularity, especially on the Western rivers. And Governor DeWitt Clinton of New York had begun to elicit legislative support for the construction of a canal (derided by his critics as "Clinton's Big Ditch" or "the Governor's Gutter") that would stretch across the state for 340 miles from Albany to Buffalo, through thick forests and disease-ridden swamps, connecting the Hudson River with the Great Lakes.

Manufacturing was poised to expand as well. When the recent war temporarily deprived American consumers of British goods, New England merchants and entrepreneurs provided financial backing for scores of small-scale domestic textile "manufactories" that produced a total of $24 million worth of cotton goods and provided employment to nearly a hundred thousand men, women, and children. Americans produced an additional $19 million worth of woolen goods in 1815, and the Boston Manufacturing Company, headed by Frances Cabot Lowell, had recently completed the nation's first integrated textile factory along the Charles River in Waltham, Massachusetts.

In the aftermath of war, a new spirit of nationalism swept over the United States. For the past twenty-five years, the nation had been riven by deep divisions over domestic issues—primarily Alexander Hamilton's economic proposals—and the war in Europe. The disagreements produced the first two political parties in the United States: the Federalists, led by Hamilton and John Adams, who were horrified at the disorder and excesses of the French Revolution; and the Democratic-Republicans, who shared Thomas Jefferson's dislike of a strong central government, and Madison's distrust of Great Britain.

Lately, however, many Republicans had come to accept much of the Federalist domestic agenda; a powerful central government seemed less threatening if they controlled it, as they had since 1801. (Madison, however, had grown no more fond of Britain since the king's troops burned the President's Mansion in Washington; in early 1816 Madison was living in a private dwelling on the corner of New York Avenue and 18th Street known as the "Octagon House," while workmen repaired and repainted the mansion, this time with white rather than gray paint.) Moderate Federalists who could recognize a lost cause were deserting to the opposition in increasing numbers. And a series of costly missteps by the dwindling band of hard-core Federalist stalwarts—including vocal opposition to the war effort and a thinly veiled threat by New England political leaders in December 1814 to secede—destroyed any hopes the Federalists may have entertained to regain power on the national level.

Partisan rancor thus subsided, although it did not entirely disappear when the Fourteenth Congress concluded its regular session in the spring of 1816. Legislators spent much of their time debating economic issues. In early April, Congress approved the first protective tariff in the nation's history. Several weeks later, legislators voted to establish a second Bank of the United States, to provide a uniform, stable currency and a source of credit for business ventures.

Yet there remained many congressmen and voters, especially from rural areas, who distrusted the power of a central bank independent of popular control. These same critics demanded that the federal government cut taxes now that the war had ended. Since military expenditures during the war had sent the federal debt soaring to nearly $124 million, Congress hesitated to slash taxes and decrease revenue too rapidly. It did repeal all duties on domestic manufactures, but it retained several other minor taxes, including those on carriages and postage. Administration officials estimated that the new, higher tariff rates would bring in at least $25 million per year, which they claimed would be sufficient to pay the government's routine civil and military expenses, fund annual increases in the size of the navy (which had proven woefully inadequate during the recent hostilities), and pay off the remaining debt in about twelve years.

Before Congress adjourned, it also voted itself a pay raise. Since the first Congress convened in 1790, legislators had received six dollars per diem in lieu of a regular salary. Although the cost of living had increased by at least 75 percent over the past twenty-six years, their remuneration had not changed. Hence congressmen felt justified in approving the Compensation Act, which granted them an annual salary of $1,500. Few realized at that time that this measure would destroy many members' political careers.

As lawmakers departed Washington at the end of April, they congratulated themselves on accomplishing their tasks in an unusual display of good feelings. "Among the most auspicious appearances of the times, is the obliteration of party spirit," declared a Southern representative. "No question at the present session of congress has been discussed or determined on the ground of party. . . . Let us then cherish these feelings; let us emulate each other only in serving our country with the more zeal, and the more fidelity."

* * *

ON April 29, Americans noticed a large, irregular spot on the surface of the sun when they glanced skyward. One observer compared it to "a spider, having parts extending from the main body," while another claimed that "its general appearance is not unlike that of a cluster of islands . . . surrounded by a belt of rocks." A representative of the National Mathematical Academy in Philadelphia estimated the length of the spot at just under 40,000 miles, with a breadth of nearly 3,000 miles. It lay just north of the center of the sun's surface, and its stationary nature over the course of a week led a group of American astronomers to dismiss their initial hypothesis that it might simply have been the planet Mercury moving across the face of the sun. Instead, they decided it was probably a wandering comet pulled in by the sun's gravitational force.

In its May 1816 issue, the *North American Review* cited the theories of Sir Frederick William Herschel, a British astronomer, who argued that the spots were "chasms in the [sun's] atmosphere, occasioned by ascending currents of gaseous fuel." Since there appeared to be "a variable emission of light and heat, intimately connected with the appearance and disappearance of spots," Herschel theorized that "seasons of uncommon heat and cold, of fertility and barrenness, so far as they depend upon the supply of heat, are to be traced not so much to accidental causes near at hand, as to the inconstancy of the fountain." (Herschel, a legendary figure in the history of astronomy, made numerous important discoveries, including Uranus and its two moons, but also believed the sun was inhabited, along with all the other planets and stars. He speculated that the sun's surface was actually cool enough to support life; only the outer solar atmosphere was hot.)

Others suggested that the sunspots were volcanoes on the surface of the sun, or "burning mountains of immense size; so that when the eruption is nearly ended and the smoke dissipated, the fierce flames are exposed, and appear as luminous spots." Yet another explanation proposed the spots to be "a kind of excavation of the luminous fluid supposed to envelope [sic] the opake [sic] and solid body of the sun." Even those who supported this concept found it difficult to imagine how any gap within a liquid could remain unfilled; one contributor to the *Gentleman's Magazine* in Britain likened it to "no less a miracle than the passage of the Israelites through the Red Sea." Perhaps, suggested a writer in the *Baltimore American*, "the Sun has cast forth several immense bodies, and . . . there is a danger of one of them coming in contact with our little tiney [sic] globe, when, in the horrible crash, we may experience another deluge, or suffer a terrible conflagration!"

No one in 1816 understood that sunspots are formed by variations in the strength of the magnetic field that surrounds the sun. Occasionally, a portion of the magnetic field grows strong enough that the field coils back on itself and punctures the surface of the sun, a process which inhibits the fusion reactions that produce solar energy. This in turn reduces the temperature of the sun's surface at the point of the puncture. Since the brightness of the sun's surface is proportional to its temperature, the sunspots appear darker than the rest of the sun.

Scientists in Europe and the United States had regularly recorded sunspot activity with telescopes since the early seventeenth century, when several astronomers, including Galileo, first observed them. Most of the earliest sunspot observations were taken during the period now known as the Maunder Minimum—named for the English scientist Edward Maunder—that extended from 1645–1717, when sunspot activity was at an unusually low level. The near disappearance of sunspots in the 1650s puzzled astronomers, as did their sudden reemergence in the second decade of the eighteenth century.

While individual sunspots occur almost randomly, the total number of spots follows a fairly predictable eleven-year cycle (a cycle that was discovered in 1844). But sunspot activity also varies over much longer periods of time which are less predictable and less regular than the short-term cycle. The eruption of Tambora coincided with another minimum in sunspot activity—the Dalton Minimum of 1790–1830. The Dalton Minimum was shorter and less intense than the Maunder Minimum, but it still resulted in a notable decrease in sunspot activity; hence the surprise exhibited by the appearance of a large sunspot in April 1816.

According to one contemporary account, no sunspots of this magnitude had been witnessed in the United States since 1779. Moreover, observers could stare at the spot without the usual protection of shaded glasses, because the atmosphere lately had been filled with a curious thick haze—"a fine dust," reported a Virginia newspaper, "very injurious to respiration." "It had nothing of the nature of a humid fog," noted an American physician. "It was like that smoking vapour which overspread Europe about thirty years ago." And while sunspots typically are visible to the naked eye only when the sun is barely above the horizon, when the atmosphere has scattered much of the sunlight, this spot could be seen throughout much of the day. In fact, the aerosol haze from Tambora may have lengthened by as much as five times the usual window for viewing sunspots after sunrise and before sunset.

Since most Americans had never witnessed the sunspots that routinely move across the face of the sun, this highly visible spot— much larger than usual—generated more apprehension than the haze. Some feared it was an omen of impending apocalypse, a "calamitous sign in heaven," or a warning that "the sun may, in time . . . become wholly incrusted" with spots, "so as to plunge us at once into the unutterable darkness that characterized the primitive chaos." Others predicted the huge spot would weaken the sun's rays and permanently cool Earth's atmosphere. While the editors of the North American Review dismissed such speculation, they did admit that "the observation . . . that the light of the sun is less brilliant and dazzling than usual, is unquestionably well founded. We have remarked at different times during the present season, on days when the sky was perfectly clear, that there was a degree of feebleness and dimness in the Sun's rays, not unlike the effect produced by a partial eclipse."

Yet the first four months of 1816 were not noticeably colder than normal in the Eastern United States. In New England, the winter had been one of the mildest in a decade, with significantly less snow than usual. "The winter was open," noted Noah Webster in his diary at Amherst, Massachusetts. "A snow in January, which was sufficient for sledding, was swept away in a few days. The ground was uncovered most of the winter." Judging by the measurements of several amateur meteorologists at Northeastern colleges, January's temperatures appeared to have been slightly above normal, with a warming trend at the end of the month. In Maine, the days were so pleasant "that most persons allowed their fires to go out and did not burn wood except for cooking." Similarly, the Connecticut Courant reported that "January was mild—so much so as to render fires almost needless in sitting rooms." (Thomas Jefferson, on the other hand, wrote to a friend from his retreat at Monticello, just west of Charlottesville, Virginia, shortly after New Year's Day that he was "shivering and shrinking in body from the cold we now experience.")

February brought generally mild temperatures with only a few snowstorms. "The first of March was very warm," noted Adino Brackett, a farmer and schoolteacher in Lancaster, New Hampshire, "and almost all the snow went off." The weather then turned clear and cold for several weeks, but the month ended with another warm spell and a rare appearance of early spring thunderstorms in the Northeast. There had been sharp cold snaps along the East Coast in mid-March, however, including a bout of sleet in Richmond, Virginia, that left fruit trees covered in icicles. As winter departed, the first week of April was slightly warmer than usual in New England, with very little precipitation.

Although it appears counterintuitive, the stratospheric aerosol cloud from Tambora was partly responsible for both the mild winter of 1815–16 in North America and the stormy conditions across central Europe. The aerosol cloud not only scattered sunlight, preventing it from reaching Earth's surface, it also absorbed some of the incoming energy, reradiating it as heat. This warmed the stratosphere immediately above the cloud. If the aerosol cloud had warmed the stratosphere evenly around the globe, its effect would have been minimal. In the depths of winter, however, the high northern latitudes are plunged into continual darkness for several months. Without sunlight to absorb, the aerosol cloud could not heat the Arctic stratosphere; yet it continued to heat the stratosphere in the sunlit middle and lower latitudes.

A strong, cyclonic vortex forms near the North and South poles each winter. Strong west-to-east winds surround the vortex and expand to cover much of the high latitudes. These winds are created by the difference in winter temperatures between the sunlit middle and perpetually dark high latitudes: Air always flows from warmer temperatures toward colder ones, but Earth's rotation turns the air off its path, towards the right in the Northern Hemisphere and the left in the Southern, to produce westerly winds. These westerly winds prevent cold, polar air from moving into the middle latitudes. When the vortex is particularly strong, lower atmospheric pressures exist near the pole; higher pressures are found in the middle latitudes; and the westerly winds provide an effective barrier. Should the vortex weaken, the pressure rises near the poles and falls in the middle latitudes, leading to frequent outbreaks of polar air. In the Northern Hemisphere, scientists have defined the North Atlantic Oscillation index to describe this seesaw of pressures between the poles and the middle latitudes, with a high index associated with a strong vortex.

Because the aerosol cloud from Tambora heated the stratosphere in the middle latitudes, but not in the Arctic, it enhanced the stratospheric westerly winds around the polar vortex. This effect soon made its way from the stratosphere to the troposphere, strengthening the barrier to Arctic air and leading to a stronger than normal high-pressure system in the Atlantic Ocean near the

Azores Islands. The unusually warm winter throughout New England likely resulted from fewer incursions of polar air into the region. Data from tree rings and other proxies for temperature indicate that the average winter temperature in 1815–16 was as much as three degrees Fahrenheit warmer than normal in a band extending southwest from Alaska through central and southern Canada, across the Great Lakes, and into New England.

By strengthening the polar low and the Atlantic high-pressure system, the aerosol cloud also accelerated the trans-Atlantic westerly jet stream that steers weather systems from North America towards Europe. The jet stream also shifted north, bringing more systems to central and northern Europe and fewer to the Mediterranean Sea and North Africa. The westerly inflow of air from the Atlantic provided a steady source of moisture for these systems, which released that moisture over Europe in a series of snow- and rainstorms. The aerosol cloud effectively increased the North Atlantic Oscillation index; as weather forecasters are well aware, high values of this index are often associated with stormy winters across northern and central Europe. Using climate models to simulate the effects of past volcanic eruptions, scientists have found a consistent link between large eruptions and increases in the index the following winter, with the models producing a nearly constant stream of storms across the Atlantic as a result. The unsettled conditions across Europe in the winter of 1815–16 were likely the result of the aerosol cloud's effect on the North Atlantic Oscillation.

Although the primary effect of the aerosol cloud was to cool global temperatures, its strengthening of the wintertime Arctic vortex delayed the appearance of severely cold temperatures in the United States. Once the long, polar winter night ended, however, the vortex weakened. Sunlight returned to the Arctic, and the aerosol cloud began to heat the stratosphere there as well as at lower latitudes. The westerly wind barrier around the vortex largely vanished, and cold air became free to move away from the pole—south, towards the United States and Europe. The cooling effects of the aerosol veil again became dominant, setting the stage for a chilling spring and a disastrous summer.

Nevertheless, the short-term effect of the mild winter of 1815–16 in the United States was to fuel the ongoing debate over whether American winters were growing warmer. Renowned Puritan cleric and naturalist Cotton Mather had first advanced this hypothesis in the late seventeenth century, less than a hundred years after the first English settlers arrived in Massachusetts Bay. "Our own Winters are, observably as Comfortably Moderated since the Land has been Peopled, and Opened, of Late Years," wrote Mather. "Our Snows are not so Deep, and Long . . . and our Winds blow not such Rasours, as in the Days of our Fathers when the Hands of the Good Men would Freeze unto the Bread upon their Tables." (Occasionally Mather veered into flights of hyperbolic excess in describing the rigors of winters past; he once claimed that when his grandfathers tossed water into the air, it "would be Turned into Ice e're it came unto the Ground.") Mather ascribed the changing climate to the settlers' destruction of forests and their cultivation of ever-greater tracts of land, which presumably allowed the sun's rays to better penetrate and warm the earth.

Nearly a century later, Thomas Jefferson seconded Mather's deforestation theory, although the two men would have agreed on little else. An obsessive record-keeper who spent a lifetime searching for meaning in America's physical environment, Jefferson faithfully recorded the temperature nearly every day—and often twice a day—for fifty years. (He even noted the weather in Philadelphia on July 4, 1776, when members of the Continental Congress signed the Declaration of Independence: 76 degrees at one o'clock in the afternoon.) Based upon his personal observations and anecdotal evidence, Jefferson suggested in 1781 that Virginia's climate was indeed changing. Not only were winters less severe than they had been several decades earlier, but summers were cooler than before. "Both heats and colds are become much more moderate within the memory even of the middle-aged. Snows are less frequent and less deep. . . . The elderly inform me the earth used to be covered with snow about three months in every year. The rivers, which then seldom failed to freeze over in the course of the winter, scarcely ever do so now." Twenty-five years later, this notion apparently had become so widespread that Jefferson could write that "it is a common opinion that the climates of the several States, of our Union, have undergone a sensible change since the dates of their first settlements; that the degrees both of cold and heat are moderated."

Among those who concurred were French historian and philosopher Constantin-François de Chasseboeuf (who renamed himself the Comte de Volney). After traveling through the United States in 1795–98, Volney attributed the perceived climate change in North America to deforestation. To support his theory, he quoted an early history of Vermont, which claimed that conditions "in the cultivated part of the country" had changed dramatically since English settlers first arrived in New England: "The seasons are different, the weather more variable, the winter become shorter, and interrupted by great and sudden thaws. Spring is a scene of continual vicissitude . . . Summer is not so hot, but it lasts longer. Autumn is most tardy in beginning and ending . . . nor does winter become settled and severe before the end of December."

"It is a popular opinion that the temperature of the winter season, in northern latitudes, has suffered a material change, and become warmer in modern, than it was in ancient times," concluded Noah Webster in a speech to the Connecticut Academy of Sciences in 1799. "This opinion has been adopted and maintained by many writers of reputation"—Webster cited Jefferson, Dr. Samuel Williams, a weather expert and former Harvard professor, and Massachusetts physician Edward Augustus Holyoke—"indeed, I know not whether any person, in this age, has ever questioned the fact." Webster himself believed that "the weather, in modern winters, is more consistent, than when the earth was covered with wood, at the first settlement of Europeans in this country." The warm weather of autumn, he argued, extended further into the winter months due to "the greater quantity of heat accumulated in the earth in summer, since the ground has been cleared of wood, and exposed to the rays of the sun." Similarly, "the exposure of its uncovered surface to the cold atmosphere" allowed frost to penetrate the ground to a greater depth in winter, which appeared to delay the advent of summer weather.

Nonsense, countered William Dunbar, a Scottish-born scientist who had emigrated to Pennsylvania in 1771. Dunbar, who frequently exchanged meteorological observations with Jefferson, claimed that deforestation actually made summers and winters more extreme. "I would enquire," he wrote in an article published in the *Transactions of the American Philosophical Society*, "whether a partial clearing extending 30 or 40 miles square, may not be expected to produce a contrary effect by admitting with full liberty, the sunbeams upon the discovered surface of the earth in summer, and promoting during winter a free circulation of cold northern air."

Timothy Dwight, a Massachusetts cleric and educator who, like his contemporary Jefferson, loved to collect weather data, also rejected the argument that American winters were growing milder. Dwight pointed to numerous very cold and snowy winters in the thirty years since independence that rivaled any of the formidable seasons of the seventeenth or early eighteenth centuries. Besides, discussions of changing climates seemed pointless to Dwight without adequate statistical data. "Few, if any, registers were kept in former times," Dwight noted, and fewer still had been published. "Hence the comparisons of our present climate with that of former periods must be extremely defective."

Climate scientists now know that deforestation of large areas can cause prolonged droughts and exaggerate seasonal variations in temperature, such that summers become much warmer and winters much colder. Dunbar was partially correct in his conclusions, although he failed to understand how forest canopies maintain the climate beneath them. Forests insulate their environment not only by reflecting sunlight but also by trapping moisture; plant roots help to retain water in the ground, while the canopy prevents water vapor from escaping into the air above. Remove the forest, and the moisture in the soil quickly escapes; winds then transport the water vapor hundreds or thousands of miles away. This starts a vicious cycle: Less water in the soil leads to less evaporation into the air, which can lead—when applied to an area of hundreds of square miles or more—to less rainfall, which in turn leads to less water in the soil. What rain does fall will often be unable to penetrate into the dry, hard soil, further increasing the risk of devastating droughts.

Summers become hotter in deforested areas not only because more sunlight reaches the surface, as Dunbar argued, but also because there is less moisture in the soil to cool the ground through evaporation. Water in the soil performs the same function as sweat does in humans; with little moisture to evaporate, bare ground quickly warms in the sunlight. Without the insulating effects of the forest canopy, winter temperatures can drop rapidly as the heat stored in the soil is lost to the atmosphere. There is no evidence to support Dunbar's link between deforestation and stronger northerly winds, although generally forests do act as a brake on the local wind speeds, regardless of the direction. The effects of deforestation on local temperatures and rainfall can be mitigated where the forests are replaced with other ground cover, such as shrubs or crops, instead of simply left as bare soil.

If deforestation had, in fact, transformed their climate, Americans were ambivalent about the desirability of that change. On the one hand, the early colonists viewed the virgin North American forests as dangerous and evil places, the preserve of the devil (and, not coincidentally, Native Americans). They and their descendants believed they had a duty to level what Nathaniel Hawthorne termed the "heathen wilderness." Turning a dense and dark forest filled with "stagnant air" and "rank vegetation" into productive farmland to support a Christian community seemed to fulfill God's plan for the New World. Yet by the early nineteenth century, Americans in the Eastern states increasingly viewed the landscape less as a threat than a source of beauty and natural wonder. Alarmed at the ravages wrought by the "savage hand of cultivation," they worried that their slashing and burning of the wilderness despoiled God's handiwork and disrupted the natural harmony between heaven and earth, and that violent and erratic weather patterns comprised their punishment.

Certainly, chauvinistic New Englanders who prided themselves on their hardiness had no desire to escape the bracing rigor of their winters. Months of subfreezing temperatures accompanied by occasional blizzards built the rugged New England character, they believed, inculcating the virtues of prudence, foresight, diligence, and cooperation in farmers from Connecticut to Maine. "Of all the scenes which this climate offers," wrote St. John de Crevecoeur in an essay on the American farmer, "none has struck me with a greater degree of admiration than the ushering in of our winters . . . a rigour which, when once descended, becomes one of the principal favors and blessings this climate has to boast of." Without such a challenge, New Englanders feared losing their unique identity and growing as weak and soft as they perceived the European character.

Popular anxiety about a general warming trend faded, however, as the nation entered the second decade of the nineteenth century, the coldest ten-year period on record in the history of North America. Even before the eruption of Mount Tambora, aerosol veils from a series of volcanic eruptions were cooling temperatures around the world. In 1809, a very powerful volcano erupted at an unidentified location—probably somewhere in the tropics, based on the recent discovery of large amounts of volcanic sulfuric acid in ice cores in the Arctic. Three years later, Soufrière ("Sulfur Mine") on Saint Vincent erupted over a six-week period, followed by Awu on Sangihe Island, slightly northeast of Tambora. In February 1814, the eruption of Mount Mayon in the Philippines killed over 2,000 people on the island of Luzon. Some of each of these aerosol clouds, particularly the latter two, would have lingered in the stratosphere in 1815. (The lifetimes of stratospheric clouds vary from eruption to eruption, but three- to five-year spans are common, with a decreasing fraction of the original cloud remaining each year.) The devastating global cooling from Tambora, an eruption more powerful than the three earlier ones put together, was likely amplified by the existing cooling trend from these previous eruptions.

In the United States, 1812 brought significantly cooler temperatures and greater precipitation than usual; at Middlebury College in Vermont, Professor Frederick Hall noted that "crops were destroyed by the coldness and wetness of the season," and observers in New England reported frosts in late August and snow in September. The following two years were only slightly colder than normal, but the growing season of 1815 in New England was cut short by May snows and early September killing frosts. In eastern Canada, the province of Quebec suffered devastating losses to its harvests in 1815. The relatively mild North American winter of 1815–16, therefore, generated few complaints.

Then April arrived. After a mild start, the weather took a decidedly nasty turn in the middle of the month. On April 12, nearly a foot of snow fell on Quebec City, and it continued to snow for the next five days. "The country has all the appearance of the middle of winter," noted a news report on April 18, "the depth of snow being still between 3 and 4 feet. We understand that in many parishes the cattle are already suffering from a scarcity of forage." The same storm hit Albany, New York, a day later, leaving the roofs of houses and the nearby hills completely covered with snow. To the west of the city, "the country in many places had the appearance of winter; the hills being as white as in the month of January." Further west, the storm surprised settlers in the town of Chillicothe, then the capital of Ohio. On April 18, one correspondent reported "a temperature extraordinary at this season of the year. In the latter part of last week, the weather was excessively cold—on Sunday, snow fell to the depth of several inches; and since that time the weather has been clear, but nearly as cold as it was in February."

But the advent of a heat wave at the end of the month raised farmers' spirits; by the time the sunspots appeared in late April, Vermont farmers—who already had planted some of their crops— were sweltering under highs in the low 80s.

COOLER temperatures also settled across the European continent in 1810, ushering in a decade that would be the coldest in several centuries for much of western and central Europe. From 1810– 1815, the difference was felt mainly during the autumns and winters; the summers were not unusually frigid. In 1812, central Italy experienced snow and a highly atypical hard freeze in April, followed by a very cold autumn; harvests in Germany, Switzerland, and the Netherlands also suffered from the cold. After relatively normal weather in 1813, exceptionally low temperatures returned in 1814—the coldest year on record for much of central Europe. Conditions did not improve significantly in 1815: Switzerland, Italy, Germany, and Austria (especially in the southern provinces of Styria and Carinthia) all endured heavy precipitation and a colder than usual autumn, resulting in poor harvests which sent the price of wheat sharply higher. Weather during the winter of 1815–16 was unsettled across much of Europe; in Germany, strong winds and a lack of snow cover blew wheat seeds off the soil, forcing farmers to replant their fields.

In Britain, 1810 marked the start of the coldest decade in Great Britain since the 1690s, with average temperatures one to two degrees Celcius colder than normal, frigid enough to provoke a change in women's fashions. During the 1790s, English women had adopted revealing styles of undergarments from France; as temperatures dropped, however, they covered up their cleavage with the more modest and far warmer shifts known as "bosom friends" to help fend off the chilling winds.

Despite the cooler weather, British farmers enjoyed a very good harvest in the autumn of 1815. The following winter began colder than usual in Britain, with highs in the upper 30s and low 40s in January and February. March brought spells of warmer weather, but significantly more precipitation; it snowed or rained for nearly half the days, and one storm dropped a foot of snow on Lancashire. Sleet and snow returned on April 9, along with sub-freezing temperatures that kept several inches of snow on the ground in southern England. Four days later, heavy snow along the east coast prevented travelers from leaving Dover for the continent; more snow fell on April 14. By the last week in April, highs were back in the mid 60s, and farmers could finally plant their crops, but the growing season already had been delayed. In Ireland, too, the spring was abnormally late.

Scotland fared worse. In Aberdeenshire, frost and snow from mid-November through mid-March froze the turnips used for cattle fodder, and the plants rotted in the alternating frosts and snow. "We never experienced a worse winter for feeding," complained the *Aberdeen Journal*. Farmers began taking their cattle to market much earlier than usual, driving down the price of beef. The remainder of March in eastern Scotland was "stormy in the extreme; in consequence of which . . . very little ploughing was got done." April was cold and dry. Virtually nothing was growing by the beginning of May: "Even on the coast, there is yet no appearance of vegetation." Conditions improved little in May. "Throughout the whole of this month," noted a report from Midlothian, just south of Edinburgh, "the weather has been unusually barren, from a continued cold, sharp, dry wind, generally from the north. . . . The fields, in general, are backward and in great want of warm sun, especially the grass and wheat, which is near a month later than ordinary, and are weak and unpromising at present."

Across most of western and central Europe, spring was lost in the waves of cold weather that swept over the continent in April and May. Travelers to Calais in mid-April encountered a storm that brought "a considerable quantity of snow" to northern France. In the Abruzzo region of central Italy, farms in the higher elevations still had so much snow on the ground in late May that farmers could not sow their wheat, and the price of grain was rising. There were late frosts in Austria, and the stormy winter and cold spring already had created a shortage of grain and higher prices in south-western Germany, as well.

On May 12, sleet pelted English fields and towns. "Never was there such a backward season," muttered the English reformer and part-time farmer William Cobbett. "The extreme changeableness of the weather which has prevailed so long, still continues," reported the *Royal Cornwall Gazette*. "Every flattering prospect of genial warmth has been quickly succeeded throughout the spring, with the reverse of a chilling and searching, or damp atmosphere." Particularly in northern England, oats had "a yellow and unhealthy appearance," and wheat looked so sickly that many farmers simply ploughed up their fields and resowed their lands with barley. Pastures and meadows seemed barren and backward. "Such an ungenial season has necessarily been unfavorable to all the production of the earth," concluded the *Gazette*, "giving the assurance of a late harvest, so full of risk and experience in the northern parts."

This news did not please Lord Liverpool, the prime minister, an unimaginative, no-nonsense Tory who had led His Majesty's Government since the assassination of his predecessor, Spencer Perceval, in 1812. "Led" perhaps was too strong a word; Liverpool, whom Benjamin Disraeli later referred to as "the arch-mediocrity," was the titular head only of the Conservative Party. His subordinates, including Foreign Secretary Lord Castlereagh, regularly took turns usurping his authority.

Royal authority was exercised in 1816 by the Prince Regent, the eldest son of King George III, although the king was still alive. Beginning with a brief attack in 1765, George III experienced periodic bouts of madness that appear to have been the result of porphyria, a rare blood disorder. His symptoms included delusions, hallucinations, severe abdominal pains, insomnia, confusion, and muscular weakness. His physicians' inability to determine the cause of his illness, and their understandable reluctance to hazard a guess about the likelihood of any recovery, had contributed to a constitutional crisis when the king suffered a second, prolonged attack in 1788. Parliament waited more than six months for George to recover; finally the House of Commons passed a Regency Act to transfer authority to the Prince of Wales. But as the Lords debated the measure, the king suddenly and unexpectedly recovered, and remained in good health until the next attack in 1801. A fifth and final attack in 1810 convinced parliamentary leaders to approve another measure to permit the Prince of Wales to rule in place of the seventy-two-year-old monarch, although fleeting glimpses of sanity in the first year or two kept alive hopes of the king's eventual recovery.

By January 1816, his doctors had given up hope. "It is the opinion of the medical gentlemen attending him," read their official statement to the public, "that nothing far short of a miracle can bring about a recovery from his afflicting malady." For the remainder of his life, George III resided in a suite of thirteen rooms in Windsor Castle. Although the king initially enjoyed walking on the terrace around the castle, by 1816 he was virtually blind and no longer ventured outside, although his coterie of attendants still dressed him every day for dinner (roast beef on Sundays) at 1:30 in the afternoon.

The Prince Regent, meanwhile, had achieved a well-deserved reputation as an indolent gambler and womanizer who ran up immense debts. One newspaper estimated that by March 1815, the Prince Regent had accumulated debts worth 1,480,600 pounds sterling during his lifetime. He also was known as a heavy drinker in an age when London gentlemen routinely consumed four or five bottles of port in a single evening. Not surprisingly, he suffered severely from gout. Whenever he wished to ride a horse, the Prince Regent sat in a special chair fitted with rollers, which was wheeled up a ramp to a platform; then a horse was passed underneath, and the prince was lowered gently into the saddle.

Partly to assuage parliamentary anxieties about his numerous illicit liaisons, and partly as the price of a deal with Parliament to pay off part of his debts, the prince had married Princess Caroline of Brunswick in 1795. They took an instant dislike to each other, and separated soon after the birth of their only child, Charlotte, a year later.

Before he assumed his father's authority, the prince had befriended Whig politicians, largely because they were not his father's friends. Once he became the Prince Regent, however, he aligned himself firmly with the Tory party, and with Liverpool's ministry from 1812. If that did not make the government more popular, the successful prosecution of the war against Napoléon did.

Nevertheless, Liverpool entered 1816 facing a host of problems as Britain made the transition from war to a peacetime economy. A trade recession caused in part by the termination of wartime contracts forced numerous businesses to cut wages or lay off workers, and others to declare bankruptcy. The ranks of the unemployed swelled further as the government rapidly demobilized the army, throwing more than a third of a million more men into the labor market. "The nation," wrote one observer, "was in the condition of a man who, after struggling with some deadly fever, has crept out of the contest, bankrupt of energy."

Although British farmers enjoyed a bountiful harvest in 1815, grain prices remained relatively high due to the Corn Laws which Parliament had passed at the end of the year. (In the early nineteenth century, the British used *corn* as a generic term for grain.)

These measures, hotly debated and greatly resented by English liberals at the time, prohibited the importation of foreign wheat unless the price of domestic grain fell below a specified price. They were intended to protect English landowners, especially those who had brought marginal lands under cultivation during the recent war, when Napoléon denied Britain its normal sources of supply on the continent. The government feared that if it removed these price supports, grain prices would plummet and landowners, tenant farmers, and rural laborers alike would suffer ruin. Given that most English voters—and even more certainly most Members of Parliament—belonged to the landowning class, repeal of the Corn Laws seemed unlikely for the foreseeable future.

Yet a high price for wheat wrought great hardship on the urban working classes. In normal times, a poor laboring family might spend half its meager income on food, primarily bread. When harvests failed or other disasters caused the price of grain to rise, workers found themselves hard-pressed to purchase enough food to survive, never mind spending on clothes or other manufactured goods. The same logic dampened the spending of middle-class consumers as well, which exacerbated the trade recession.

Parliament, meanwhile, kept howling for the government to cut spending and reduce taxes now that the war had come to a successful conclusion. "The main root of the evil is in the taxes," grumbled a typical landowner, and hundreds of petitions poured into Parliament to abolish the income tax which had been passed as a wartime emergency measure. "Economy is more the order of the day than war ever was," complained Lord Castlereagh in early 1816. "Endless debates upon economy and a sour, discontented temper among our friends." It was, Castlereagh informed the Duke of Wellington, "one of the most disagreeable political experiences through which he had ever passed." The foreign secretary found it necessary to trim his European policies to fit a British public reluctant to spend any money in peacetime on continental affairs. As one observer has noted, "With Napoléon safely locked away in Saint Helena, the great majority of English people were completely indifferent to what went on in Europe."

Parliament did, however, manage to find funds for the wedding of Princess Charlotte of Wales, the Prince Regent's only legitimate child (and therefore the heir apparent), and Prince Leopold of Saxe-Coburg, who were married in London on May 2. In the spring of 1816, Charlotte enjoyed far more popularity with the British public than her father, especially after she rejected an arranged marriage with the Prince of Orange, who was nearly as dissolute as the Prince Regent. The House of Commons granted the couple an income of 60,000 pounds sterling per year, plus 40,000 pounds for furnishing their house, an additional 10,000 pounds for the princess's wardrobe, and another 10,000 pounds for her new jewelry. (One disgruntled critic pointed out that Saxe-Coburg would "drain the people of England of a sum more than eight times as much as the President of the United States of America receives from the people of that country, for attending to all their affairs, and presiding as the Chief Magistrate of a vast and free country, containing ten millions of people.") The gifts may have compensated Charlotte for the enmity of her father; it was said that the Prince Regent disliked her primarily because she was the daughter of his wife.

Four days later, a riot broke out in the town of Bridport, in West Dorset. Angered by the combination of high rural unemployment and a fifty percent increase in the price of wheat since January, a mob smashed the windows of several bakers and millers. On May 16, a similar disturbance occurred more than 200 miles away in Bury St. Edmunds, forcing the sheriff of Suffolk to rush to London to beg the home secretary for troops.

Disorder quickly spread throughout East Anglia. The population of the region had swelled during wartime; now the return of demobilized soldiers coincided with the demise of the cottage spinning industry to produce widespread joblessness. In some villages, the unemployment rate reached 50 percent. For those fortunate enough to find work, wages sometimes sank to the pitifully low rate of three to four shillings per week. The rioters typically demanded higher wages and cheaper food—wheat at half a crown a bushel, and a pound of choice meat at fourpence—and often targeted labor-saving farm machinery, such as threshing machines, for destruction.

One group of demonstrators in Norfolk, reportedly numbering about fifteen hundred, armed themselves with bludgeons studded with short iron spikes, and hoisted a flag with the legend "Bread or Blood" before smashing the windows of shops and the homes of the gentry. They wrecked farm machinery and broke into mills and carried away sacks of flour, some of which (in a fit of absence of mind) they dumped into the river. A mob in Norwich destroyed as much property as they could with axes, shovels, spades, and saws before the militia arrived; then they stoned the soldiers.

On May 22, hundreds of villagers—some of whom were quite inebriated—gathered at the Globe Inn in Littleport, Cambridge-shire, and commenced to rampage through the streets. They began by plundering the house of a magistrate, proceeded to empty the cellars of public houses, and carried on by robbing wealthier residents (many of whom fled for their lives), demolishing their furniture, and hurling less portable possessions into the street. The following day the mob moved on to the town of Ely, where they demanded amnesty and a minimum wage tied to the price of flour. The local magistrates initially consented, and provided beer to the demonstrators as a token of good faith. But a small group of rioters returned to Littleport and resumed their depredations. When a detachment of royal dragoons and a troop of yeoman cavalry appeared to subdue them, the rioters barricaded themselves in the George and Dragon Inn. After a brief sort of skirmish in which one rioter was shot dead, the rest surrendered. More than eighty people were arrested; twenty-four were convicted, and five were hanged.

Alarmed, nearby villages began swearing in special constables, and the authorities in Cambridge briefly considered arming university students to help defend the town. Neither they nor Liverpool's government in London had any way of knowing that the British economy—already battered by a trade recession and rising unemployment—would soon suffer the shock of a disastrous growing season that would send the price of bread soaring even higher, and further fuel the discontent of the poorer classes.

3.

COLD FRONTS

"The most gloomy and extraordinary weather ever seen . . ."

MAY DAWNED COLD and dry over the northeastern United States and eastern Canada. A news report from Quebec described "large quantities of snow" in the fields, ice in the St. Lawrence River, and a hard frost on the evening of May 2. In Maine it seemed as if winter had returned, and parts of New York State were still covered with six or more inches of snow. The *New York Evening Post* blamed the frigid temperatures on "the unusual long spell of cold westerly winds which have prevailed since the spring set in. . . . Vegetation at this season of the year was never more backward."

Soon things got worse. On May 12, strong winds swirling down from Canada brought snow and freezing temperatures to New England, killing the buds and leaves on fruit trees. Two days later, Albany, New York, reported that "the ground was covered with snow, and the temperature of the weather during the day more like that of March than May. Rarely has vegetation been

more backward at this season of the year than it is now in this city."
Residents of Trenton, New Jersey, awoke to find a "heavy black
frost" that had frozen the ground half an inch deep.

On May 14, the cold wave struck crops in Virginia (the *National Register* reported frost in the vicinity of Richmond), and by
one account reached as far south as Tennessee, ruining substantial
quantities of cotton. The severe cold exacerbated the effects of a
prolonged drought throughout the mid-Atlantic and Southern
states, a highly unusual occurrence at that time of year. In Virginia,
the *Norfolk Beacon* reported that farmers were "ploughing up and
re-planting the corn. The temperature of the weather with us
is very fluctuating—the evenings and mornings generally so cold as
to render a fire quite agreeable." As the cold persisted, ice formed
nearly an inch thick on rivers and ponds from Maine to Buffalo.
"The season continues extremely unfavorable to Agriculture,"
mused a Quebec correspondent. "Masses of snow still lie in the
fields, and very little wheat has yet been sown in this district."

Seasonably warm temperatures returned on May 19, but only
briefly. Nine days later, another front swept down upon Quebec
from the northwest, bringing more snow and leaving ice a quarter
of an inch thick. As the cold advanced through New England, it
killed corn in the fields in central Maine. Snow fell in Vermont;
the "remarkable cold" froze the ground an inch deep. Cattle could
not forage in the pastures, and farmers had to use part of their
corn supplies as fodder. "The last spring and the present," noted
the *New England Palladium*, "are certainly the most backward of
any for the last 25 years." Again the frost reached as far south as
Richmond, and as far west as Cincinnati, where blossoms shriveled
on the fruit trees.

David Thomas, a farmer in Cayuga County, New York, left his
home on May 21 on a journey to explore the lands along the Wabash River in the territory of Indiana, which had recently applied
to Congress for admission as a state. As he departed, Thomas
wrote in his journal that "the season has been unusually cold, and

vegetation proportionally retarded." Two days later, he noted that "the morning was rainy, cold, and uncomfortable, with wind from the north," the sort of wind by which "our deepest snows have been borne along." As he approached the town of Buffalo, he felt a breeze "so damp and chill that instantly we stopt, and put on our great coats." The following morning (May 25), "was so cold that we shivered in a winter dress, with great coats and gloves." According to local residents, the spring had been so frigid that the ice along the shore of Lake Erie had disappeared only five days earlier.

Conditions did not improve as Thomas continued westward. He found Chautauqua Lake "wrapt in the drapery of winter," and a cold rain delayed him for three hours as he neared the border with Pennsylvania on May 28. "This morning was very frosty," he wrote in his journal on May 29, "and ice covered the water one-fourth of an inch thick." A brisk breeze from the northeast convinced Thomas to don his great coat again. The next morning he observed "a severe frost"; then "the clouds rolled on heavily to the eastward, and portentously to those who have neither home nor shelter."

"When the last of May arrived," wrote a Maine chronicler, "everything had been killed by the cold," although not much had been planted anyway. "The whole of the month has been so cold and wet," complained New Hampshire farmer Adino Brackett, "that wheat could not be sown 'til late and then the ground could not be well prepared." "Everybody complains of the present 'strange weather; this unnatural weather; this unseasonable weather,'" noted the *Chambersburg* [Pennsylvania] *Democratic Republican*. Spring was "at least a month later than usual." Instead of the usual warm, nourishing showers of April and May, the Eastern United States was experiencing "general aridity, the mountains are covered with snow, the valleys with ice, and the fruits of the earth are stunted and withered. Weather-wise people are at a loss to account for this 'strange weather.'"

* * *

PARIS, too, shivered through a cold and wet springtime, but in May 1816 Louis XVIII appeared to face considerably more pressing problems than the dreary weather. Following Napoléon's defeat at Waterloo, the Allied sovereigns had reinstalled the corpulent Louis on the throne of France; critics jibed that he had been "brought back in the baggage of the Allies." But they also had imposed upon Louis the stringent terms of the second Treaty of Paris. France was reduced to its borders of January 1790, which meant the loss of about 5,000 square kilometers and 300,000 citizens; the French people would also have to repay all foreign debts incurred by previous French governments—including, of course, Napoléon's. Far more damaging were the reparations France would have to pay the Allied victors: 700 million francs over a period of five years, plus the entire cost of feeding and sheltering an Allied occupation force of 150,000 (stationed mostly in eastern France) for at least three years. Adding the annual costs of the indemnity and the occupation troops to the regular budget, Louis's government in the spring of 1816 was facing short-term obligations of nearly 1,500 million francs, a sum which would require both substantial tax increases and cuts in government spending.

Compounding Louis's financial woes was the presence of a zealously reactionary Ultra-Royalist majority in the Chamber of Deputies. Led by the Count d'Artois—the king's brother, who was barely on speaking terms with Louis—the Ultra-Royalists were determined to seek out and punish the "accomplices" of Napoléon, and especially his most vocal supporters during the Hundred Days. Famously "more royalist than the king," the Ultras knew they could not count on the indolent Louis (whom they privately mocked as "a crowned Jacobin, a King-Voltaire, a dressed-up comedian") to carry out a thoroughgoing purge of French society. Accordingly, in late October 1815 the Chamber seized the initiative and passed the first of a series of measures that launched the "White Terror," authorizing the arrest of individuals suspected of plotting against the restored monarchy, and the establishment of special courts to try them.

Doubtless the results disappointed the deputies. Authentic antiroyalist conspiracies were few and far between. "There are continual reports of insurrections and plots," reported a British military officer in Paris in the spring of 1816, "but it is now well known that the most of them are 'got up' by the Ultras to entrap the unwary. The French people seem sunk in apathy and to wish for peace at any rate; nothing but the most extreme provocation will induce them to take up arms." Meanwhile, the clergy sought to restore the Roman Catholic Church to its privileged pre-Revolutionary position, including the return of real estate that formerly belonged to the Church. Priests whipped up popular sentiment against the alleged enemies of the Church, reportedly forging communications from the Holy Ghost or claiming to have received letters dropped from heaven by Jesus. The result was a series of attacks by Catholic mobs on Protestants, particularly in the south of France; in Nimes, a mob massacred sixteen Protestants during a two-day riot.

Such tactics succeeded mainly in arousing anxiety among the populace, most of whom were willing to tolerate Louis but opposed any attempt to resurrect the Ancien Régime, particularly if it meant returning real estate to the Church. Fearful that the vengeful actions of obdurate reactionaries would alienate the French public to the point of threatening his throne yet again, Louis and his ministers repeatedly opposed the majority in the Chamber, until the nation was treated to the spectacle of Ultra-Royalists defending the prerogatives of the legislature against the king. After beating back an Ultra attempt to abolish divorce, the government at last decided to prorogue the Chamber. On April 29, the king declared the legislative session closed, and his ministers began to plan for new elections in the fall.

A week later, a lawyer named Jean-Paul Didier launched an abortive uprising in Grenoble that collapsed almost before it began. Supported by a force of several hundred peasants and retired soldiers, Didier purportedly sought to overthrow Louis and replace him with Napoléon's infant son, the King of Rome. Government troops easily quashed the feeble uprising and executed twenty-one alleged conspirators, including a sixteen-year-old boy; Didier, who fled to Savoy, was subsequently captured and executed on June 8. Meanwhile, the police in Paris claimed to have uncovered another plot, this one led by a small group of working men.

To make matters worse, the price of bread was rising due to a shortage of grain from the war and the need to provision the Allied army of occupation. Well aware that he could ill afford to alienate the poor of Paris, who depended upon cheap bread, Louis issued an ordinance permitting foreign vessels to import grain without paying the usual duties. Then he hoped for a plentiful harvest.

"The uneasiness of the court is indescribable," reported an American correspondent in Paris, "the palace at night may be said to exhibit the aspect of a camp or of a besieged palace. A double line of guards surround it on all sides." Patrols of gendarmes and the national guard kept watch in every street; coffee houses were cleared at 11 P.M. The London *Star* reported that ships bound for the United States from French harbors were full of prospective émigrés. "There was a strange feeling of unrest in the country," concluded one observer, "and there were rumours of the return of Napoléon and of the massacre of nobles and priests."

WHEN Mary Wollstonecraft Godwin arrived in Paris on May 8, she found her French hosts less than congenial. "The manners of the French are interesting, although less attractive, at least to Englishmen, than before the last invasion of the Allies," she wrote to a friend; "the discontent and sullenness of their minds perpetually betrays itself." Doubtless their resentment stemmed from the humiliation of 150,000 foreign troops on French soil, but Mary saw no reason why "they should regard the subjects of a Government which fills their country with hostile garrisons, and sustains a detested dynasty on the throne, with an acrimony and indignation of which that Government alone is the proper object."

Mary was traveling with her lover, Percy Bysshe Shelley, their infant son, William, and her stepsister, Claire (nee Clara Mary Jane) Clairmont. Nineteen years old in the spring of 1816, Mary Godwin had met Shelley in 1813, and the two fell in love at once. The daughter of William Godwin, a writer notorious for his free thinking and philosophical anarchism—Godwin believed advancing human knowledge and morality would eventually render government obsolete—and noted feminist Mary Wollstonecraft (who died shortly after Mary was born), Mary grew up reading widely in the works of the *philosophes*, poets William Blake and Samuel Coleridge, and, of course, her parents.

For his part, Shelley was a child of privilege who attended Oxford until the authorities expelled him for his public defense of atheism. In 1811, at the age of nineteen, he had married Harriet Wentworth, then only sixteen herself. Shelley soon tired of monogamy and began to spend much of his time at the home of William Godwin, whose philosophy he admired and whose daughter he subsequently pursued. When he learned that his daughter had fallen in love with a married man, Godwin decided to fall back upon conventional morality and forbade Mary to see Shelley. In late July 1814, the lovers ran off to Europe. By the time they returned in early 1815, Mary was pregnant. The child, born premature, lived only eleven days; Mary later dreamed she could bring her daughter back to life.

Burdened by financial problems and wounded by the critical dismissal of an early poem, "Alastor: Or, the Spirit of Solitude," published in February 1816, Shelley decided to leave England. Accordingly, he and Mary (accompanied by Claire and three-month-old William) crossed the Channel in early May. Originally Shelley had planned to visit either Italy or Scotland, but Claire—who recently had become the lover of George Gordon, Lord Byron—convinced them to stay in Geneva instead, because that was where Byron would spend the summer. Shelley agreed; at least the cost of living in Geneva was lower than in England.

Their journey by coach from Paris to Geneva took them across the Jura Mountains; Shelley, like Mary, did not regret leaving France and the "discontent and sullenness" of Frenchmen. The weather in the middle of May was far worse than Mary expected. "The spring, as the inhabitants informed us, was unusually late," she wrote to a friend, "and indeed the cold was excessive; as we ascended the mountains the same clouds which rained on us in the valleys poured forth large flakes of snow thick and fast." Initially the snow stuck only to the overhanging rocks, but as the coach climbed higher it started to freeze on the road.

Evening fell; the party pressed on, snow pelting against the carriage windows as darkness descended. Then Mary could see Lake Geneva and, far in the distance, the Alps. "Never was scene more awfully desolate," she noted. "The trees in these regions are incredibly large, and stand in scattered clumps over the white wilderness; the vast expanse of snow was chequered only by these gigantic pines, and the poles that marked our road."

They settled in a secluded villa known as the Maison Chapuis, a pleasant if humble two-story cottage on the south edge of the lake, facing what Mary termed the "dark frowning" Jura range. On the infrequent evenings that were pleasant and clear, they would sail upon the lake. "Unfortunately," complained Mary in early June, "an almost perpetual rain confines us principally to the house. . . . The thunderstorms that visit us are grander and more terrific than I have ever seen before." One night a brilliant streak of lightning lit up the lake, "the pines on Jura made visible, and all the scene illuminated for an instant, when a pitchy blackness succeeded, and the thunder came in frightful bursts over our heads amid the darkness."

As a member of a consortium of New England college professors who regularly made weather observations, Professor Chester Dewey of Williams College kept a thermometer suspended on the north side of his house, well protected from the sun. Three times a day (7 A.M., 2 P.M., and 9 P.M.), Dewey noted and recorded the temperatures, deducing the mean temperature each day from his observations. In the first few days of June, Dewey noticed the temperatures fluctuating wildly, as if on a roller coaster. June 1 and 2 were quite warm; the following two days were much cooler. June 5 brought sweltering heat: At noon Dewey's thermometer soared to 83 degrees.

It was not an isolated reading. Montreal reported "hot and sultry" weather on June 5. To the east, Boston experienced a high of 86 degrees; at Waltham, the mercury reached 90 degrees; and at Salem, 92 degrees. The *Vermont Mirror* reported from Middlebury that June 5 was "the warmest day that has here been experienced during the season," and the *Rutland Herald* noted "the intense summer's heat."

"The mild influence of the sun," wrote a newspaper editor in eastern Massachusetts, "gave us fond anticipations (tho' our seeds were but just springing out of the ground,) of a plentiful harvest." A wave of thunderstorms passed through in the afternoon, cooling the region briefly before unusually high temperatures returned. At ten o'clock that evening, Albany recorded a temperature of 72 degrees, 15 degrees warmer than the normal overnight low temperature. A reporter in Danville, Vermont, could see heat lightning in the distance. "The night was so warm," noted a resident of Bangor, Maine, "that one blanket was sufficient to keep a person comfortable." Overnight, a steady rain developed.

The warm, humid air and rain in New England preceded a strong low-pressure system that was making its way across the Great Lakes on June 5. In the Northern Hemisphere, the winds around low-pressure systems spiral counterclockwise; as lows move from west to east, the winds drag warm air from the south ahead (i.e., to the east) of the low-pressure centers. When this warm air meets colder air, such as was present across New England on June 3 and 4, the warm air slowly rises, resulting in steady rain and

occasionally in thunderstorms. While these warm fronts are usually benign, lows are often followed by sharp cold fronts, due to
the winds pulling cold air from the north. It is cold fronts that
most often cause thunderstorms and tornadoes, as the sudden in-
flux of cold air causes the existing warm air to rise quickly.

Highly unseasonable, frigid air lurked behind the cold front of
the low that crossed the Great Lakes on June 5. In a weather pattern more typical of winter than summer, a polar high-pressure
system was following the low. In summer, Arctic air is usually
contained north of Hudson Bay by the subpolar jet stream: strong
westerly winds high in the troposphere that effectively form a barrier to weather systems. Occasional southward excursions of this
jet stream in winter can produce frigid, but often clear days across
the Great Plains and Eastern United States. First in May and then
again in June 1816, however, the jet stream dipped far to the south,
forming a U-shape and allowing Arctic air to flow from northern
Canada as far south as the Carolinas. The collision of this air with
the warm, moist air masses that normally prevail in New England
and eastern Canada produced powerful storms.

Limited weather observations from the early nineteenth century and the chaotic nature of the atmosphere make it difficult to
determine with certainty why the jet stream moved so far south.
One explanation is that a broad area of high pressure, a "blocking
high," had developed in late May in the central Atlantic. These
systems impede the normal west-to-east flow of the jet stream,
causing it to shift north and south to avoid the block. The effect
then cascades backwards and forwards along the jet stream in
waves, disrupting the jet stream for thousands of miles in each
direction and forming the type of U-shaped bends that affected
eastern North America in 1816. As with water moving through a
clogged pipe, the block slows the movement of weather systems,
stagnating the weather and allowing extreme conditions to persist
for longer than they might otherwise. A slow, meandering jet stream
is consistent with the impact of Tambora's aerosol cloud on the

North Atlantic Oscillation—a weak polar vortex and frequent in-cursions of Arctic air into the middle latitudes—in the summer of 1816. The aerosol cloud did not necessarily cause the early June storm that struck New England, but the stratospheric veil almost certainly cooled the air behind the storm and set the atmospheric circulation pattern that allowed the air to penetrate so unseason-ably far south.

When the low-pressure center and its trailing cold front passed Lake Erie on June 5, several Royal Navy ships stationed there reported strong northwesterly gales as the polar air rushed in. In New Brunswick, central Ontario, the noontime temperature was only 30 degrees. Thunderstorms formed where the air moving be-hind the cold front began to meet the air brought in by the warm front, bringing heavy rain to western New York and southern On-tario. The low-pressure center continued to move east, while the subpolar jet slipped ever farther south.

Late on the morning of June 6, the cold front and its powerful northwest wind suddenly struck Quebec, turning rain to snow. For more than an hour, snow fell thickly on the city streets. When the sky cleared in the afternoon, residents could see the mountaintops to the north covered with snow, "the most distant apparently to the depth of a foot." Flocks of birds hitherto found only deep in the forest swarmed into the city in search of warmth, "and were to be met with in every street," reported the *Quebec Gazette*, "and even among the shipping. Many of them dropped down dead in the streets, and many were destroyed by thoughtless or cruel persons. The swallows entirely disappeared for several days." In the country-side, newly shorn sheep perished from the cold.

That night the ground around Quebec froze; the following day the thermometer never rose above freezing, and more snow fell. With the summer solstice less than two weeks away, "the roofs of the houses, the streets and squares of the town, were completely covered with snow," observed the *Quebec Gazette*. On the morning of June 8, "the whole of the surrounding country was in the same state, having . . . the appearance of the middle of December." More snow fell that day, and more on June 9. An unfortunate traveler about a dozen miles outside of Quebec struggled to plow through snowdrifts that rose up to the axletrees of his carriage. Every night the ground froze, and the wind continued to blow strongly from the northwest, "driving before it an immense mass of lowering clouds, which constantly concealed the sun." When the sun finally returned on June 10, the land west of the Chaudière River was still covered with snow, in some places about a foot deep.

Montreal received less snow, but on June 7 "the frost was sharp, ice as thick as a dollar [coin], which has injured tender as well as hardy plants." Since wheat farmers already had planted much of their supply of seeds, the *Montreal Herald* advised its readers to share their dwindling supplies with their poorer neighbors—and plant as many potatoes as possible, in case the wheat crop failed completely. "Early this morning some snow fell," the *Herald* noted on June 8, "and the frost was as severe as on yesterday morning."

As the low-pressure system tracked across New England on June 6 and 7, the cold front caused temperatures to drop by 30 degrees or more and the winds shifted from mild southwesterlies to gale-force northwesterlies. With Quebec and Montreal already enveloped in snow, a second band of precipitation—first rain, then snow—formed south of the Saint Lawrence River and spread from west to east. In Danville, Vermont, a piercing, cold wind made it seem like November. Snow and occasionally hail began around 10 A.M. on June 6 and continued until evening. "Probably no one living in the country ever witnessed such weather," claimed the Danville *North Star,* "especially of so long continuance." A heavy snow fell in and around Waterbury, about twenty miles north of Montpelier, but much of it melted as it hit the ground, which was still near its normal summer temperature. In the hills outside of Middlebury, however, the snow piled up three inches deep, and Rutland presented "a novel spectacle, to see the ground covered with snow on the 6th of June, and the Green Mountains whitened with the same for two or three successive days." Some Vermont farmers who had recently shorn their sheep reportedly attempted to tie the fleeces back on the unfortunate animals, but many froze to death anyway. As in Quebec, wild birds flew into barns and houses to flee the cold; "you could pick up numbed hummingbirds, yellow birds, martins, and 'scarlet sparrows' in your hand," recalled one writer, "and many were found dead in the fields."

At Bennington, a farmer named Benjamin Harwood noted in his diary that "it had rained much during the night and this morning [June 6] the wind blew exceedingly high from NE, raining copiously, chilling and sharp gusts." It began to snow about 8 A.M., and continued desultorily until early afternoon until about an inch and a half lay on the ground. By the time it was done, "the heads of all the mountains on every side were crowned with snow," and five of his family's sheep had been lost in the storm. It was, Harwood concluded, "the most gloomy and extraordinary weather ever seen."

Snow commenced in Bangor between two and three o'clock in the afternoon. It fell "in beautiful large flakes," by one account, "some of which as they struck the ground covered spots two inches [in] diameter," continuing for an hour and a half. The oversized flakes were likely due to the very moist, summertime air that the low-pressure system had pulled up from the Gulf of Mexico. From Jackson, Maine, came a report that June 6 brought "a violent and heavy storm from the west North West, blowing very hard, accompanied with heavy cold rain and snow." If the precipitation had consisted entirely of rain, it might have totaled six inches or more.

A group of men in Sanbornton, New Hampshire, began the day by assembling timber to build a new schoolhouse. As the cold front passed through, they blew on their hands to keep warm, then stamped their feet and flapped their arms against their sides, and finally cursed the cold as a band of snow forced them back indoors. Eighty miles to the north, bricklayers in the town of Bath quit working on a brick house because their mortar froze. In Waterford, Maine, one elderly gentleman spent the day chopping wood with a heavy coat on, the snow flying in squalls around him.

At Concord, New Hampshire, recently elected Governor William Plumer delivered his inaugural address on the afternoon of June 6 at the local meetinghouse. "The wind blew a gale, with an occasional shower of snowflakes," recalled one member of the audience. During the ceremonies, "our teeth fairly chattered in our heads, and our feet and hands were benumbed." As the guests departed town that evening, gusts of wind threatened to overturn their carriages as they crossed Concord Bridge, and when they reached their hotel "we shivered round a rousing fire, complaining of the cold room."

Throughout New York State, towns at higher elevations reported heavy snow and freezing temperatures on June 6. In Elizabethtown, about 130 miles north of Albany, the rain changed to snow around seven thirty in the morning and continued for three hours, followed by flurries on a strong westerly wind. "The severity of the cold was such as to freeze the ground," read one report, "and destroy most of the garden vegetables." Travelers who made it into Albany from the west that day reported a storm "as severe from half an hour to an hour." At Geneva, "a considerable quantity of snow fell," and the Catskill Mountains in the southeastern part of the state were covered in snow.

At Williamstown, where it snowed on and off on June 6, Professor Dewey saw that "on the mountain to the west . . . the ground was white with snow—travelers complained of the severity of the N.W. wind and snowstorm." Residents of the Berkshires found enough snow to go sledding. Waltham also received snow, strong wind, and rain. In Boston, the mercury dropped forty degrees in less than a day, and snow flurries swirled through the city.

When residents of Waterbury, New York, arose on the morning of June 7, they found ice everywhere. "The situation here, as in other parts of the country, has been uncommonly cold," noted one correspondent. "But this morning, at 6 o'clock, the thermometer was at 30. Ice three-eighths of an inch thick—and at this moment, 12 o'clock (at noon) ice still in the shade."

Temperatures hovered around freezing across most of New England on June 7. Towns across Vermont reported ice between half-an-inch and one-inch thick on shallow ponds. "The surface of the ground was stiff with frost," reported Harwood. "The leaves of the trees blackened . . . snow remained on Sandgate and Manchester Mountain past noon or as late as that. Wind extremely high night & day and the cold abated but little in the P.M. . . . Mended fences with greatcoat and mittens on."

In the Hudson Valley, vegetables were entirely destroyed by frost; in Middlebury, the cold and wind wreaked severe damage on fruit trees. "I well remember the 7th of June," wrote Chauncey Jerome, a clockmaker in Plymouth, Connecticut, years later. "While on my way to work, about a mile from home, dressed throughout with thick woolen clothes and an overcoat on, my hands got so cold that I was obliged to lay down my tools and put on a pair of mittens which I had in my pocket." Maine farmers who chose to contribute their labor maintaining county roads in lieu of paying local taxes also found it necessary to don overcoats and mittens.

A severe frost destroyed nearly all the corn planted in Jackson, Maine, about fifty miles north of Augusta. "In the evening," wrote a correspondent, "the atmosphere [was] so intensely cold, that the small birds, our annual visitors from the southward, sought for shelter in people's homes and barns, many of them, with the Swallows have been found starved and frozen to death." The frozen ground also helped kill recently sheared sheep who could find no forage—"the fields as bare of herbage, as usually in the month of November, and the verdure of the forest has the appearance of Fall instead of Summer."

Crops in Massachusetts also suffered damage. Professor Dewey reported that the ground in Williamstown remained frozen. "Moist earth was frozen half inch thick, and could be raised from round Indian corn [maize], the corn slipping through and standing unhurt. Had not the wind made the vegetables very dry, it is not improbable that they would have been frozen also."

Cold and frost extended all the way down to New York City. "This morning, the 7th of June, we are told there was ice on this island," declared a Manhattan newspaper. "Yesterday and to-day our thermometer stood at 50 within doors, the wind is gale and air much colder without; and in the garden we found the vegetables changed in their appearance, and we fear much injured."

As darkness fell on June 7, another storm brought more snow. This time Vermont sustained a direct hit. Accompanied by bitterly cold winds, snow and sleet began falling Friday night and continued until noon. The town of Cabot received between a foot and eighteen inches of snow, and nearby Montpelier nearly a foot. Drifts outside of Danville piled up to twenty inches. "The awful scene continued," wrote Benjamin Harwood grimly. "Sweeping blasts from north all the forepart of the day, with light snow squalls."

On the morning of June 8, temperatures at or just below freezing combined with wind speeds near 30 miles per hour to produce wind chills of 10 degrees. "Still uncomfortably cold, squally, and blustering," read one Vermont news report. "Winter fires, and winter groups around them." Farmers donned mittens to work in the fields; others found that the ground was frozen too solid to work at all. One farmer built a fire near his field of corn and enlisted help in keeping it going every night, to keep his crop from freezing. "6th, snowed in considerable quantities," wrote Adino Brackett, a New Hampshire farmer and teacher, in his diary. "7th also snow. 8th snow. This is beyond anything of the kind I have ever known."

Snow was reported on the hills outside Amherst, Massachusetts, in the town of Salem, and on the high ground around East Windsor, Connecticut. A traveler who came through western Massachusetts saw "large icicles pending, and the foliage of the forests was blasted by the frost." A Boston newspaper announced that "snow fell in this town on Saturday [June 8]; and at Wiscasset, and other places, it snowed for several hours in succession. The occurrence is uncommon . . ."

"I can find no person who has ever before seen snow on the earth in June," claimed a correspondent in Waterbury, Vermont. "This part of the country I assure you presents a most dreary aspect; great-coats and mittens are almost as generally worn as in January; and fire is indispensible." The Danville *North Star* agreed. "The weather was more severe [on June 8] than it generally is during the storms of winter. It was indeed a gloomy and tedious period."

As the low-pressure system finally began to move out to sea, the subpolar high became entrenched across New England and southern Quebec and Ontario. The high drove Arctic air deep into the valleys, from which it would not be easily extracted. Across Maine, it snowed for three hours on the morning of June 8. The following day temperatures rose slightly, "but still frost and ice—the wind still blowing from N.N.W. and remarkably cold for the season." Anyone traveling even a short distance needed greatcoats and mittens. Another "most severe frost" struck Maine on the morning of June 10, "that destroyed the blossoms and even leaves of the apple trees in certain directions, accompanied with ice . . . thicker in proportion, than any night last winter." As he began to plant his corn that day (considerably later than usual), Joshua Whitman, a farmer in central Maine, noticed numerous birds dead in the fields from the cold. "It has frozen very hard for four nights past," he wrote. "The ground freezes and is raised by the frost."

In Middlebury, Vermont, the morning of Sunday, June 9 was "severely cold and . . . the mountains, not more than two miles east of this village, were completely covered with snow." News accounts reported icicles nearly a foot long. Moved by the extraordinary weather to an excess of poetic sentiment, the *Vermont Mirror* claimed that "the very face of nature still appears to be shrouded in a death like gloom, and as she weeps, which well she may, for the barrenness of her fields and for the chilling blasts that whistle through her locks from an unpropicious [sic] clime, her tears freeze fast to her cheeks as they are seen to flow."

Farther south, visitors to Salem, Massachusetts, found ice in the well at the toll house on the turnpike on the morning of June 9, and frost again in the evening. Fearing the worst for his congregation in South Windsor, Connecticut—and for his own crops—the Reverend Thomas Robbins decided to preach a sermon that morning on the parable of the Barren Fig Tree (Luke 13: 6–9): "A certain man had a fig tree planted in his vineyard; and he came seeking fruit on it, and found none." Two days later, Robbins concluded that the corn in his fields had been "killed to the ground."

"Another frost, cold day," noted Benjamin Harwood in his diary on June 10, "indeed obliged to thrash our hands while hoeing." Harwood's corn, which had emerged less than a week earlier, was "badly killed—difficult to see it—gloomy weather." Professor Dewey, too, recorded a severe frost on June 10: "Indian corn, beans, cucumbers, and the like, cut down." The morning temperature in Malone, New York, dipped to 24 degrees, the coldest temperature recorded during the entire storm. Even towns along the New England coast reported below-freezing temperatures for eight of the first twelve nights in June, and the snow flurries that swirled into Boston on June 7–8 were the latest recorded seasonal instance of snowfall in the city's history.

David Thomas was in Pittsburgh, Pennsylvania, when the cold front arrived on June 6. "For three days we had brisk gales from the north-west, of unusual severity for summer," he wrote in his journal. "The surface of the rivers was rolled into foam, and each night was attended by considerable frost." As Thomas made his way through the farmlands of Washington County the following week, he encountered extensive orchards of apple and peach trees, "but the fruit has been chiefly destroyed by the late frosts"—the only year it had failed in the past decade. The orchards in southeastern Ohio fared no better; the frosts of June 6–10 left them nearly barren of fruit. "We saw neither peaches nor apples till we approached this [Little Miami] river; and, indeed even here, these fruits are scarce. Dead leaves, in tufts, are hanging on the papaw, and on most other trees—the first growth of this spring having been entirely destroyed. This remark will apply to much of the state where we travelled."

When warmer weather finally returned late on June 11 (following another frost in the morning), farmers took stock of the cold wave's cost. "The trees on the sides of the hills, whose young leaves were killed by the frost, presented for miles the appearance of having been burned or scorched," wrote Chester Dewey. "The same appearance was visible through the country—in parts, at least, of Connecticut—and also, on many parts of Long Island, as I was told by a gentleman of undoubted veracity, who had visited the island." From Dutchess County in the Hudson Valley came a warning that "the crops of wheat and rye, in this county, which are usually so abundant are almost entirely destroyed." In Albany, the editor of the *Daily Advertiser* feared that "great damage has been done by the frosts, which have been so severe as to make ice of considerable thickness. . . . The prospect to the farmer, as far as we have heard in the country, is, at present, very gloomy."

Maine farmers reported corn crops "totally destroyed . . . and even of the sheep that had been shorn, many perished," even though they had been sheltered in barns. In Portland, the *Eastern Argus* reported that "a check is given to all vegetation, and we fear the frost has been so powerful as to destroy a great portion of the young fruit that is put forth." Central Maine suffered significant damage to fruit blossoms, and "in some instances the corn is totally destroyed, the plant being frozen to the seed; in most places it has been cut off to the surface of the ground," although residents hoped it could still sprout again.

"What is to become of this country, it is impossible to divine—distressing beyond description," wrote a correspondent from Jackson. "Farms that usually cut from Thirty to Forty tons of Hay, by their present appearance will not cut Five, and to all appearance, this part of the Union is going to suffer for bread and everything else." In Worcester, Massachusetts, "expectations have in a measure been blasted . . . and the frost has cut down and destroyed many very valuable fruits of the earth. . . . A destruction of the crops of grain as also of every species of fruit is fearfully anticipated." The *Brattleboro Reporter* agreed that "the most gloomy apprehensions of scarcity are entertained by those who witnessed the phenomena."

To emphasize the unprecedented nature of the cold spell, news reports repeatedly asserted that the oldest living residents in their community could not remember such violent winter storms in the month of June. The *Albany Argus*, for instance, declared that "the weather, during the last week, has exhibited an intensity of cold, not recollected to have been experienced here before in the month of June." In Rutland, Vermont, "the oldest inhabitants in this part of the country do not recollect to have witnessed so cold and unfavorable a season as the present," and in Middlebury, "never before, we are informed, was such an instance known, by even the oldest inhabitants now living amongst us."

In the absence of reliable weather statistics, individual human memory—and the collective recollections of a community—were the only means of comparison to previous seasons. But this method clearly had its limitations; as the editor of the *Albany Daily Advertiser* pointed out, "we are very apt to misrecollect the state of the weather from time to time. Memory is certainly not safely to be relied on relative to this subject, for any great length or time." Hence the *Advertiser* urged that regular journals of weather observations should be kept throughout the nation. "A great mass of useful information might be collected concerning our climate, and seasons," the editorial concluded, "if gentlemen who possess the necessary instruments, would be careful to devote a few minutes in each day to mark the state of the weather, and the temperature of the atmosphere." Even a modest effort on the part of these individuals, the *Advertiser* predicted, would provide data which "would be of great and lasting importance."

A number of Americans (besides Jefferson, of course) already had made sporadic attempts to collect weather statistics in a systematic fashion, although a lack of uniformity in instrumentation and methodology limited the usefulness of their data. In the 1740s, Dr. John Lining—a Scottish-born physician living in Charleston, South Carolina—began tracking changes in the weather with variations in his own physical processes, to try to determine the relationship between climate and public health. "I began these experiments," Lining wrote, "[to] discover the influence of our different seasons upon the human body by which I might arrive at some certain knowledge of the cause of our epidemic diseases which regularly return at their stated seasons as a good clock strikes twelve when the sun is on the meridian." Several other physicians in the United States maintained their own records comparing weather and public health data in the late eighteenth and early nineteenth centuries, but there was little coordination of their efforts.

In 1778, Jefferson succeeded in compiling parallel weather observations between Monticello and the College of William and Mary in Williamsburg, Virginia, courtesy of the president of the college, who agreed to take daily readings of the temperature, winds, and barometric pressure. The effort lasted for only six weeks, however. Although Jefferson persistently encouraged the establishment of a national system of meteorological observation throughout the last decades of his life, the best he could achieve was an occasional exchange of information with like-minded souls in cities from Quebec and Philadelphia to Natchez and London. The closest the nation came to achieving a coordinated program of weather measurements before 1816 was the thrice-daily observation system established by the consortium of New England colleges—notably Middlebury, Williams, Yale, and sometimes Harvard—of which Chester Dewey was a member.

Such an accumulation of concrete statistical details was precisely the sort of empirical scientific task that appealed to Americans in the early nineteenth century. As Gordon Wood has pointed out, Americans were forsaking the Enlightenment's fascination with metaphysical principles and abstract generalities in favor of a harder-edged and utilitarian approach to science. By 1816, science in the United States no longer was the preserve of gentlemen with sufficient leisure to contemplate the moral grandeur of natural laws, or pursue knowledge purely for its own sake. Anyone could gather data (assuming one was armed with the proper measuring instruments), or make sense out of statistics accumulated by others. When introducing his *Picture of Philadelphia*, a detail-laden snapshot of the city published in 1811, physician James Mease declared that "the chief object ought to be the multiplication of facts, and the reflections arising out of them ought to be left to the reader." Americans increasingly believed that these collections of scientific data should serve a useful purpose; the study of chemistry, for instance, should produce better cider, cheese, or methods for marinating meat. Perhaps the compilation of meteorological data might result in more efficient agricultural practices. And if scientific investigations helped Americans in their ceaseless pursuit of material wealth, so much the better.

IN the early nineteenth century, most meteorological instruments in the United States and Europe were owned by gentleman scientists, who collected data for their private diaries or to share with their colleagues in learned societies. Many of the rest of the instruments were located on ships: British Royal Navy vessels, for instance, were required to measure the air temperature, ocean temperature, wind speed and direction, and the fraction of the sky covered by cloud four times a day. (In a testament to British military discipline, navy logbooks reveal that ships continued to make regular readings even when taking enemy fire.) Barometers and thermometers were the most common instruments, having been developed over the previous 150 years. While some of the earliest models provided results of questionable accuracy, by 1816 the designs of both instruments had been refined so that they were able to provide precise and reliable measurements of the atmospheric pressure and temperature, respectively.

Anemometers (for measuring wind speed) and hygrometers (for measuring humidity) were far less common and less accurate. There was no standard method for measuring wind speeds until Sir Francis Beaufort's eponymous scale, developed in 1805, was adopted by the Royal Navy in the 1830s, and wind forces would not be related to anemometer measurements until the 1850s. It is nearly impossible to compare the readings from earlier anemometers, since the designs of the instruments and the scales applied to their measurements varied so widely. Most hygrometers of the early nineteenth century were simply the combination of two thermometers: one kept dry and the other immersed in water. As the water naturally evaporated, it cooled the wet thermometer; the temperature difference between the two thermometers could then be used to determine the humidity. In 1783, the Swiss physicist Horace-Bénédict de Saussure demonstrated the first hygrometer based on the contraction and expansion of human hair due to changes in atmospheric moisture. While his design would later become very popular, in 1816 it had not yet been widely adopted. (Currently, the most accurate hygrometers are polished mirrors that are cooled until water condenses onto them, an adaptation of a technique pioneered by the British chemist John Frederic Daniell in 1820.)

Although barometers and thermometers were in widespread use throughout Europe and the United States throughout the eighteenth and into the nineteenth centuries, many weather diaries remained private; those records that have been published often contain long gaps or end abruptly. The meteorological community was primarily composed of amateurs, albeit enthusiastic ones, rather than professionals. Governments had not yet established official agencies with the responsibility for monitoring or understanding the weather—the Royal Meteorological Society in Britain, for example, was not founded until 1850—and, as during the French Revolution, those that did exist could be disbanded if they became politically unpopular. The information we have today about the climate of the period is the result of the painstaking, meticulous reconstitution by modern climatologists of fragmented data from disparate sources around the globe.

Those nineteenth-century scientists who had access to instruments and kept detailed, regular records would have been aware of the connections between the variations in temperature and pressure and the variations in local weather patterns. Such variations had been noted for nearly two hundred years. Evangelista Torricelli, the Italian physicist and mathematician who invented the mercury barometer in 1643, soon recognized that the atmospheric pressure changed from one day to the next. Four years later, famed French philosopher René Descartes made two identical paper scales for a barometer; one he kept, the other he sent to his friend Marin Mersenne "so that we may know if changes of weather and of location make any difference to [the readings]." In 1648, the French mathematician and philosopher Blaise Pascal carried out a series of experiments on mountain peaks, with the help of his brother-in-law, to demonstrate that air pressure decreases with altitude. His findings astonished most contemporary scientists, who assumed the atmosphere's composition remained constant throughout its depth.

While the amateur meteorologists of the early nineteenth century understood the links between their own atmospheric measurements and immediate changes in their weather, they were unable to forecast the weather more than an hour or two in advance. Having developed reliable, if elementary instruments and a rudimentary understanding of atmospheric physics, there remained three key challenges that would make accurate weather predictions impossible for another 150 years. The first was the speed at which meteorological data could be transferred and collected at a central location. Forecasting the weather requires accurate information about the current state of the atmosphere. A crude, but often effective prediction technique is to simply use the weather from a nearby location upwind of the location for which one is forecasting. If the wind moves at a greater speed than the information, however, even this technique is useless. Not until the development of a widespread telegraph network in the mid nineteenth century could scientists collect meteorological data quickly enough to make these basic forecasts for a few hours ahead, or warn of the approach of severe weather.

To move beyond the simple, upwind forecasting method, meteorologists must understand the circulations of and interactions between air masses around the globe. As scientists continued to develop meteorological instruments through the seventeenth, eighteenth, and nineteenth centuries, they also developed hypotheses to explain the changes in the readings they obtained. Aided by the instruments aboard ships, many mathematicians and "natural philosophers" turned their attentions to the causes of the direction and strength of the transoceanic winds. These projects carried significant potential benefits to them and their government sponsors, since knowledge of the seasonal variations in the paths of the strongest winds would allow merchant vessels and warships to cross the ocean more quickly than their competitors and enemies.

As the British Empire and the Royal Navy expanded during this period, British scientists engaged in a fierce debate over the origin of the east-to-west trade winds (named for their importance in conveying goods-laden ships to the Americas) that blow steadily across the Atlantic and Pacific in both the Northern and Southern Hemispheres. Some supported Galileo's earlier hypothesis that the winds were caused by Earth rotating more quickly in the tropics than at the poles; the tropical atmosphere could not "keep up" with the spinning Earth below, they argued. To one standing on the ground, rotating to the east with Earth, the wind would indeed appear to blow from east to west. Others, such as the late-seventeenth-century astronomer Edmund Halley, believed that the winds blew from the east because the sun's energy flowed from east to west during each day. Halley argued that the sun's energy heated the air, which rose to form a wind; the sun's movement caused this wind to appear to blow from the east. Halley's explanation became canon and was widely accepted in the early nineteenth century.

It would be another twenty years after the eruption of Tambora before scientists acknowledged the true explanation for the trade winds. First advanced—with some inaccuracies—by the British lawyer and amateur meteorologist George Hadley in 1735, the theory stated that the trade winds are caused by air trying to flow from each hemisphere towards the equator. When viewed from the perspective of someone standing on the rotating Earth, however, the winds—which are not rotating—appear to curve to the right in the Northern Hemisphere and to the left in the Southern, giving east-to-west winds in both hemispheres. For his contributions, climatologists still refer to the circuit of winds between the equator and the middle latitudes as the Hadley Cell.

Hadley's theory was often discussed, but the idea of Earth as a rotating frame of reference was difficult for scientists to grasp. Hadley's principle did not gain meaningful traction until Gaspard-Gustave Coriolis conclusively demonstrated in 1835 the actions of the various forces acting in a rotating reference frame. (Coriolis, incidentally, thought his work would be most useful for those who built waterwheels, or played billiards.)

Many other fundamental principles of atmospheric science relevant to weather forecasting were developed in the decades following the eruption of Tambora, but remained unknown or as working hypotheses to those attempting to explain the cooling climate and extreme weather after 1815. The Navier-Stokes equations, which describe the three-dimensional flow of viscous fluids, including the atmosphere, were derived in 1845, when George Gabriel Stokes updated Claude-Louis Navier's 1822 formulation. These equations are crucial to describing the ever-evolving state of the atmosphere; today they form the basis for the computer simulations of Earth's climate that make it possible to predict the weather days and sometimes weeks in advance. Similarly, the Clausius-Clapeyron relationship, which explains that a greater quantity of water vapor can exist in warmer air, was advanced by its namesakes in the mid-1830s. Without the understanding of the global circulation of the atmosphere that these theories provide, the gentleman scientists of the early nineteenth century lacked the knowledge to understand that volcanic eruptions would affect the world's weather patterns; certainly they could not have forecast the disruption that the eruption of Tambora would create.

Even with speedily transmitted data by telegraph and comprehension of physical laws that govern the atmosphere, meteorologists failed to produce reliable, useful weather forecasts until after the Second World War due to the third and final hurdle: computational speed. The Navier-Stokes equations and the other key atmospheric formulae require computers in order to generate timely forecasts. The human brain simply is not sufficiently powerful, as the early-twentieth-century British mathematician Lewis Fry Richardson discovered when he tried to apply the equations developed in the nineteenth century to real weather observations. It took Richardson nearly three years—working part-time while serving as an ambulance driver during the First World War—to make a six-hour weather forecast for France, a forecast that turned out to be spectacularly inaccurate.

In the absence of data, theories, and computers, amateur meteorologists of the early nineteenth century fell back upon the centuries-old method of pattern recognition when attempting to forecast the weather and climate. They looked for signs from nature—larger than normal berries on trees, an early appearance of acorns, even the thickness of onion skins—as forewarnings of the coming seasons. (Thin onion skins supposedly meant a mild winter.) Links between these signals and the subsequent climate, whether real or imagined, became established in "weather lore" and provided the basis for many almanacs. Such sayings often thrived due to their adherents' selective memories, attaching greater importance to the instances in which the lore proved accurate than to those (often more frequent) times when it failed. Some meteorologists of the era also proposed associations between the seasons themselves, such as a cold winter following a warm autumn. In some cases modern science has proven these relationships to be correct, but only because the abnormal conditions in both seasons are caused by the same variation in the atmospheric circulation.

4.

THE HANDWRITING OF GOD

"The atmosphere still seems as cold as in March or November . . ."

O N JUNE 5, President Madison (annual salary: $25,000) left his temporary dwelling in Washington, D.C. (annual rent: $1,814), and headed for Montpelier, his home in Orange, Virginia, about 50 miles south of the nation's capital. (No one voluntarily spent the summer in the hot, muggy, mosquito-infested District of Columbia.) Since Congress adjourned on April 30, the president had spent much of his time negotiating with Britain a reduction in armaments on the Great Lakes. Through the United States ambassador at the Court of St. James's, John Quincy Adams, Madison also informed Foreign Secretary Lord Castlereagh that the U.S. intended to obtain equal commercial access to export markets—primarily for American grain—in the British West Indies.

Before he left Washington, Madison sailed down to Annapolis to inspect a new U.S. warship; since the president decided the trip was not, strictly speaking, official business, he insisted on paying out of his own pocket the twenty-five-dollar fee due to the sailors who took him down the Potomac. Then a messenger arrived with a letter from the Dey of Algiers, whom the American public regarded as one of the widely despised "Barbary Pirates." The Dey's letter was written in Turkish and translated into Arabic, but since no one in the president's immediate circle could decipher either language, the letter sat, unread, for two months until a translator could be found.

Madison reached Montpelier just in time for the arrival of the cold wave that was devastating New England's crops. Freezing temperatures had settled over New Jersey and Pennsylvania on June 6 and 7; then frost struck the fields of central Virginia, damaging corn, wheat, and vegetables. "This is an extraordinary spring," declared a Richmond newspaper. "On Thursday morning last we had a *frost* in this city." To make matters worse, the effects of the springtime drought were felt even more strongly in the south than in New England; Charleston, South Carolina, suffered through eight weeks without rain in March and April. "We do not recollect to have witnessed a more distressing drought, than that which at this time visits every portion of our country," lamented the *American Beacon*, published in Norfolk. "The temperature of the weather with us is very fluctuating—the evenings and mornings generally so cool as to render a fire quite agreeable. The Earth is so parched . . ."

There was no shortage of explanations put forth by self-appointed experts to account for the recent extraordinary weather. News of the eruption of Mount Tambora had reached the United States by June 1816, but no one had yet published a theory to link Tambora's ash cloud to the frigid temperatures in North America. Instead, numerous newspaper stories attempted to connect the cold wave with the previously sighted sunspots. "The sun is no doubt the great fountain of caloric, or heat, as well as of light," mused a typical report, "and it is very rational to suppose that the objects which exhibit to us the appearance of spots on the sun, by intercepting the *calorific rays*, may have deprived the earth of some part of the quantity which it usually receives." Although sunspots visible to the naked eye had largely faded from view by the end of May, they suddenly reappeared during the first week of June. One enterprising amateur astronomer tried to revive the hypothesis by suggesting that even weakened sunspots might have combined with a total lunar eclipse on the evening of June 9—which left New Englanders in darkness for sixty-seven minutes—to somehow enable the moon's gravitational pull to disrupt the normal flow of winds around Earth.

Skeptics remained unimpressed. "The alarm from spots on the Sun proves the small progress of science and of the advantages nominal science has over superstition and prejudice and ignorance," sniffed Reverend William Bentley of Salem. "We think the alteration took place before the spots were observed," scoffed *Niles' Weekly Register,* "but it is foolish to be positive about any opinion in a question of this kind."

Perhaps. But the proponents of the sunspot theory were correct in presuming a connection between sunspots and temperatures and weather patterns on Earth, albeit not in the manner they suggested. The spots on the sun's surface appear darker than the rest of the sun because less heat from the sun's fusion reactions reaches the surface there. While this would suggest a reduction in the energy emitted by the sun, the opposite is in fact the case: An increase in sunspot activity is associated with an *increase* in the energy leaving the sun.

Although the sunspots are cooler than the remainder of the sun, they are surrounded by warmer, brighter areas that are often more difficult to notice against the background of the sun itself. The net effect of the cool sunspots and the warmer regions around them is to slightly increase the total amount of energy that the sun produces. These changes in solar energy may affect temperature and precipitation patterns on Earth, but temperature variations associated with sunspot activity are considerably less than those caused by volcanic eruptions. The aerosol cloud produced by Tambora likely reduced the amount of solar energy reaching Earth's surface by 0.5 percent, an effect ten times stronger than that caused by a normal minimum in the eleven-year sunspot cycle, and more than three times stronger than the Maunder Minimum, the period of lowest sunspot activity on record. While the coincidence of Tambora and the Dalton Minimum probably increased the cooling effect of the aerosol cloud on Earth's climate, the volcanic ash was the primary and proximate cause for the exceptionally cold and wet summer of 1816.

An understanding of the relationship between sunspot activity and solar energy lay more than thirty years in the future, however. Not until 1848 did Joseph Henry, the first director of the Smithsonian Institution, demonstrate that sunspots were cooler than the surrounding sun. It is not surprising, therefore, that a number of incorrect and conflicting theories over the origins and effects of sunspots circulated as North America's weather began to change in 1816.

Other Americans attributed the snow and frigid temperatures to the unusually large concentrations of ice still floating in the Great Lakes and—according to British merchant sailors—in the North Atlantic, off the coast of Newfoundland. These immense fields of ice purportedly absorbed substantial quantities of heat from the atmosphere, and thereby reduced its temperature. Critics noted, however, that if this hypothesis were true, coastal areas in New England (specifically, Maine, eastern New Hampshire) would have endured deeper snows and lower temperatures than inland regions such as Vermont, more than one hundred miles from the ocean. But they had not. Perhaps the afflicted inland regions were cooled by the ice on the Great Lakes; yet this argument seemed to go only round in circles. "Very cold weather produced great quantities of ice," concluded one skeptic quite properly, "and great quantities of ice, at their dissolution, were the cause of uncommon cold weather."

Yet another theory linked disturbances in the atmosphere to a series of earthquakes that struck the lower Mississippi River Valley in 1811–12. From the Ohio River to the Mississippi, 1811 was known as "The Year of Wonders." The sequence of exceptional events began with spring floods in the Ohio Valley, followed by the appearance of the Great Comet of 1811 (the brightest comet to cross the heavens in several centuries), an unusually cold summer with occasional hailstorms, and an epidemic of fever that swept across the frontier. In the fall, settlers were treated to the ominous sight of a total eclipse of the sun, then vast flocks of pigeons in the sky, and finally immense swarms of squirrels—tens of thousands, by one account—in a solid mass, heading south, altogether unafraid of humans, many drowning when they tried to swim across the Ohio River. (Squirrels are notoriously poor swimmers.) "The word had been given to them to go forth," wrote one elderly pioneer, "and they obeyed it."

In retrospect, these "wonders" seemed portents to many Americans of the shock that struck the region on December 16, 1811. An earthquake of magnitude 7.7, centered in northeast Arkansas, shook the earth from Cairo, Illinois, to Memphis, Tennessee. Settlers along this frontier—then the forward edge of American settlement—felt the ground rise and fall, and heard "a very awful noise resembling loud but distant thunder, but more hoarse and vibrating, which was followed in a few minutes by the complete saturation of the atmosphere, with sulphurious vapor, causing total darkness." Fissures opened in the earth, throwing out sand and water, and swallowing up huge chunks of land. "At the same time," recalled an eyewitness, "the roaring and whistling produced by the impetuosity of the air escaping from its confinement, seemed to increase the horrible disorder of the trees which everywhere encountered each other, being blown up cracking and splitting, and falling by thousands at a time."

Initially the Mississippi River appeared to recede from its banks and flow backwards, taking with it stands of cottonwood trees; then immense waves arose and capsized boats on the river, or washed others ashore. Cliffs along the riverbank caved and collapsed into the river; entire islands vanished. Log cabins crumbled as far away as St. Louis, Cincinnati, and towns throughout Kentucky and Tennessee.

A series of aftershocks caused nearly as much destruction. A second major shock occurred on January 23, 1812, then a third on February 7, completely destroying the town of New Madrid, Missouri, the largest settlement on the Mississippi between St. Louis and Natchez. In all of these shocks, clustered around M 8.0, "the earth was horribly torn to pieces," and the Mississippi littered with trees and the wrecks of ships.

Washington Irving claimed that this combination of earthquakes, pestilence, and extreme weather events produced "a feverish excitement" in the minds of many Americans, "and filled the imagination with dreams of horror and apprehensions of sinister and dreadful events." To millennialists, the sequence of natural disasters appeared a portent of the apocalypse, and evangelistic preachers warned that the world would soon end.

Others of an ostensibly more scientific inclination argued that the earthquakes had altered the American climate by disrupting the normal exchange of electricity between earth and sky, thereby denying the Eastern United States the heat necessary to grow crops. "It is perfectly understood in South America," claimed one newspaper editor, "that those natural convulsions [i.e., earthquakes] always produce effects on the weather." Several years earlier, two European writers working independently—Scottish jurist and amateur climate scientist John MacLaurin (Lord Dreghorn) and French journalist Simon-Nicholas Henri Linguet—had advanced a similar theory. MacLaurin claimed that the weather in Scotland had turned colder since the famous Lisbon earthquake of 1755, and Linguet confirmed that in both Champagne and Picardy, vintners had been unable to grow the same grapes or make the same wine as they could before the earthquake.

In an essay published in the *Daily National Intelligencer*, Dudley Leavitt, a New England teacher of mathematics and natural philosophy, attempted to explain not only the snowstorms of June but the entire series of cool summers in the Eastern United States in the years immediately preceding 1816. Leavitt attributed the below-average temperatures to "the extensive forests in North America [which] naturally have an effect to prevent the sunbeams from reaching the ground." Not only did the sun fail to heat the ground, but the process of evaporation of water from leaves and plants exerted a cooling effect on the atmosphere, particularly during periods of above-average precipitation. "On this principle," Leavitt reasoned, "the increased coldness of our summers for several years past may be, in a great part, accounted for, since, as our summers lately have been . . . very wet, the consequent evaporation has greatly contributed to cool the air, and of course the seasons have become colder." Leavitt predicted that a drier summer would thus increase the atmospheric heat, "unless the fire of *Nature* is really *going out*, which there is no sufficient reason yet to believe is the case."

While Leavitt blamed the frigid summers on precipitation and vegetation, the *Brattleboro Reporter* took precisely the opposite view, claiming that the destruction of virgin forests by American and Canadian settlers created a cooler climate. Reversing earlier generations' theory that widespread razing of woodlands created warmer temperatures, the *Reporter* proposed that chopping down forests simply allowed cold winds from Canada to swoop down unhindered into New England. David Thomas concurred. "A few years ago, our fields were sheltered by woods," he observed, "and every farmer has observed the difference, in spring, between vegetables growing in bleak [that is, colder] and in secluded situations." Thomas further speculated that repeated plowing of the soil in long-settled regions was turning up "paler coloured subsoil," which presumably retained heat less efficiently than the black surface soil of virgin forests.

During his travels through Pennsylvania and Ohio, Thomas repeatedly heard local residents offer their own unique explanation for the recent series of unusually cool summers. They suggested that a solar eclipse in 1806 was responsible for the subnormal temperatures; some claimed that the eclipse had administered some type of powerful shock to the atmosphere, while others believed that "a pernicious vapour [had] escaped from the shade of the moon."

While many Americans sought explanations for the unusually cold weather in the physical world, others looked to God, or at least Providence. In colonial times, Americans (particularly New England Puritans) were prone to interpret meteorological events in theological terms. Weather was a physical manifestation of the Divine Will in all its majesty and capriciousness, and as one historian has noted, storms represented "the very handwriting of God: whatever transpired in the heavens was a direct communication from on high, with a special significance for them and them alone."

American farmers prayed for the weather they needed to prosper; if it failed to appear, they endeavored to reform to obtain it. Occasionally superstition overtook theology, as when ministers sometimes rang church bells during lightning storms to ward off evil demons. (No statistics exist on how many clerics were struck by lightning while engaged in this task.) But for the most part, American colonists kept their eyes on the heavens, and the popular belief in theological meteorology lingered long past the Revolution, despite the influence of Enlightenment thought and particularly Newtonian mechanics. Certainly many members of the revolutionary generation understood exactly what Thomas Prince spoke of in his 1749 sermon, "The Natural and Moral Government and Agency of God in Causing Droughts and Rains": "When the Vapours rise and gather in thick Clouds, and the Lightning flashes with irresistible Power; let us lift up our believing Eyes and see God in them."

On this matter, at least, Americans saw no conflict between science and faith. God worked through natural means to carry out His will. Providentialism incorporated the latest scientific knowledge and used it to explain how God worked in the world; a recent study of Chesapeake society has made it clear that Americans' belief in the workings of natural laws "supplemented rather than replaced the idea that God sent natural calamities as a warning."

In diaries, journals, and private correspondence, early-nineteenth-century Americans, regardless of region or socioeconomic status, demonstrated that they still believed that God controlled all aspects of the natural world. Providence was the working of God's will in human affairs, and even religious skeptics accepted the presence of a providential power, albeit in a lower case. It was one means by which they made sense of the sometimes baffling world around them. As the editor of *Harper's* suggested, Providence was "the most general, pervasive, ineradicable feeling in the hearts of our countrymen."

"All things are known to God, & all that He does is right & we learn that not even a sparrow fallith [sic] to the ground without his notice, so I leave all in his hands," wrote a Southerner emigrating to the west. "The Wheel of Providence is constantly moving," agreed the wife of an Ohio farmer; "nothing impedes its progress." Upon the birth of a child, a Massachusetts father exulted that "The King Providence has granted us a lovely daughter." And a New York teenager took time to record in his diary that "the Lord in his goodness has spared me 16 years and has given me health and strength."

Whatever happened, happened because God willed it. On a national level, Americans typically looked to the future with optimism and confidence, convinced that God had chosen the United States to regenerate the world. "I always consider the settlement of America with reverence and wonder," acknowledged the eminently rational John Adams, "as the opening of a grand scene and design in providence, for the illumination of the ignorant and the emancipation of the slavish part of mankind all over the earth." Yet the average American also displayed a clear sense of resignation about temporary setbacks or losses in the present and the immediate past. God's inscrutable will worked itself out in the natural world, in Americans' personal lives, and they had no choice but to accept whatever joys and tragedies came their way.

Americans saw God's hand especially in unexpected events that affected an entire community, such as hurricanes, epidemics, earthquakes ("peculiar Tokens" of God's anger), and famine. Destructive frosts and snowfalls in June came from God as well. One Vermont newspaper could even cite scripture from the Old Testament to explain the recent cold wave: "Perhaps we can assign no other cause than that the fiat of the GREAT FIRST CAUSE," the editors wrote, "and the wisest philosophers will be ready to exclaim with Elihu, the friend of Jub, 'By the breath of God frost is given, and the breadth of the waters is restrained.'" Or as a Connecticut farmer confided to his diary, "Great frost—we must learn to be humble."

Learn to be humble, because the snow and the frost may have signified God's displeasure. Repent and reform, as Anglican minister Joseph Bend instructed his Baltimore congregation when an epidemic of fever struck nearby Philadelphia in 1793: "By fasting, humiliation, & prayer to stay the hand, which afflicteth your brethren, & to avert from yourselves the calamity, under which they are mournfully groaning." Perhaps Americans were growing too materialistic, too obsessed with the manufactured goods that became more readily available each year. As cities grew and civilization encroached upon the wilderness, more Americans lost contact with nature. Notions of civic virtue, of self-sacrifice for the good of the nation seemed to have become passé. Social extravagance, once the preserve of the wealthy, was filtering down into the middle class, widening divisions among citizens. Perhaps the virtuous, agrarian American republic was beginning to resemble the decadent nations of Europe.

Religious revivals—particularly along the frontier—had commenced in the 1790s. Now, in the spring and summer of 1816, they gathered strength and spread into more settled areas, especially into western New York state. "The revivals in these years

[1816–1817] were more numerous, and of greater extent, than in former years," wrote a nineteenth-century historian of the region. Between 1812–1815, the Presbyterian churches in western New York gained about five hundred new members per year; in 1816, that number rose to more than a thousand; in 1817, to nearly two thousand. Congregations of various denominations in Buffalo, Binghamton, Ithaca, Auburn, Onondaga, Geneva, and Palmyra experienced substantial increases in membership. In the town of Norwich, where more than sixty new members joined the Congregational Church, "all classes were subjects of the work; the old, and the young; the rich, and the poor; the learned, and the ignorant; the lawyer, the farmer, and the mechanic." And the movement had barely begun.

PITTSBURGH, Pennsylvania, marked the southern limit of the June snowstorms in the United States. Western Pennsylvania received two to three inches of snow, though towns on the eastern side of the Appalachians escaped with only flurries. Frost and ice accounted for most of the damage to crops and commerce. In mid-June, a correspondent from Erie reported that "the season has been dry and frosty for weeks together. It appears as if we should have no crops in these parts—the corn has been all killed by the frost of the 9th, and until very lately lake Erie was not navigable for the ice."

Pennsylvania in 1816 was at the apex of its "golden age" of agriculture, in the midst of the transition between subsistence and commercial farming. Farmers who formerly planted a variety of crops to keep their families fed now focused upon one primary product to sell at market. Wheat remained the most common crop in most parts of the state, although farmers on the western side of the Appalachians preferred to raise corn (up to twenty-five bushels per acre), since it could be distilled into whiskey and shipped far more cheaply in liquid form across the mountains to eastern markets. Corn also was grown for family consumption, of course, and to provide feed for livestock.

With European grain production disarranged by the Napoleonic Wars, U.S. exports of both wheat and corn boomed as prices soared in the first decade of the nineteenth century. The growth of Pennsylvania's towns and cities provided an expanding domestic market, and advances in agricultural machinery helped alleviate the state's chronic shortage of farm labor. Although Pennsylvania farmers were notoriously reluctant to adopt new techniques, wealthy "gentlemen farmers" in the east pioneered new techniques that increased yields per acre, such as planting red clover as a cover crop, and spreading lime and gypsum to reduce soil acidity.

Farmers could supplement their incomes if they were fortunate enough to discover a seam of coal on their property. Often the coal lay just under the surface of the soil, uncovered the first time a plough cut through the earth. Typically a farmer would mine the coal himself whenever he could spare the time from other chores, although the lack of machinery prevented him from digging past the level where water flooded the mine. In western Pennsylvania, where coal seemed to be everywhere, it sold for six cents a bushel in the spring of 1816; local residents preferred to use it instead of wood for fuel, "the blaze being so brilliant as to supersede the use of candles, even for sewing."

Farms located near substantial deposits of iron (most often in central Pennsylvania) earned additional profits from selling wood to the ironmongers—who needed it for charcoal to smelt iron—or simply by leasing their woods to the iron manufacturers, who cut and transported the timber themselves and then returned the cleared land to the farmer. Since larger furnaces employed upwards of one hundred workers, they required a wide range of support services (food, supplies, and building materials for the walls, desks, and benches of schoolhouses) that farm families willingly provided.

Livestock, especially sheep, represented yet another opportunity for Pennsylvania farmers to augment their income, and in the summer of 1816 a speculative bubble in Merino sheep was about to burst. A fine-wool breed native to the Iberian peninsula, Merino sheep first appeared in quantity in the United States in 1810, after Napoléon's conquest of Spain loosened restrictions on their sale. A frenzied pursuit of the aristocratic Merinos ensued, as Americans frantically bid up the price of breeding stock. Merino wool tripled in value in two years; in eastern Pennsylvania's Bucks County, "full-blooded Merinos sold as high as $300 to $500 each and in a few instances they brought $1,000. . . . A man in this county sold his wheat crop, 200 bushels, at $3.00 a bushel and gave the whole of it for one sheep." Prices peaked in the early months of 1816; by June they had begun to weaken.

Prices of the imported goods that farmers purchased remained high, however. Cut off from regular sources of supply during the war against Britain, Pennsylvanians found themselves paying thirty-three cents per pound for sugar, and forty cents for a pound of coffee. (Some enterprising consumers substituted rye for coffee, and drank the brew unsweetened.) The prices of cotton and woolen goods also had skyrocketed at a time when many farm families who used to make all their own clothes—as well as their shoes, saddles, cabinets, and just about anything else they needed—were beginning to spend more time raising crops for market and less on household crafts.

Pennsylvanians were as likely as any other Americans to see God's hand in the June cold wave, although the expression of organized religion had been dampened by the effects of Enlightenment philosophy and the rationalism of the French Revolution. Moreover, several religious denominations had suffered setbacks during and immediately after the Revolution: Quakers whose pacifism led them to remain neutral in the struggle for independence often lost the respect and trust of their patriot neighbors, and never quite regained it; Anglicans—with the King of England at the head of their church—found themselves under attack by mobs and the courts during the revolutionary struggle; and Presbyterians, who overwhelmingly supported the rebel cause, lost both clergy (who served as chaplains) and members of their congregations to the military effort. But by the start of 1816, religious enthusiasm was making a comeback in western Pennsylvania, and the events of the summer would provide considerable momentum.

Pennsylvanians—and particularly the Pennsylvania Dutch—took a backseat to no one in ascribing spiritual or supernatural (the line often blurred) causes to natural phenomena. For the ordinary farmer who needed to feel at least minimal control over the fate of his crops and livestock, superstitions governed every aspect of farming. The movement of the moon, planets, and stars provided a blueprint for success, even among well-educated Pennsylvanians. "Gather apples on the day of the moon," recommended one farm journal; sow grain only when the moon was waxing; plant potatoes only in the "dark of the moon"; slaughter cattle during a full moon. Signs of the zodiac carried nearly as much weight as the moon, especially among German-American farmers who relied heavily on an almanac-like publication known as the *Kalender-Aberglaube*.

Almanacs were nearly as ubiquitous as Bibles in Pennsylvanian farm households in the early nineteenth century. Besides providing practical wisdom on agricultural and personal matters, they served as farmers' only source of weather forecasts authored by humans. (Certain animals were also afforded the power to predict the weather. If a rooster crowed after 10 P.M., or if mice or rats scurried about more noisily than usual, it would rain the following day; or if a groundhog saw its shadow on February 2, there would be six more weeks of winter. Even donkeys got into the act: "Hark! I heard the asses bray," ran one piece of prognosticative verse, "I think we'll have some rain today.") Almanac writers typically took credit for making a correct prediction, though they deferred the blame if nature proved them wrong. A farmer in southeastern

Pennsylvania who embarked upon a lengthy journey based on his almanac's forecast of fair weather found himself forced to stop short of his destination due to heavy rains. When he complained, the almanac's author replied that "although I made the almanac, the Lord Almighty made the weather."

And that included the cold wave that swept over Pennsylvania on June 7. Those days of subfreezing temperatures seemed especially ominous to those farmers who, encouraged by wartime's high prices for grain and corn during the war, had ignored the warnings of their cautious neighbors and purchased additional acreage and machinery, often with borrowed funds.

Based upon David Thomas's observations, farmers in western Pennsylvania already were walking a thin line between prosperity and disaster. "Agriculture is at its lowest ebb, both in theory and practice," Thomas wrote in his journal as he traveled through the region in the first week of June, "and we have never seen its operations so miserably conducted throughout the same extent of country." He passed scores of small farms that had been deserted, their solitary buildings (or their burnt remains) deteriorating in the saddening countryside. The emaciated appearance of pigs and dogs on the local farms—a sight which Thomas felt was "truly indicative of habitual scarcity"—confirmed his negative impressions. Thomas blamed the poverty of the region on ignorance, rather than laziness. Western Pennsylvania farmers appeared unaware of the benefits of planting clover or scattering stable manure or gypsum, and they often plowed only a few inches below the surface of the soil, preventing roots from gaining a firm hold. When cold weather struck on June 7, moisture on the surface froze and expanded, dislodging their plants.

Pittsburgh, on the other hand, impressed Thomas with its vitality and industry. Already known as the "Birmingham of America" for its manufacturing capabilities, Pittsburgh was not a lovely city—there were still many ramshackle wooden buildings scattered among the brick structures, and few of its streets were paved, so that rain turned the roads into dark, heavy mud. And the residents, according to Thomas, displayed a disconcerting proclivity to employ profanity at every available opportunity. But the city boasted a broad array of industrial enterprises: iron mills, nail factories, paper mills, cotton and woolen factories, flour mills, and glass factories, powered largely by steam and fueled by the coal mines surrounding the city. The burning coal that drove the economy also fouled the air; day and night, thick black smoke filled the atmosphere. "Often descending in whirls thro' the streets," Thomas noted, "it tarnishes every object to which it has access." Housewives who hung their clothes outside to dry sometimes had to pull them down and wash them again before they dried. But when the cold front struck Pittsburgh in June, the heat from the burning coal helped save the fruit trees around the city. "The peach, the plumb [sic], the apple and the cherry, abound on the branches," Davis remarked with surprise, "though the frosts have been very severe."

COLD rains pelted western Europe throughout June. A low-pressure system settled over northern Germany and Denmark, pulling in frigid air from the north and northwest, and sea ice still floated in the North Atlantic, off the coast of Iceland. From Lancashire in northwestern England came reports that "the character of the present season has been on the whole ungenial," with temperatures averaging five degrees colder than the previous year. "The atmosphere still seems as cold as in March or November," observed the *Lancaster Gazetteer* on June 8. "For above a week past, the weather here has been very cold for the season, with high winds and rain." Two days earlier, a storm had brought snow to the hills of northern Lancashire, "a circumstance not within the recollection of the oldest person living in that neighbourhood." On June 9, the area received another "considerable fall of snow." Parts of Bavaria received sufficient snow on June 7 to cover the ground for several days. Up and down the Italian peninsula, the cold damp weather threatened the silk harvest.

Traveling from Belgium through northern France, Lady Caroline Capel (sister of the Marquess of Anglesey, one of Wellington's leading commanders at Waterloo) found herself soaked from "the torrents of rain that have fallen every day." "France is quite dreadfull," she informed her mother, Lady Uxbridge, "& the Incessant rain, or rather Water Spouts, that fell during our whole journey till we entered this Country was really melancholy; Not a day passed that three of the party were not drenched to the skin, so that we are well off to have escaped without some real illness."

As the downpours persisted, the Ultra-Royalist pursuit of radicals in France gathered momentum, aided by clerics, prefects, and informants. Anyone who openly rejoiced in the government's difficulties was subject to arrest; some zealous reactionaries wished to make simple possession of a tricolor banner evidence of treason. Academics were not exempt from persecution. The Royal Academy of Sciences, recently reestablished by Louis XVIII, purged from its ranks "all scientists, writers or artists whose names recalled unpleasant memories of the Republic or the Empire," and launched a program designed to support the monarchy.

This was only the latest volley in the continuing battle between scientific research and politics in France, to the detriment of meteorological studies. In late-eighteenth-century Europe, Enlightenment scholars had proposed the systematic gathering of meteorological observations, hoping to discover that weather variations were the result of "predictable forms of behaviour." The primary impetus for meteorological research at this time came from the medical profession. The prevailing theory among physicians was that disease was caused in large measure by the effects of the physical environment—climate, living conditions, topography—on the human body. (When the French spoke of the "temperature" of the air in the late eighteenth century, they usually referred not to the heat in degrees, but to the "temperament" of the atmosphere—e.g., cold and wet, or warm and dry—as if it had a constitution similar to that of humans.) In an attempt to improve public health by correlating disease and the outbreak of epidemics with weather patterns, the Société Royale de Médecine established a network of weather observation stations across France in 1778. Throughout the 1780s, more than 150 provincial physicians compiled a substantial quantity of climate data throughout France; unfortunately, officials never managed to analyze the data before the Revolutionary authorities disbanded the Société Royale, along with other institutions of the Ancien Régime, in 1793.

Few were gathering statistics in early June 1816 as weeks of incessant rain in Saxony caused the Saale River to flood, threatening the inhabitants of Halle (the birthplace of Georg Friedrich Händel), and inundating the surrounding countryside. "The only object visible above water was our lofty bridge," reported one resident from Halle. "Many cattle have been drowned. The price of bread and other articles of subsistence is rising among us in the same proportion as the number of poor is on the increase."

Swiss almanacs predicted a wet, stormy summer, and to Mary Godwin's dismay, they were right. By the middle of June, Mary and Percy Shelley had settled into their château, the Maison Chapuis, in Cologny, on the southern edge of Lake Geneva. Her infrequent forays into Geneva left her in a sullen mood. There was nothing in that city, Mary wrote to a friend, "that can repay you for the trouble of walking over its rough stones. The houses are high, the streets narrow, many of them on the ascent, and no public building of any beauty to attract your eye, or any architecture to gratify your taste." A high wall with three gates surrounded the town, she added, and each evening promptly at ten o'clock the town authorities locked the gates. Shelley seemed equally unimpressed. "Geneva is far from interesting, & is a place, which for the sake of scenery I should never have made my habitation," he decided.

Mary preferred to spend hours sailing with Shelley on the lake

(Chapuis had its own private harbor) when the weather permitted, particularly in the evenings. As the days passed, however, she found herself spending less time with her lover. Percy had met Lord Byron, and the two men at once struck up an intimate friendship.

George Noel Gordon, Lord Byron, was undoubtedly the most famous and controversial celebrity in Britain in 1816. Having grown up in modest circumstances in Aberdeen, Scotland, he inherited at the age of ten the estates and title of his great uncle. The family fortune enabled him to attend Harrow and Cambridge, where he commenced the dissolute lifestyle that earned him as much notoriety as his poetry. Byron published his first poems in 1807, at the age of nineteen, and cemented his literary reputation with the publication of the semiautobiographical "Childe Harold's Pilgrimage" five years later. By that time he had completed a series of romantic affairs with older married women (including Lady Caroline Lamb and Lady Oxford) and the occasional distant relative. Meanwhile, his bank funds steadily diminished, despite the fact that even his less inspired works sold thousands of copies as soon as they were published.

Partly to restore his finances, Byron proposed in 1812 to Annabella Milbanke, the twenty-year-old daughter of a wealthy landowner. Self-absorbed, chilly, and entirely devoid of any sense of humor, Milbanke initially rejected Byron. Two years later, she accepted his renewed offer, despite the fact that he proposed by letter rather than in person. By then Byron was drinking heavily, working only desultorily (and often in the early hours of morning), and sinking more deeply into debt. And he had begun to spend a great deal of time with his half sister, Augusta Leigh. The daughter of Byron's father by a previous marriage, Augusta was wed to a cousin who preferred to spend his time at the racetrack. She and Byron found themselves quite compatible—Augusta, too, preferred pleasure to the dictates of conventional morality—and almost surely became lovers.

Despite this increasingly close relationship—or perhaps because of it, given Byron's highly developed sense of guilt and the fact that he always referred to Augusta as his sister—Byron and Annabella married on January 2, 1815. Their honeymoon was a nightmare. Annabella later claimed that as they drove away from the church, Byron confessed that the sound of wedding bells horrified him; that evening, she recalled, "he asked me with an appearance of aversion, if I meant to sleep in the same bed with him—said that he hated sleeping with any woman, but I might do as I chose. He told me insultingly that 'one animal of the kind was as good to him as another' provided she was young—and that with men, this was not any proof of attachment." Unable to sleep, Byron allegedly spent the evening pacing up and down the corridors outside their hotel room, carrying loaded pistols in his hands.

Annabella hoped that she could "save" Byron, but he grew increasingly bored and depressed, and irritated with his wife. Five weeks after their daughter, Augusta, was born on December 10, 1815, Annabella left Byron to return to her parents. In February 1816, she informed her husband that she wanted a divorce. Her petition for a legal separation cited both Byron's alleged incest, which was not a crime in Britain at the time, and sodomy, which was. (Byron likely had engaged in homosexual behavior on a few occasions, although more out of curiosity than conviction.) Unable to write, taking laudanum to alleviate the pain of a liver ailment, contemptuous of Lord Liverpool's Tory ministry (they reciprocated his enmity), unable to repay his creditors—bailiffs frequently camped outside his house at Piccadilly Terrace—and harassed by the British public who, as J. B. Priestly noted, "never really knew what it was all about but was ready to hiss that villainous Byron in the streets or the theatre," Byron decided to make a fresh start. On April 25, 1816, Byron left England, never to return. He was twenty-eight years old at the time.

Traveling in a carriage modeled upon Napoléon's (one of his idols), Byron made a brief stop at Waterloo to inspect the battle-field before arriving in Geneva on May 25. He was accompanied by an Italian physician and aspiring writer named Dr. John W. Polidori. Twenty-one years old in the spring of 1816, Polidori had obtained a sizable advance from Byron's publisher to keep a jour-nal of their travels in Europe, but his task was complicated by the constant browbeating he suffered from the poet. Byron sneered at Polidori's literary ambitions, and dismissed him as "exactly the kind of person to whom, if he fell overboard, one would hold out a straw to know if the adage be true that drowning men catch at straws."

Shelley, however, earned Byron's respect for his poetry, his wit, and his iconoclastic attitudes. Even though Shelley's poems were little known among the general English public, Byron knew "Queen Mab" (which Shelley had sent to him), and thought it quite good. The two men found common ground both in their art and their disdain for bourgeois society. And in the summer of 1816, few places in Europe seemed more conventional than Ge-neva, partly because of the vestigial Calvinism that lingered in the city (it had a well-deserved reputation as the most morally conser-vative city on the continent), but also because it was overrun with wealthy English tourists, whom one observer claimed had "turned Geneva into an English watering-place."

Most of his fellow countrymen received Byron quite coldly. "The English in general are very harsh towards him," noted one of Byron's few admirers in Geneva. "They are thrilled to have an excuse to treat with an air of superiority a man who so clearly towers above them all." For his part, Byron returned the contempt of his Swiss hosts and their English guests. "Switzerland is a curst, selfish, swinish country of brutes, placed in the most romantic re-gion of the world," he wrote. "I never could bear the inhabitants, and still less their English visitors. . . . I know of no other situation except Hell which I should feel inclined to participate with them."

Mary Godwin had met Byron earlier that spring, in England, and the two appear to have hit it off well. Certainly Byron admired Mary's father for his radical writings. But Shelley's obvious preference for Byron's company rather than her own caused Mary considerable dismay, particularly since she was perfectly capable of holding her own in their literary conversations. The situation was complicated by Polidori's jealousy of Shelley, who was monopolizing the attentions of his idol, Lord Byron, and the presence of Claire Clairmont, who was pregnant with Byron's child (she had thrown herself at Byron shortly before he left England) and desperate to rekindle the sexual spark between them.

Tensions rose; so did the frequency of the storms that swept across Lake Geneva. "We watch them as they approach from the opposite side of the lake," wrote Mary, "observing the lightning play among the clouds in various parts of the heavens, and dart in jagged figures upon the piny heights of Jura, dark with the shadow of the overhanging clouds." Forced to abandon their excursions on the lake, the group gathered at Byron's rented villa. Often they discussed "the nature of the principle of life," as Mary explained, "and whether there was any probability of its ever being discovered and communicated." Galvanism—the use of electrical shocks to jolt an inanimate being into life—was a popular topic in Europe and the United States at the time, as was the topic of atmospheric electricity, including lightning and the interplay of electrical currents between earth and sky. Certainly Polidori, Shelley, and Mary were well acquainted with recent scientific experiments in the field of galvanism. Perhaps, thought Mary, a corpse could be reanimated, or "the component parts of a creature might be manufactured, brought together, and endued with vital warmth."

On other occasions the conversations were less intellectual. "The season was cold and rainy," Mary later recalled, "and in the evenings we crowded around a blazing wood fire, and occasionally amused ourselves with some German stories of ghosts, which happened to fall into our hands." On the evening of June 16, Byron decided to regale his friends with several stories from a collection of German horror stories entitled *Phantasmagoriana, or Collection of the Histories of Apparitions, Spectres, Ghosts, etc.* One of these concerned "the story of a husband who kisses his new bride on their wedding night, only to find, to his horror, that she has been transformed into the corpse of the woman he once loved." An interesting choice, considering Byron's reticence on his own wedding night.

"These tales excited in us a playful desire of imitation," noted Shelley, and so he, Byron, and Mary agreed to each write a story "founded on some supernatural occurrence." When the group gathered again on the evening of June 18, they resumed their talk of ghosts and horror, each trying to outdo the other. Shortly after midnight, Byron read Samuel Taylor Coleridge's poem, "Christabel," with its lines about a mysterious stranger (perhaps a witch) who had been abducted in her youth:

> *Then drawing in her breath aloud,*
> *Like one that shudder'd, she unbound*
> *The cincture from beneath her breast:*
> *Her silken robe, and inner vest,*
> *Dropt to her feet, and full in view,*
> *Behold! her bosom and half her side—*
> *A sight to dream of, not to tell!*
> *O shield her! shield sweet Christabel!*

For a moment everyone remained silent. Then Shelley suddenly shrieked, put his hands to his head, and ran out of the room. Polidori followed and threw cold water in Shelley's face, then administered a dose of ether. Staring at Mary, Shelley said that he had "suddenly thought of a woman he had heard of who had eyes instead of nipples, which, when taking hold of his mind, horrified him."

That evening, in her bedroom with its dark parquet floors, and moonlight struggling to penetrate the closed shutters, Mary thought of a creature, "manufactured, brought together, and endued with vital warmth." Gradually, over the remaining months of 1816, Mary Godwin's creature would emerge in a form far more famous than any character created by either Shelley or Byron.

5.

DAY AFTER DAY

"This end of the World Weather is sadly against me . . ."

AT THE INDEPENDENCE Day celebration in Boston, John Adams glanced around at the assembly of four hundred guests in the main hall of the State House, and discovered that he was the only signer of the Declaration of Independence present. For that matter, few members of the Revolutionary generation remained alive in New England. "Death is sweeping his scythe all around us," the eighty-one-year-old Adams wrote that summer, "cutting down our old friends and brandishing it over us."

Adams spent much of his time reading, especially history. He recently had finished (for the second time) Mary Wollstonecraft's sympathetic chronicle of the French Revolution, scribbling his dissenting opinions—often at voluminous length—in the margins of his book. It would be all very well, he argued at one point, if the "empire of superstition and hypocrisy should be overthrown; but if all religion and all morality should be over-thrown with it, what advantage will be gained?" Clearly optimistic about his own future—a reporter on July 4 noted that the former president "still retains the appearance of health and cheerfulness"—Adams embarked upon a new reading project: a sixteen-volume history of France.

Thomas Jefferson, on the other hand, was feeling the effects of time. "Here a pivot, there a wheel, now a pinion, next a spring will give way," Jefferson grumbled in a note to Adams. He could no longer walk very far, although he tried to ride two or three hours a day. He needed glasses to read at night (and during the day for small print) and, Jefferson admitted, "my hearing is not quite so sensible as it used to be." Having recently sold his personal library to Congress to replace the books burned or purloined by British troops when they sacked Washington in 1814, Jefferson was trying to rebuild his literary collection at Monticello, just outside Charlottesville. In the meantime, he had his hands full supervising the care of his gardens. Although his plants had survived the June cold wave, the persistent drought threatened to destroy everything. "In June, instead of $3\frac{3}{4}$ inches, our average of rain for that month," Jefferson informed a friend, "we only had $\frac{1}{3}$ of an inch."

Thirty miles away, President Madison hosted an Independence Day banquet for ninety guests at Montpelier, with dishes spread out along a long table on the lawn under an arbor. It was a nearly all-male affair; Dolley and the president's mother, sister, and niece were the only women present. Dressed in his customary black coat, black breeches with buckles at the knees, and black silk stockings, Madison was determined to enjoy the last few months of his presidency. (In fact, his four-month stay at Montpelier in 1816 remains the longest continuous absence of any president from Washington.) Madison's reputation as a gracious host was based partly upon his generosity with his collection of fine wines (especially Madeira, which he imported by the case and stored in the hollow pediment of his front portico), partly upon the vivacious personality of his wife, and partly upon the excellent fare served up by his French cook. "One could not be in a company more amiable, better versed in good manners, and possessing to a higher degree the precious and very rare art of leaving to the persons who pay them a visit, the comfort and freedom they enjoy in their own home," claimed Attorney General Richard Rush.

Twenty-two years earlier, Jefferson had persuaded Madison to keep a record of the weather at his home, so Jefferson could compare atmospheric temperatures between Monticello and Montpelier. Madison and members of his family had dutifully compiled detailed weather statistics from 1784–1802, but apparently they discontinued the practice shortly after Madison joined Jefferson's first administration as secretary of state. Jefferson, however, continued his own observations on meteorological events while he was president, including notes on the depth and duration of every snowfall in the nation's capital.

Scarcely had the dishes been cleared from Madison's Independence Day repast when a company of four French diplomats, including the recently appointed ambassador, Jean-Guillaume Hyde de Neuville, arrived at Montpelier for a visit. Although de Neuville—who had spent the last few years of Napoléon's reign in exile on an estate in Brunswick, New Jersey—appreciated Madison's diplomatic tact in not mentioning Napoléon during their conversations (pretending that "Louis XVIII had just succeeded Louis XVI"), the French minister was outraged to learn that a member of Madison's cabinet had described the reigning king of France as "an imbecile tyrant" during a July 4 toast in Baltimore. De Neuville insisted the offending official be sacked; Madison demurred. In a private note to Secretary of State Monroe (who was the only Cabinet member spending the summer in Washington), the president wondered if de Neuville "hoped to hide the degradation of the Bourbons under a blustering deportment in a distant country." Small chance, since the antimonarchical brouhaha in Baltimore was not an isolated incident.

Across the United States, the fortieth anniversary of the signing of the Declaration of Independence followed a familiar pattern of parades, public readings of the Declaration (often by elderly Continental Army veterans), and patriotic speeches. Along with Thanksgiving, it was one of only two holidays observed in all eighteen states. (Some New England communities refused to celebrate December 25 as a holiday on the grounds that no one knew for sure precisely when Jesus was born.) Fireworks were readily available in most states, although their unfortunate tendency—in the wrong hands—to set afire the roofs of houses led New York City officials to ban all but government-sanctioned public displays.

In the aftermath of the recent war against Britain (the "Second War of Independence"), the day's themes leaned heavily toward military valor and national unity. Toasts praised President Madison ("A ruler more respected for his merit, than his power, and greater in the simple dignity of his virtues than the proudest monarch on his throne"), and Jefferson ("Hc gave to this day its celebrity—On this day Freemen will ever remember him as first among the first"). They lauded the Union itself ("With it, there is strength, safety and happiness—dissolve it, discord and civil commotion would soon make us the fit subjects of a despot"), while comparing the United States favorably with the ancient republics of Greece and Rome. Speakers denounced the reactionary monarchs of Europe ("They have warred against liberty, and 'hunted virtue and valor to the tomb'") and sympathized with the unfortunate citizens of France ("degraded and abject . . . May the voice of liberty incite her to action, and lead her to glory") and Spain ("sinking back into the night of ignorance and the gloom of superstition—ruled by an idiot and a tyrant") and even England ("grinding her subjects to the earth to bribe other powers").

Temperatures in New England had rebounded nicely, for the most part, since the snowstorms of June 6 and 9. Waltham and Williamstown in Massachusetts reported highs above 90 degrees in the third week of June, and Salem reached 101 degrees on Sunday, June 23. The cold returned briefly on June 28 and 29, when Professor Dewey reported a light frost. It had been the coldest month of June ever recorded in New Haven, Connecticut, but the *Vermont Register and Almanac* cheerfully predicted "sultry hot weather" for the start of July.

It missed the mark completely. July 4 was cool across much of New England. In Plymouth, Connecticut, clockmaker Chauncey Jerome noticed a group of men pitching quoits at midday in bright sunshine, wearing thick overcoats; "a body could not feel very patriotic in such weather," Jerome recalled. Two days later, another cold front swept through from the northwest. Montreal reported snow west of the city—where the growing season already was three weeks behind schedule—and ice about the thickness of a half-dollar on ponds.

On Monday, July 8, frost struck crops from Maine to Virginia. In Franconia, New Hampshire, the cold snap destroyed the bean crop. Along the eastern shore of Lake Erie, where crops had been suffering from a lengthy drought, "the wind was N. West with some snow," and the day "so cold as to render fires necessary for comfort within, and great coats over woolen clothing" outdoors. In Richmond, frost was clearly visible on the ground. "Our climate is far from having ripened to the Summer heat," noted the *Richmond Enquirer*, "the nights and mornings are yet surprisingly cool." The morning of July 9 brought even colder temperatures and hard frosts across New Hampshire, much of Vermont, and western Massachusetts. One Connecticut farmer who had recently burned off part of his land showed a visitor a log that was "frozen down, about 4 feet in length, and 8 or ten inches in breadth; I saw the ice cut up with an axe, and it appeared solid as in winter."

Although this cold wave did not have the devastating impact of its predecessor, it did sufficient damage to raise warning flags of impending scarcity up and down the East Coast. Even though most crops survived, the growth of young plants was sufficiently retarded to make them vulnerable to early autumn frosts. Accordingly, the governor of Lower Canada (including Quebec and Montreal) issued a proclamation "in consequence of the backwardness of the season" prohibiting the export of wheat, flour, beans, and barley until September; simultaneously, he opened Canadian ports to the importation of grain from the United States, free of tariff duties.

Most of Maine's early crop of hay—used as fodder for livestock—perished, and the July freeze killed beans, squash, and cucumbers. In much of Vermont and New Hampshire, the first crop of hay was only half its usual size. As far as wheat and rye were concerned, one observer confirmed that "the most gloomy apprehensions are entertained for the latter harvest. Indeed, if the present cold and dry weather continues a very little longer, the Indian corn, potatoes, beans, &c. cannot escape the autumnal frosts." The *New-Hampshire Sentinel* agreed. "Season very unpromising," it noted. "We begin to despair of corn, hay will come extremely light." The *New-Hampshire Patriot* claimed to have heard "fears of a general famine."

Similar reports came from Worcester, Massachusetts, where the weather had cut the crop of hay in half. Without hay, farmers would either have to slaughter their livestock in the fall or keep them alive through the winter with other crops such as oats and Indian corn, which would require another two months of warm weather to ripen. In eastern Ohio, the crop of hay also had failed, but there was still time for a second cutting if warm weather returned. Farther south, "the effects of an atmosphere thus cool and dry, are visible in our corn-fields," reported the *Richmond Enquirer.* "The plant wears generally a stinted look. From present appearances, the crop threatens to be a very short one." On the bright side, the cool weather had destroyed several summer pests that usually plagued the wheat in Virginia.

Speculation on the cause of the July frost centered on the sunspot theory, whose advocates claimed that diminished solar heat also explained the prolonged drought. On July 4, noted a letter to the *Stockbridge Star,* one large spot was surrounded by sixteen others, "and there was a considerable space around them which appeared less light than other parts of the sun." As the New Hampshire *Farmer's Cabinet* pointed out, however, "we have had several days of uncommon heat, and it is remarkable that these hot days have happened at the precise time when the sun has exhibited the largest spots; and the days which throughout the country have been the coldest, have been at the time when no spots were visible."

Warm weather returned to the East Coast by July 11, but the drought continued. Keene, New Hampshire, went twelve weeks without rain. Northern Vermont was halfway through a four-month summer drought with no precipitation except snow. "Think I never saw our street so dry," muttered a minister in East Windsor, Connecticut.

THOMAS Stamford Raffles returned to England on July 11, 1816. At the request of the directors of the East India Company, the British government had returned Java to the Dutch, now that the Netherlands had regained its independence from France. "The possession of Java, so far from yielding the advantages expected to arise from it, has proved a heavy burden on the finances of the parent State," explained a member of the East India Company's council to Raffles. Four years of administering Java and the surrounding islands had cost the company more than 7 million rupees, according to its own estimate.

Raffles protested the decision, which he considered remarkably shortsighted in its neglect of Britain's long-term strategic and commercial interests in South Asia. Java "cannot longer be kicked about from one place and authority to another like a shuttlecock," he argued. "All our interests in this part of the world are sacrificed." To no avail. Lord Castlereagh and the East India Company had their hands quite full governing the territories they had acquired in India, and had no intention of adding any responsibilities in that region, especially considering Parliament's insistence upon slashing government expenditures.

Raffles spent his last months in Java touring the island, examining the ruins of ancient Hindu temples and statues, and continuing his study of Java's geography and wildlife. Although his health deteriorated toward the end of his tenure ("Anxiety soon pulls a man down in a hot climate," Raffles acknowledged), he undertook a series of initiatives to restrict the importation and sale of opium in Java, and to encourage exports of the island's sugar and coffee to Europe. And he gathered the information forwarded by the residents at the company's stations throughout the islands in response to his inquiries about the effects of Tambora's eruption. Once he had assembled their replies, he asked a colleague to prepare them for publication.

Tambora was still rumbling desultorily when Raffles departed Java on March 25, 1816. As the island faded into the distance, tangible evidence of the eruption still floated in the seas around Raffles' ship. Immense pumice rafts, some as large as three miles across, littered the Java Sea, moving steadily to the west on the South Equatorial Current.

While passing through the South Atlantic, Raffles stopped at Saint Helena for a brief conversation with Napoléon Bonaparte. The former emperor greeted Raffles and a friend, Captain Travers, rather brusquely and then—after he asked Raffles to repeat his name more distinctly—began peppering Raffles with rapid-fire questions that barely gave him time to answer. Where had he been born? Had he spent much time in India? Had Raffles served in the British military force that captured Java five years earlier? How fared the local spice plantations on the islands? How did the king of Java (there was no king of Java) spend his time? Was Britain also returning the Spice Islands to the Netherlands? And which coffee was best—Java or Bourbon?

Raffles answered as best he could, until Napoléon (who remained hatless throughout the interview) finally grew bored and gave a slight nod of his head to let his guests know their time was up. Uncertain how to salute their host—should they call him

"General"? "Emperor"?—Raffles and Travers merely bowed and made their way back to their ship.

Upon landing at Falmouth on July 11, Raffles spent a few days resting in Cornwall before setting off for London. "Although I am considerably recovered," he informed a friend, "I yet remain wretchedly thin and sallow, with a jaundiced eye and a shapeless leg." The countryside through which Raffles traveled was beginning to show evidence of the deepening economic downturn. Ironworkers and the colliers who worked in the iron trade were especially hard-hit. Before the recession, ironworkers' wages were high enough that the men could rent small cottages and provide their families with a modest degree of material comforts, sometimes even saving a small percentage of their earnings. But as the furnaces shut down and coal pits closed in the postwar years, the workers were forced to sell their furniture and leave their homes, often wandering about the country searching for relief from private charities.

Parliament remained in a contentious mood, still unwilling to raise taxes and doggedly unsympathetic to the growing ranks of the unemployed. On July 2, the speaker of the House of Commons informed the Prince Regent that while the government had provided some relief to distressed rural workers, it would do little more. After all, hard times were to be expected after a lengthy war, "and for the remedy for which they trusted much to the healing influence of time." In reply, the Prince Regent lamented "the distresses of some classes of the people, [and] trusted that they would bear them with fortitude and energy."

Following the tumultuous "Bread or Blood" riots in East Anglia in May, protests during June and July remained remarkably well-mannered, despite the steadily rising price of grain and what William Cobbett called "the miserable state of things in England." The most famous incident involved a delegation of colliers and laborers from Bilston, about 125 miles northwest of London, who embarked on a march to the city to present a petition to the Prince Regent detailing their difficulties. Carrying placards that read

"Willing to work, but none of us to beg," the marchers dragged several carts full of coal behind them as a gift to the prince. They covered about twelve miles a day, subsisting on gifts of food and money from the residents of towns along the way. Since the colliers did not beg, they were not subject to the restrictions of the Vagrancy Act; moreover, they were exempt from turnpike tolls, since the turnpikes imposed tolls only on vehicles drawn by horses or other beasts.

But the government would not permit them to complete their mission. There would be no audience with the Prince Regent, for there could be no admission that either Liverpool's ministry or the Crown bore any responsibility for the nation's economic difficulties. As they neared London, the colliers—who conducted themselves "with the most perfect order"—divided into two columns: one was met by magistrates and police at Henley-on-Thames, and the other at St. Albans. The magistrates explained that the processions could advance no farther, but they offered to purchase the coal and distribute it among the poor; then they treated the marchers to beer and gave them money for their journey home.

Through it all, the summer remained stubbornly cold and wet, even by English standards. Spring temperatures had been nearly three degrees colder than average, and June and July started off even further below the norm. In Northamptonshire, just north of London, the high temperature had risen above 67 degrees only twice in the first three weeks of July; most nights the lows sank into the 40s. "The season has been so unusually and constantly cold that fires have been kept without intermission in almost every house," wrote United States Ambassador John Quincy Adams in his diary. Adams, who had been meeting regularly with Castlereagh in London to implement the details of the Treaty of Ghent, knew a thing or two about cold weather, having spent much of his early life in Massachusetts. Yet even this native New Englander claimed that "I have not yet ventured to throw aside my flannel waistcoat, nor as yet for one night to discard the blanket from the bed." Across the greater part of Europe, he concluded, "the weather has been equally extraordinary."

Indeed it had. The strong trans-Atlantic westerly winds that provided so effective a barrier to Arctic air during the mild winter of 1815–16 began to slow during the spring. Like a river whose course has been disrupted by fallen rocks or trees, the Atlantic jet stream began to develop wide meanders to the north and south of its usual track. Where the jet stream dipped south, Arctic air and frequent storms spilled into the lower latitudes. In the ridges between these troughs, mild air flowed from the south, higher pressure dominated, and conditions remained relatively stable. These ridges formed what meteorologists call "omega blocks"—the distortion of the jet stream around them resembles the Greek letter omega (Ω)—and stalled the progress of cyclones.

An analysis of weather records by H. H. Lamb suggests that one such block existed across the central Atlantic in the summer of 1816. A second formed in eastern Europe near the Ukraine, which experienced exceptionally hot conditions that were likely due to the stagnant air that persisted within the ridge of high pressure. Between these ridges, the jet stream veered far to the south, allowing air from Greenland and Iceland (where ice-covered seas persisted into June) to sweep across Britain and Ireland and into central Europe. Low-pressure systems cascaded down from Iceland along this stream. Unable to penetrate the block to the east, they would continue to wreak havoc over Europe for much of the summer. A second prolonged dip in the jet stream formed upwind of the Atlantic block, affecting eastern Canada and New England; the June snowstorms in that area resulted from a particularly severe southward excursion of the jet stream.

The weaker trans-Atlantic westerly winds and meandering jet streams signaled a reduced North Atlantic Oscillation Index. During the winter, the aerosol cloud from Tambora had strengthened the Arctic cyclonic vortex; by springtime it had begun to have the opposite effect on Atlantic pressure systems, and hence on the

North Atlantic Oscillation Index and the jet stream. As the aerosol cloud reflected sunlight, the temperatures of the land and ocean cooled gradually, due to the heat stored under their surfaces. By the summer, more than a year after the eruption, this cooling most likely had begun to overtake the stratospheric warming. Since the tropics cooled more than the Arctic, the temperature difference between the two narrowed, leading to reduced trans-Atlantic westerly winds, a weaker and meandering jet stream with several blocks, and frequent intrusions of Arctic air into North America and western Europe.

Computer simulations of the effects of volcanic eruptions on climate provide evidence for this strengthening of the Atlantic jet stream in the first winter after the eruption, with a delayed weakening of the jet that can last for up to a decade, depending on the strength of the eruption and the lifetime of the stratospheric aerosol veil. The timing of the weakening varies among the simulations, however, even for the same volcanic eruption. While all simulations produce global cooling and a weaker Atlantic jet, some produce stronger cooling than others or delay the appearance of the negative North Atlantic Oscillation. The disagreements between these studies on the precise details of the climatic response to volcanic aerosols demonstrates that, even almost two hundred years after Tambora, there are still unanswered questions about how strongly the eruption affected the weather. A study by Drew Shindell and his colleagues, for example, concluded that the negative North Atlantic Oscillation Index did not emerge until two or three years after Tambora erupted. The exceptionally cold and stormy weather in Europe and North America in the summer of 1816, combined with the jet displacements noted by H. H. Lamb, however, argues that Tambora caused a transition to a negative North Atlantic Oscillation Index and a meandering jet stream within one year.

As July slid and splashed to its sodden conclusion, British newspapers echoed the concerns of their American counterparts about the effects of the unusual weather on the coming harvest.

"The continuance of the present very unseasonable weather has been attended with the most baneful effects in various parts of the country," reported *The Times* of London on July 20. In the southern counties, incessant rain already had ruined the hay and clover crops. Farmers in that area feared that if the heavy rains continued, their wheat crops might fail as well, "and the effects of such a calamity and at such a time [i.e., during the economic downturn] cannot be otherwise than ruinous to the farmers, and even to the people at large." As in the United States, reliable historical temperature records were scarce, and so *The Times*, too, resorted to comparisons through anecdotal evidence: "Such an inclement summer," it ventured, "is scarcely remembered by the oldest inhabitant of London or its environs." And on the Corn Exchange in London, the price of wheat continued to rise due to "the quantity of fine Wheat at market being small, and the weather continuing unsettled."

From Sweden to northern Italy, and Switzerland to Spain, great rain-bearing clouds seemed to darken the skies every day. "Melancholy accounts have been received from all parts of the Continent of the unusual wetness of the season," mourned the *Norfolk Chronicle*; "property in consequence swept away by inundation, and irretrievable injuries done to the vine yards and corn crops." Some of the worst damage occurred in the Netherlands. In the province of Guelderland, a region of rich grasslands crisscrossed by numerous rivers that was already suffering from the postwar agricultural depression, the rains had destroyed so much of the hay and grain crops usually used for fodder that farmers already had begun to kill their livestock, knowing they could not feed the cattle through the winter. Nor was there sufficient food for the human population. "An indescribable misery has taken place," reported one observer, "so that the lower classes of people have been obliged to feed on herbage and grains." Facing insufficient supplies of bread and potatoes, the governor of the province asked local magistrates to establish relief kitchens (at public expense) to provide their

needy residents with what was known as Rumford's soup—an inexpensive, filling, and reasonably nutritious concoction made from
dried peas, vegetables, and sour beer. (Rumford's soup had been
invented about twenty years earlier by an American physicist and
entrepreneur named Benjamin Thompson, who lived most of his
adult life in Europe under the name Count Rumford.)

During the first week of July, the Rhine rose at Arnhem "to
the almost, at this season, unparalleled height of 15 feet, 7 inches,"
and still the rain poured down. "In every part of the neighbouring
country, where the lands are rather low, they are in a state of inundation," read a report in *The Times* of London. The districts along
the Maas and Waal Rivers were almost entirely under water. In
Zutphen, northeast of Arnhem, farmers reportedly had given up
any hope of saving even a portion of their crops. "Our rich grass
lands are already under water," reported one correspondent, "and
the grass which is not yet spoiled can only be got at by mowing in
boats, for the immediate use of the cattle, which we have been
obliged to stall."

Along the river Yssel, "the grass which was cut on Tuesday last
the farmers have been obliged to pick up with boats on the following day, to give their cattle food: in many places they have been
obliged to cut the corn for that purpose: and as there is no fodder,
such corn as can be got at must be cut, or the cattle will have nothing to subsist on." Some desperate farmers reached into their
stores of winter seed corn to feed their cattle, thereby endangering
next year's harvest as well. Dispatches from Overyssel and Friesland
provinces were equally alarming. "Even if the weather were to
take a favourable turn," noted *The Times* of London, "the injury
already sustained, and the calamitous consequences of a summer
inundation, cannot be repaired. . . . This appears certain—that an
unusual scarcity and high price of all provisions must be the consequence."

Conditions were no better in most of the German states. "We
continue to receive the most melancholy news from Germany on

the extraordinary weather which afflicts nearly the whole of Europe," noted a correspondent in Paris. "The excessive abundance of rain has caused disasters almost every where." Crops in Saxony and Würzburg failed, leaving farmers "in utter despair." To the south, Upper Franconia—famous for its breweries and grain—lay waste under "continual rains, torrents the like of which we have never before seen, [and] storms followed by hail." The Rhine and the Neckar Rivers rose nine and a half feet above their usual level, flooding the area around Manheim and leaving whole villages under water. "The hopes of a very fine harvest have been almost ruined," wrote one witness to the devastation. "The loss in hay, corn, tobacco, and pulse is incalculable."

Switzerland fared even worse. Frances, Lady Shelley (no relation to the poet), left Paris in early July and headed for Switzerland with her husband, Sir John Shelley, an English nobleman notorious for his self-indulgent lifestyle and his friendship with the Prince Regent. As they approached the Swiss border after eight days of incessant rain, Lady Shelley noted that "the country was flooded, and the crops everywhere suffering from the unusually wet season. The hay in many places has been washed down the stream." On July 15 they reached Lac de Bienne, where Jean-Jacques Rousseau had lived, and found "the whole country . . . completely inundated, and the three lakes now form but one. The season has been calamitous. All the crops were destroyed, and much of the beauty of the scenery has been spoiled by the wintry aspect of the meadows."

From the canton of Glarus, a center of textile production in eastern Switzerland, came word that the inhabitants, due largely to "the severity of the present season, are sunk to the last degree of wretchedness." The only glimmer of hope came from a private charity which was trying to build a settlement for the poor on the banks of the river Linth. In the plains of the canton of Basel, fields of wheat and potatoes lay submerged in water as the Birsig overflowed its banks; only the crops planted on higher ground held out any hope of survival. As the prospect of famine increased, the government of the canton of Bern issued an ordinance prohibiting the export of bread, flour, and grain.

Things seemed a little brighter in Austria. A report from Vienna on July 12 noted that "the harvest, which has been delayed in Austria by the continuation of the cold and bad weather, has at length begun every where." Although the grain had been damaged by late frosts and damp weather, it appeared as if the yield of wheat, barley, and oats might actually exceed the diminished expectations in some regions. But the region from Calabria to Tyrol was already suffering from "an unexampled dearth" of grain, while the grape harvest throughout Austria "does not give any hopes either with respect to quantity or quality."

Vineyards in Burgundy were faring no better, as the Saône River flooded its banks: "All the fine plain of the Saône is covered with water." In Chancey, about one hundred and fifty miles north of Geneva, rivers reportedly rose so high that rafts could pass over the bridges. Facing a shortage of grain in the province of Lorraine, the prefect of La Meurthe forbade the brewing of beer or the use of grain to make distilled liquor. In Montauban in southwestern France, unusually large hailstones pelted crops in mid-July and "completely destroyed the hopes of the harvest wherever this storm reached." And throughout France, landowners resigned to minimal harvests resisted the collection of the land tax, which in turn exacerbated the government's budget difficulties.

Like their American counterparts, many Europeans assumed that God could alter the weather if He wished. As reports of the damage to grain and vineyards poured into Paris—where the Seine rose eight feet over several days—priests directed their flocks to pray for an end to the deluge, and so the cathedrals of Paris were filled with suppliants praying for dry weather. John Quincy Adams similarly reported that "the churches and chapels have been unusually crowded" in both England and France. In Sweden, too, prayers were "offered up in the churches daily to the Deity for a favourable change."

The same sunspots that fascinated Americans in the spring and summer of 1816 created even more consternation in Europe. Sometime in the late spring, an astronomer in Bologna (alternately referred to in some news reports as "a mad Italian prophet") proclaimed that the extraordinary size and number of sunspots meant that the sun would soon be extinguished, an event that would bring life on Earth to an end on July 18. The forecast provoked so much anxiety among the local populace—already shaken by darkly colored snow and unusually cold, wet spring weather—that government officials reportedly locked the astronomer in jail to silence him.

Other self-appointed prophets sounded similar alarms. In Naples, a priest announced that the city would soon be destroyed by a rain of fire that would last for four hours, "and those who escaped the fire were to be devoured by serpents." He, too, was placed under arrest.

Nevertheless, news of the prediction spread rapidly throughout Europe, prompting a variety of panicked responses. "Old women have taken the alarm," scoffed *The Times* of London on July 13, "and the prediction is now a general subject of conversation." Outside Vienna, frightened residents of several towns gathered together for protection; afraid that the crowds signaled the start of an insurrection, local authorities dispatched troops to prevent any disorder. From Ghent came a report of frightened women crowding into churches, "to prepare themselves against this dreadful catastrophe." On the evening of July 11—"the weather was gloomy, the thunder roared, and flashes of lightning furrowed the dark clouds accumulated over the town"—a regiment of cavalry which had recently arrived in Ghent sounded the retreat at 9 P.M. by several blasts of trumpets, as usual. Nervous bystanders, however, thought the sounds had come from the Seventh Trumpet, the apocalyptic signal prophesied in the New Testament Book of Revelation. "Suddenly cries, groans, tears, lamentations, were heard on every side," recalled a witness. "Three fourths of the inhabitants rushed forth from their houses, and threw themselves on their knees in the streets and public places. It was not without infinite trouble that the cause of this extraordinary terror was discovered." On the same day in Liège, "an enormous mass of clouds appearing . . . in the shape of a huge mountain over the city" created a similar panic.

Nor were France and Britain exempt from the hysteria. "In France as well as in this country, and generally throughout Europe," acknowledged *The Times*, "the prediction of the mad Italian prophet, relative to the end of the world, had produced great dread in the minds of some, so that they neglected all business, and gave themselves up entirely to despondency." And in Britain, the newspaper's editor claimed, anxiety over the sunspots— "added to the severe distress to which the country is otherwise reduced"—had "infused into the minds of the people generally the greatest apprehension and alarm." In the United States, the prophecy received considerably less publicity, although one writer in the *Atheneum* noted that it had "fairly frightened some of our own old women out of their lives."

Newspapers published scholarly articles from professors and professional astronomers to reassure their readers, but to no avail. As the panic spread, skeptics mocked the gullible public. On July 9, the *London Chronicle* dismissed the prophecies as "outrageous fooleries," and later lamented that "the multitude are more ignorant and credulous than in the most barbarous times." *The Times* of London referred to "the Italian mountebanks" who circulated the prophecy, and hinted that they had darker motives, perhaps attempting to foment revolution. The London *Examiner* agreed that the prophecy was "not unconnected with political circumstances, and the naturally wondering spirit to which the events of the time have given rise." *The Times* also pointed out that the prophecy was most likely false, because everyone familiar with the Book of Revelation knew that "the end of the world is to be announced by the Anti-Christ, and there are yet no accounts of his appearance." On July 17, numerous papers in London and Paris published satirical guides with outlandish recommendations on how to prepare for the end of the world. For his part, Samuel Taylor Coleridge lamented to a friend that "this end of the World Weather [i.e., more cold rain] is sadly against me by preventing all exercise."

Credulity sometimes brought tragic results. In London, an elderly cook who was prone to bouts of depression decided to hang herself "in a fit of melancholy," as John Quincy Adams observed, "at the prospect of the world's coming to an end. Such is human credulity!" (The coroner's inquest brought in a verdict of insanity occasioned by the notorious prediction.) And on the morning of July 18, an eight-year-old girl living in Bath chose to awaken her aunt, a devout believer in the prophecy, by screaming "Aunt, Aunt, the World's at an end!" The words so startled the poor woman that she fell into a coma, and remained insensate throughout the following day.

Any sighs of relief when July 18 came and went were short-lived; the heavy rains continued. "Another wet morning," recorded British diarist Joseph Farington. "The season very remarkable." As a severe storm approached Lancashire in northwest England on July 21, villagers in Longpark saw "a dense whitish cloud . . . which advanced with great rapidity, and, on its nearer approach, presented the appearance of the waves of the sea tumultuously rolling over each other." Within ten minutes, jagged hailstones up to one inch in diameter had shattered windows and destroyed virtually all the vegetation in the area. The nervous residents dropped to their knees and began to pray, fearing the apocalypse had arrived just a bit off schedule. The same storm produced almost total darkness in Argyllshire, Scotland, setting off a similar bout of terror of impending annihilation. And in France, a workingman in L'oise who had just returned from mass suddenly began shouting that he, too, was a prophet, and that the end of the world was indeed approaching.

* * *

ONE Vermont farmer decided to give up and head west even before the summer was over. Since 1814, Joseph Smith and his wife,
Lucy, and their nine children had been renting a farm in Norwich,
Vermont. More than a decade earlier, Smith had owned his own
land, but a bad business investment in 1803 forced him to sell and
become a tenant farmer, moving frequently with his family, back
and forth across the Vermont–New Hampshire border, looking for
the best deal. They had lived for a while in Sharon, Vermont—
where his fourth son, Joseph Jr., was born in 1805—and then in
Royalton; in 1811 they moved to Lebanon, New Hampshire, and
finally Norwich. Besides working the land they rented, Joseph and
his older sons hired themselves out as farmhands at harvest time,
or performed odd jobs in town. For a while one of the boys, Hyrum,
attended Moor's Charity School in Hanover. Lucy helped earn
extra cash by painting oilcloths used as table coverings.

The Smith family's stay in Norwich proved disappointing. In
1814, their crops failed. The following year brought another poor
harvest. "The next year [1816] an untimely frost destroyed the
crops," Lucy later recalled, "and being the third year in succession in
which the crops had failed, it almost caused a famine." And it persuaded Joseph to emigrate. Several of Joseph's brothers already had
moved to northern New York State, and the Vermont newspapers
regularly carried advertisements for land in the Genesee Valley
available for two to three dollars an acre. "This was enough," noted
Lucy. "My husband was now altogether decided upon going to New
York. He came in, one day, in quite a thoughtful mood, and sat
down; after meditating some time, he observed that, could he so
arrange his affairs, he would be glad to start soon for New York."

Joseph chose to leave alone, and promised to send for his
family—which now included a three-month-old baby, Don Carlos—
once he established himself. He settled in Palmyra, a small town of
about fifteen hundred people twenty miles south of Rochester,

where he opened a small shop that sold "cake and beer": light refreshments such as gingerbread, pies, boiled eggs, and root beer. Joseph's family joined him soon thereafter. It was a region, as Joseph Jr. subsequently pointed out, of "unusual excitement on the subject of religion. . . . Indeed, the whole district of country seemed affected by it, and great multitudes united themselves to the different religious parties."

6.

THE LOST SUMMER

"A belief begins to prevail among the many in all countries that there is something more than natural in the present state of the weather . . ."

A SEEMINGLY ENDLESS series of storms struck Ireland in July. "The month was, without, perhaps, the exception of a single day, a continuity of showers of hail or rain, and at the same time very cold," reported *The Times* of London. "A great blight in the wheat crop, particularly in Wicklow and Tipperary. The rain was so severe that scarcely any corn was left standing."

In the summer of 1816, the Irish economy was struggling to adjust to the short-term demands of peacetime and the long-term effects of five decades of economic growth. Between 1765 and 1815, prices of the agricultural goods Ireland produced—primarily wheat, oats, pork, beef, and butter—more than doubled. During the first part of this period, much of the demand for Irish foodstuffs came from the British and French colonies in the West Indies, facilitated by the increasing volume of trans-Atlantic shipping. In the latter years, trade with Britain flourished to provide food for the expanding population of factory workers in England and Scotland; between 1778 and 1798, the value of Ireland's exports (including linen, its main industrial product) shipped across the Irish Sea quadrupled. The Napoleonic Wars brought even more prosperity to Ireland, as the British government sought food for its armies while the normal supplies of agricultural produce from the Continent were cut off.

Rising food prices led to the cultivation of ever-greater quantities of land throughout Ireland. Landlords drained boglands and planted crops on mountainsides that were only marginally productive. As in England, much of this expansion was carried out with borrowed funds. So long as prices remained high, the benefits outweighed the costs, but Irish landlords, like their English counterparts, carried an increasing load of debt.

Ireland's expanding economy also contributed to a substantial increase in population, as the island's birthrate rose and the death rate fell. In 1767, Ireland's population totaled 2.5 million; by 1816 it neared 6 million. A disproportionate share of this growth occurred in the poorer classes, and primarily in rural areas.

In the early nineteenth century, more than 80 percent of the Irish population depended on agriculture for a living. Nearly all of the land was owned by the Anglo-Irish gentry, who spent the bulk of their profits building grand houses on vast estates. Overwhelmingly Protestant, the great landowners dominated Irish political, economic, and social affairs. They often served as the only employer in the area surrounding their estates, hiring artisans, servants, and day laborers; sometimes they also owned the grain mills to which their tenants would bring their harvest. Tradition demanded that the gentry lighten the burdens of their neighbors by providing occasional entertainment to their community, and so they hosted parties and organized hunting and fishing expeditions; as their expenses mounted, many landlords found themselves sinking even deeper in debt. Tradition also expected the gentry to fulfill the social obligations of the propertied classes, notably by providing charity to the poor in times of need, but in early-nineteenth-century Ireland these duties were increasingly ignored.

Just below the landlords on the social scale came the substantial tenant farmers, who lived comfortably and displayed their wealth through a variety of household furnishings and tailored clothing (waistcoats, knee britches, warm stockings, and sturdy boots). If a prosperous farmer was a Protestant, he might hope that his son would rise into the legal or medical profession, or perhaps obtain a position in the Anglican Church. Catholics, on the other hand, were prohibited by the penal laws (passed by Parliament a century earlier) from attending British universities or serving in Parliament, and were likewise excluded from careers in the civil service, the law, or the armed forces. Hence the priesthood or a position as a schoolteacher seemed the only avenues for their advancement.

The great majority of Ireland's rural population—probably between 75 and 80 percent—resided in the poorer classes of small tenant farmers, cottiers, and laborers. They typically lived in mud cabins, the meanest of which consisted of "a single room, a hole for a window with a board in it, the door generally off the hinges, a wicker-basket with a hole in the bottom or an old butter-tub stuck at one corner of the thatch for a chimney, the pig, as a matter of course, inside the cottage, and an extensive manufacture of manure . . . [taking place] on the floor." Straw often sufficed for beds; the only cooking utensil a large iron pot; and stumps of fir trees for chairs. The walls and roof usually consisted of "rough stones and clay mortar; a few rough sticks, procured generally out of the bogs, which serve to support a bad covering of straw; sometimes interlined with heath for want of a sufficiency of straw, and seldom renewed while it is possible to inhabit it." Those slightly better off might live in a four-room cabin, with a handmade table and wooden kitchenware, and a wardrobe of serviceable, albeit well-worn and patched, clothing. Their less fortunate brethren owned no overcoats at all, and women and children went barefoot all year-round.

Opportunities for members of different social classes to mix were limited primarily to public occasions such as markets, fairs, feast days, weddings, or county funerals. Even during these events, however, it proved difficult for the wealthier Irish to communicate with the poor, since most of the laboring class (semiliterate at best) still spoke only Irish, and most of the landed classes spoke English—increasingly the language of politics and business. The bane of public gatherings in the early nineteenth century was the faction fight, an organized brawl in which two opposing sides assaulted each other wielding clubs, blackthorn sticks, stones, or, less frequently, swords. The factions might have divided along family lines, or parishes, or by trade, or religion; motives for fighting included arguments over property, family vendettas, personal insults or perceived slights, tensions between competing economic groups, or religious antagonism. A few notorious fights involved several thousand combatants; most numbered several hundred. Enough men died or suffered serious injuries during these brawls that the Catholic Church stoutly condemned the custom and threatened to excommunicate anyone who joined in. Nonetheless, landlords sometimes encouraged faction fights as a safety valve, to allow their laborers and tenants to vent their frustrations and anger on other members of the lower class.

Irish diets improved along with the economy, although the rising standard of living set the stage for future disaster. Laborers and the poorest farmers subsisted entirely on potatoes and water, and occasionally a bit of salt fish or meal; those who could afford a more varied diet typically added milk, then oatmeal and wheat bread. Whiskey, beer, and tobacco also were relatively inexpensive. But potatoes remained the foundation of the Irish peasantry's diet; indeed, it was one of the main causes of the increase in population in the late eighteenth and early nineteenth centuries. Spanish merchants had introduced potatoes to Europe in the late sixteenth century, but widespread public resistance to their cultivation and consumption restricted their use to animal fodder for more than a century. (Some Europeans feared the ugly tubers were the fruit of the devil, while others scorned any food that grew under the soil.) By the late eighteenth century, however, physicians and government officials recognized their exceptional nutritional value (high in potassium and vitamin C), and potatoes became a staple of the Europeans' diet, particularly among the poor. Even a child could cultivate them, and they required little effort to cook or store. No wonder that Adam Smith, the renowned Scottish philosopher and classical economist, concluded that potatoes were "particularly suitable to the health of the human constitution."

Hence the population of Ireland embarked upon a dramatic increase, as did much of western and central Europe. Potatoes provided significantly more nutrients than the Irish peasantry's previous grain-based diets, and since a family of five or six could subsist for a year on the potatoes grown on a few acres of land, Irish peasants began to marry earlier and produce more children. And since a potato diet mitigated the prevalence or effects of many of the diseases that afflicted the Irish peasantry—scurvy, dysentery, tuberculosis—the infant mortality rate and the overall death rate both declined.

Prosperity brought new complications in its wake, however. As the Irish population swelled, and the price of agricultural products rose, the value of land soared as well. Many landowners raised their rents accordingly; others evicted their tenants and enclosed their lands as pasture for even more profitable sheep or cattle. Tenants who found themselves unable to pay the higher rents were thrown off their land, and a steady stream of dispossessed farmers headed for the cities—by 1816, Dublin's population had grown to about 200,000 residents—where they joined unemployed rural laborers who had lost their jobs to farm machinery or the new water-powered textile looms in the linen industry. Still, most of the unemployed remained in the countryside. And many of those who did have jobs were underemployed; in an average year, by one estimate, nearly half a million Irish were employed for six months or less.

Parliament's recent decision to bind Ireland more tightly to Britain created additional problems. The Act of Union of 1800, which established the United Kingdom of Great Britain and Ireland, disbanded the Irish Parliament and provided seats for Irish representatives in both the House of Commons and the House of Lords. This removed one of the few reasons for the Protestant gentry to spend any time whatsoever in Ireland; accordingly many of them settled in England and became absentee landlords. Distance diminished their sense of responsibility for the welfare of their tenants—it was said that they traded their Irish sympathies for English prejudices—and in many cases their estates in Ireland deteriorated from neglect. For its part, Parliament preferred to ignore Irish affairs altogether whenever possible. Since their only representatives were Protestant members of the propertied class, the Irish people at large were left with no voice in their government at all.

Under these conditions, a rapidly growing population living on land already cultivated to its maximum extent was courting disaster. Holdings were subdivided repeatedly from one generation to the next; by the first decade of the nineteenth century, any perceptive observer could see that the average size of a peasant's holding soon would barely suffice to feed a family even with a generous potato harvest. And in both towns and countryside, the oversupply of labor kept wages depressed as the price of commodities rose, further driving down the standard of living for those whose margin for survival already was razor thin.

An expansion of trade had provided profitable foreign markets for Irish goods, but Ireland's commerce was growing dangerously unbalanced. Across the Atlantic, the products of American farms replaced Irish crops, leaving Ireland heavily dependent upon the English market; by 1816, approximately 85 percent of Irish exports went to Britain. Prospects for further economic development appeared dim, due to a lack of capital for investment in either industry or agriculture. Already Irish cotton and wool manufacturers—who had enjoyed an edge from lower labor costs— were losing ground to English mills due to a widespread failure to employ the latest developments in technology. Landowners could obtain additional capital only by raising their rents or enclosing their lands, but both options would have increased unemployment. And if the government lowered taxes to allow landlords to acquire more capital, the laboring classes would suffer from reductions in the funds available for poor relief.

Whenever Irish harvests failed and famine threatened, primary responsibility for humanitarian relief—such as public works projects—and the preservation of order typically devolved upon the local authorities: magistrates (drawn from the ranks of small farmers and prosperous tenants), sheriffs, and the parish vestry. Since these officials were nearly always Protestant, they often allocated a disproportionate share of relief funds to the minority Protestant community. Other times they failed to carry out their responsibilities at all due to corruption or incompetence. Nor did the landlords—more concerned with order than charity—step in to fill the vacuum; as one observer noted, the Irish gentry "had neither the will nor the way to carry the same administrative burden as their English counterparts." In either case, local authorities typically failed to provide adequate services to the needy, thereby earning the distrust of the poorer classes, most of whom were Catholic.

That left responsibilities squarely in the hands of private charities and the central government in Dublin, headed by the viceroy—formally, the lord lieutenant—appointed by Parliament. In the summer of 1816, relations between His Majesty's Government and the Irish masses were still troubled as a result of the bloodshed of 1798, when Irish nationalists launched a poorly planned and ill-coordinated uprising that ended with perhaps twenty thousand Irish rebels and civilians dead, along with six hundred British soldiers, and much of the Irish countryside laid waste. Most of the Irish casualties were the product of the vicious tactics employed by British forces—following the orders of Castlereagh, then chief secretary for Ireland—in quelling the rebellion. If authorities in London intended the Act of Union to bind Ireland more closely to Britain, it succeeded only in deepening Irish resentment of their English masters, and fueled sectarian hostility.

Few capable or ambitious politicians in London sought the office of lord lieutenant. The unique challenges presented by governing Ireland posed far greater risks than benefits to a politician on the rise. Consequently the viceroys were often second- or third-raters. A case in point was the lord lieutenant in 1816, Lord Whitworth, appointed in 1811 only after months of fruitless searching for a more widely known or respected candidate; as one historian put it, Whitworth's appointment "generated universal amazement." He was notorious largely as a reputed lover of Catherine the Great of Russia (which he probably was not) during his tenure as British ambassador to Russia, and for his marriage to a wealthy widow, the Duchess of Dorset, a match which made him seem a social climber. Despite the elevated status bestowed by his marriage, Whitworth remained so far down the ranks of the British aristocracy that the king felt compelled to grant him an earldom upon his appointment as lord lieutenant in Dublin, to boost his personal authority. Despite society's doubts, however, Whitworth was not without executive ability; one of his colleagues claimed that Whitworth possessed a "cool and sure intellect . . . good sense, temper, firmness, and habits of business."

Certainly Whitworth had the good sense to rely upon his chief secretary, Robert Peel, for the day-to-day administration of Irish affairs. The son of a successful textile manufacturer, Peel had been educated at Oxford—where he distinguished himself in his studies of the classics, mathematics, and physics—before embarking on a career in law. He entered Parliament in 1810, at the age of twenty-two, and subsequently was appointed under-secretary for the Colonies in Spencer Perceval's administration. When Liverpool assumed power two years later, following Perceval's assassination, he named Peel chief secretary for Ireland.

As chief secretary, Peel was responsible primarily for maintaining order in Ireland (a daunting task in the best of times), and for upholding Protestant rule. For the past several decades, Parliament had witnessed a series of campaigns in favor of Catholic emancipation—the repeal of the penal laws that denied certain civil rights to Catholics in Ireland. The Whig opposition in the House of Commons openly favored emancipation, and a faction of Tories (including Liverpool) privately supported it. But King George III and the House of Lords resolutely refused to consider emancipation, and Peel (who sided with the Tory majority) never wavered from the party line.

In normal times, reports crossed Peel's desk in Dublin recounting one instance after another of smuggling, banditry, kidnapping, murder, arson, theft (generally of food or weapons), rape, faction fighting, sedition, grave robbing, nonpayment of rent, assault of revenue collectors, and disturbance of the peace. Local magistrates and the county police often found themselves powerless to deal with these outrages, since intimidation of witnesses and brutal retaliation against anyone brave enough to give testimony discouraged cooperation with the authorities. Shortly after taking office, Peel informed a colleague that "the country is in a very distracted state in many parts. . . . It is very difficult to conceive the impunity with which the most horrible crimes are committed in consequence of the fears even of the sufferers to come forward to give evidence."

Under the unique conditions of Irish life, with its deep-rooted tensions between the Protestant gentry and their Catholic tenants, this litany of felonies actually served, as Norman Gash put it, as a form of "intermittent social warfare." Peel harbored no illusions about his ability to ameliorate the situation. "The enormous and overgrown population of Ireland is (considering the want of manufactures or any employment except agricultural) a great obstacle in the way of general improvement," he wrote, "and an obstacle which much wiser men than I am will find it very difficult to remove."

Peel's initial response was to urge the establishment of a full-time body of police in Ireland to assist local authorities in maintaining order. Parliament, wary of the expense and distrustful of the precedent of a professional police force, grudgingly passed the requisite legislation in July 1814. The force grew slowly, partly because of a shortage of competent candidates, but it eventually took hold and became known as the Royal Irish Constabulary, or (after Sir Robert) "Peelers" or "bobbies."

The outbreak of peace at the end of the Hundred Days in June 1815 brought Whitworth and Peel fresh troubles. As European governments demobilized their armies, foreign demand for Irish foodstuffs and textiles declined. And foreign sources of supply increased as agricultural production revived on the Continent. The price of Irish grain dropped by 50 percent; beef prices slid even more. Marginal lands brought under cultivation during the Napoleonic Wars turned unprofitable. Tenants failed to earn enough to pay their rent; artisans and manufacturers lost their jobs as factories suspended operations. One ray of hope stemmed from an increase in exports of agricultural goods to the United States over the winter of 1815–16, but those sales were the result of Irish prices being so low (and unsustainably so) that they undercut domestic American production.

Distress bred more disorder. In January 1816, Peel wrote to the prime minister informing him of a rash of crimes in Tipperary that amounted to a virtual rebellion. Many cases involved combinations of tenants avenging themselves upon anyone paying what they considered an excessive rent for land. The local magistrates responded harshly, condemning thirteen of the convicted men to death, with fourteen more transported to penal colonies. "You can have no idea of the moral depravation of the lower orders in that county," complained Peel. Actually, Liverpool believed he could. "In truth," the prime minister wrote, "Ireland is a political phenomenon—not influenced by the same feelings as appear to affect mankind in other countries—and the singular nature of the disorder must be the cause why it has hitherto been found impracticable to apply an effectual and permanent remedy."

Springtime brought a brief respite, perhaps because the cold, wet weather of April and May dampened any hostile impulses among the citizenry. Whitworth believed that he and Peel deserved credit for the lull, based upon the forceful measures they had encouraged in recent months. "The people see that there is something stronger than themselves, from which they cannot escape," the lord lieutenant concluded. "They have been taught respect, or at least dread of the law, and that is the instruction most wanted." One of the more curious reports came from County Clare, where a band of moonshiners distilling illegal whiskey had barricaded themselves in a castle to avoid arrest. Local authorities asked the chief secretary to send artillery to demolish the castle; Peel urged them to try less drastic measures instead.

Calm continued into the summer, but so did the rain and the cold. "Eight weeks of rain in succession," grumbled one writer. "Hay and corn crops in a deplorable state. The grains of corn in many places are covered with a reddish powder like rust"—probably a fungus which thrived in wet weather—"which has proved very destructive to the crop." Especially in the western counties, "the fields of corn presented a lamentable appearance, in many places being quite black."

DAVID Ricardo believed he knew the solution to Ireland's economic woes. A successful stockbroker and economic theorist—his most recent work, *An Essay on the Influence of a Low Price of Corn on the Profits of Stock* (1815), had introduced the law of diminishing marginal returns—Ricardo was in the process of turning himself into an English country gentleman in the summer of 1816. Two years earlier, he had purchased Gatcombe Park, an estate in Gloucestershire in southwest England. In early July 1816, Ricardo spent several days at Gatcombe entertaining Thomas Robert

Malthus, England's other foremost political economist. "We were held prisoners by the weather," Ricardo confided to a friend, but the constant rain provided the two men with an opportunity to discuss economic theory and the challenges currently confronting the government in London.

Malthus, an ordained Anglican priest who served as Professor of Modern History and Political Economy at the East India College in Haileybury, just north of London, had initially gained fame through the publication of his *Essay on the Principle of Population* in 1798. A reaction against the Enlightenment notion that human society could improve itself endlessly, Malthus' essay suggested that a society's population always had a tendency to expand beyond the available supply of food. Unless individuals voluntarily slowed the rate of population growth by "preventive checks" such as postponing marriage and practicing celibacy, nature would dispose of the "surplus population" through "positive checks," including starvation and plague. In his original essay, Malthus argued that any attempts to ameliorate the condition of the poor through charitable donations would fail, since the increased income would be absorbed by even more offspring. Five years later, however, Malthus published a revised edition of his essay, in which he suggested that the poor could be taught to practice "moral restraint" and "virtuous celibacy"—delaying marriage until they could reasonably expect to earn an income that would allow them to support their (smaller) families at the level they wished to live. Once they became accustomed to a higher standard of living, Malthus believed the lower classes would continue to voluntarily limit the size of their families and thereby help keep the population in check.

This, Ricardo argued in July 1816, was precisely what Ireland required: "a taste for other objects besides mere food," and less passion for mindless activities such as faction fighting. Any stimulus, Ricardo wrote, that would "rouse the Irish to activity which should induce them to dispose of their surplus time in procuring luxuries for themselves, instead of employing it in the most brutal pursuits, would tend more to the civilization and prosperity of their country than any other measures which could be recommended."

Ireland was one of the few subjects upon which Ricardo and Malthus agreed, however. Their differences were especially sharp on the issue of Britain's Corn Laws. Ricardo steadfastly opposed protectionist legislation, believing that the artifically high price of grain kept too much marginal land in production and reduced the profits of business owners, thereby hindering Britain's economic progress. Although Malthus originally had opposed the Corn Laws, by 1816 he had reversed his position. The need for Britain to maintain self-sufficiency in food production, Malthus claimed, outweighed any deleterious economic effects of the legislation. But both men foresaw serious trouble ahead if the dismal summer weather continued, threatening Britain's harvest.

ENGLISH tourists continued to flood into Switzerland—ten thousand, by one estimate. One British correspondent complained that Geneva was so full of his fellow countrymen that English families who wished to send their children there for an education in a foreign culture "could not find a family to place them in where there were not other English boarders."

"I hear old England is to be quite deserted this summer," wrote Lady Caroline Capel. Her daughter Georgy agreed: "I should think England was the only part of the world now where there was a lack of English. Lausanne is full of them, there are several here, in short it is quite amazing!" Lady Capel and her family had rented the Château Bel Air ("too small for our size . . . but very well furnished") about half a mile outside Vevey, on the north shore of Lake Geneva, and were having a splendid time touring local historical sites—including the notorious Castle of Chillon, the former fortress/arsenal/prison built on an island in the lake—and scrambling about the hillsides surrounding their house when the weather permitted.

But it seldom did. For nearly the entire month of July, the rain had "been violent & incessant with the exception of 4 or 5 days." Prices for produce in the local markets were rising rapidly, complained Lady Caroline. "It is being rather out of Luck, for the Oldest Man in the Country does not remember the price of Bread so high as it is at this time." She blamed the exorbitant prices on "the dreadfull & tremendous rains which have now continued so long." The vineyards, too, were "totally spoilt as well as the Corn, & the greatest scarcity is apprehended. The same accounts are received from Italy & your letter mentions the bad Weather in England— Heaven defend Us from a Famine! Sometimes I have the most gloomy forebodings."

Farther down the lake, Percy Bysshe Shelley crammed as much travel into the summer as he could. Following the evenings of ghost stories at Lord Byron's villa in late June, the two poets had embarked on a weeklong tour of Lake Geneva. They intended to visit a number of sites made famous by Jean-Jacques Rousseau, the eighteenth-century philosophe who was a native and sometime resident of Geneva, and whose books were eventually banned by the local authorities. The trip was something of a pilgrimage for Shelley, who spoke in awed tones of "the divine beauty" of Rousseau's imagination. "In my mind," Shelley wrote to a friend in London, "Rousseau is indeed . . . the greatest man the world has produced since Milton."

Following the geography set out in Rousseau's 1761 historical novel, *La Nouvelle Héloïse*, Byron and Shelley began their pilgrimage at the Castle of Chillon. Shelley shuddered at the dungeons, excavated below the lake, with their iron rings, narrow cells, and the engraven names of prisoners. "I never saw a monument more terrible of that cold and inhuman tyranny, which it has been the delight of man to exercise over man," he later told a friend. The poets then moved on to Vevey, where the Capels were staying, which

Shelley considered "a town more beautiful in its simplicity than any I have ever seen."

Looking out over a magnificent view of the Alps, Shelley suddenly mused about the end of the world. "What a thing it would be," he said, "if all were involved in darkness at this moment, the sun and stars to go out. How terrible the idea!" Heavy rains subsequently forced a premature end to the poets' expedition, although they did visit the house outside Lausanne where the British historian Edward Gibbon—whom Byron admired greatly—completed *The Decline and Fall of the Roman Empire.* Before they left, Byron gathered a few acacia leaves to preserve in Gibbon's memory.

After returning to the Villa Diodati, Byron spent much of July and August writing. The dismal weather deepened his customary melancholy. "Really we have had lately such stupid mists, fogs, and perpetual density," Byron wrote to his publisher on July 22, "that one would think Castlereagh had the Foreign Affairs of the kingdom of Heaven also on his hands." Despite his weather-induced gloom (or perhaps because of it), the summer was a remarkably creative period for Byron: "The Prisoner of Chillon," the third canto of "Childe Harold's Pilgrimage," "The Dream," "Sonnet To Lake Leman," "Prometheus," "Monody on the Death of the Right Hon. R. B. Sheridan," and a poem directly inspired by the bleak summer of 1816, "Darkness."

Whenever he sought a respite from writing, Byron found congenial company at the Château de Coppet, the salon of Madame Germaine de Staël. Madame de Staël was perhaps the only woman in the world who could match Byron for notoriety in 1816. The daughter of Swiss banker Jacques Necker, who achieved fame as Louis XVI's finance minister, Anne Louise Germaine grew up in the same sort of freethinking intellectual atmosphere as Mary Wollstonecraft. Her mother, Suzanne Curchod (a former lover of Edward Gibbon), hosted the leading salon in pre-Revolutionary Paris, a gathering place for writers, artists, scientists, and diplomats. Anne Louise Germaine's marriage at the age of twenty to the Swedish ambassador to France, Baron de Staël von Holstein, quickly deteriorated, and Madame de Staël spent the remainder of her life studying, writing, and hosting her own salon. Her vocal support for individual liberties and a constitutional monarchy earned her the enmity of both radicals and royalists in revolutionary France; she was banished from Paris in turn by the Committee for Public Safety in 1795, by the Directory the following year, and in 1803 by Napoléon, who subsequently exiled her altogether from France.

After extensive travels through Europe—particularly Germany and Italy—Madame de Staël found refuge at her family estate at Coppet, on the northern shore of Lake Geneva. There she assembled a new coterie of scholars, politicians, and writers: English, French, German, Italian, Russian, and Greek. It was "the general headquarters of European thought," wrote the French novelist Stendhal, "the Estates General of European opinion . . . Voltaire never saw anything like it. Six hundred of the most distinguished people would gather on the shores of the lake: wit, wealth, the most exalted ranks came there seeking pleasure in the salon of the celebrated lady."

Among those gathered at Coppet was Charles Victor de Bonstetten, a Swiss writer and philosopher who would subsequently publish an influential study of the effect of climate on human society—*L'homme du midi et l'homme du nord: ou l'influence du climat*, a topic that also interested Madame de Staël—and the economist Jean Charles Leonard Simonde de Sismondi. Already famous for his multivolume history of the Italian republics, Sismondi was studying the deleterious effects of unpredictable disturbances (such as an exceptionally cold and wet summer) on the economy of Britain, increasingly vulnerable to such shocks due to its dependence on exports and the whims of international commerce.

On a Saturday afternoon in July 1816, Byron arrived at Coppet for dinner. As soon as he entered the room, all eyes turned toward him, staring "as at some outlandish beast in a raree-show.

One of the ladies fainted, and the rest looked as if his Satanic Majesty had been among them." Madame de Staël, immune to scandal and quite unperturbed, gave Byron a warm and gracious welcome. Between their discussions of literature, she peppered him with detailed questions about his personal life, and particularly his troubled marriage. Byron, who was practicing his melancholy public persona while pretending to be devoted to his estranged wife, took no offense at her intrusive queries. "I believe Madame de Staël did her utmost to bring about a reconciliation between us," he confided to a friend. "She was the best creature in the world."

Byron returned to Coppet frequently over the next several months. "She has made Coppet as agreeable as society and talent can make any place on earth," he told his editor. The celebrated hostess "ventured to protect me when all London was crying out against me on the separation, and behaved courageously and kindly; indeed, Madame de S defended me when few dared to do so, and I have always remembered it."

In late July, Shelley and Mary Godwin invited Byron to accompany them on an expedition into the Alps: to Chamonix, Mont Blanc (the highest peak in western Europe), and the immense glacier known as the Mer de Glace. Byron declined, perhaps because Claire Clairmont—who had informed him she was pregnant with his child—was also going. The company set out on July 21, and as they approached the mountains Mary noticed that the Arve River, which would become the symbol of power in Shelley's poem, "Mont Blanc," was so swollen by recent rains that "the cornfields on each side are covered with the inundation."

They reached Chamonix two days later, Mary and Percy registering as man and wife when they checked into a hotel. But when they set out to get a better view of the mountains, the skies opened again. "The rain continued in torrents," Mary noted in her journal, "—we were wetted to the skin so that when [we had] ascended more than half way we resolved to turn back—As we descended Shelley went before and tripping he fell upon his knee—this added to the weakness occasioned by a blow on his ascent" and he fainted. They did manage to view the Mer de Glace the following day. "This is the most desolate place in the world," Mary concluded, and filed away the awe-inspiring sight to use in her "ghost" story. When the rains resumed, they decided to end their expedition prematurely.

A week later, Lake Geneva was struck by a storm which Lady Caroline Capel described as "a Hurricane of Thunder, Lightning & Wind . . . that beat any thing I ever heard—The scene of desolation at Vevey was dreadfull, The Lower part of the Town was entirely inundated the Lake having risen with uncommon fury to an unusual height—Many Houses washed down & Trees torn up by the roots, the poor people running about in confusion wringing their hands & crying." As the lake rose seven feet above its normal level, nervous residents could see dead animals floating downstream on the Rhone. Situated on a mountainside, Lady Capel's château escaped the flood, "but felt the wind most frightfully—It tore up a large tree in the Garden & threatened to bring the House about our Ears."

In Virginia, the drought persisted through July and into August. In the absence of any reliable system of artificial irrigation, Jefferson feared that his corn crop would be ruined; the United States, he told a friend, was experiencing "seasons the most adverse to agriculture which had ever been known." At Montpelier, where President Madison spent his days and often part of his evenings reviewing official correspondence, the corn and tobacco fields were stunted.

But in New England, temperatures had moderated, reviving hopes for a bountiful harvest. After the frosts of early July, local newspapers carried stories of dangerously depleted stores of corn and grain. "On account of the extreme backwardness of the season, and severe drought, the prospects of the farmer are distressing almost beyond precedent," claimed the *Albany Argus* on July 19. "The grass in many districts does not promise a quarter of a crop; corn is very poor, and it is fearful that but very little of it will come to maturity. . . . Some of the pastures are completely dried up, and present the appearance of a brown heath." All in all, the *Argus* concluded, "the picture of distress is very much heightened by the gloomy forebodings of an increased and prolonged scarcity." Not surprisingly, merchants responded with a bout of panic buying, forcing up the price of grain and flour.

Several newspapers in New Hampshire and Maine recommended that farmers simply give up on their stunted hay crops and replant their fields, either with grains or new grass in hopes of a better harvest in the fall. "It is acknowledged on all hands," proclaimed the *Brattleboro Reporter*, "that the first crop of grass has been very light; perhaps not more than half the usual quantity. To make up for this deficiency it is recommended to farmers to plow down as much ground as convenient as soon as possible and broadcast with oats and Indian corn," which the editor hoped would be ready for harvest by the end of September—assuming the rest of the summer remained reasonably warm. In the meantime, livestock suffered from the scarcity of fodder, and cattle were turned loose in woods or even in towns to find their own forage. Farmers improvised as best they could, substituting the dried tops of potatoes, or even straw thatch off the roofs of outbuildings to feed their stock.

By the first week of August, however, fears of a general famine had subsided. According to the optimistic forecast of the *New Hampshire Patriot*, "rye is said to be better than for some years past, [and] wheat and other early grains look well and are nearly ready for harvest." While corn remained "more backward than usual," it had recovered so rapidly after several weeks of warm weather that the *Patriot*'s editor hoped "there may be great crops even of the latter."

Farmers found time to turn their attention to politics instead.

By all accounts, the most controversial issue in the summer of 1816 was the size of the federal budget, and especially the Compensation Act—the pay raise that congressmen had voted themselves before adjourning in April. Now that the nation was once again at peace, critics complained that the Madison administration and Congress should have cut federal spending dramatically; instead, it remained at levels they considered extravagant and wasteful, especially for a Democratic-Republican administration ostensibly committed to a frugal government. "It would astonish the plain honest farmer to go to Washington and witness, with his own eyes, the extraordinary and unaccountable waste and profusion that prevails," argued the editors of the pro-Federalist *Maryland Gazette*. "Unnumbered millions" of dollars had been wasted, claimed the *Gazette*, most of which had found its way into the pockets of "the inferior tribe of political pimps and panders [sic]" who infested the nation's capital.

At a time of economic troubles, when "commerce is languishing, manufactures are at a stand, the currency embarrassed, taxes heavy, and the people in difficulties," fiscal conservatives were stunned that congressmen had voted to double their own pay; their new salary of $1,500 per year was more than twice that of a skilled worker who worked six days a week, albeit less than the wages of some government clerks. In one state after another, Federalist and Democratic-Republican voters alike vented their outrage toward their representatives. They held public meetings to denounce the Compensation Act; grand juries condemned it; state legislatures passed resolutions censuring Congress; and in Georgia, a crowd actually burned in effigy their representatives who had voted for the pay raise.

"There has never been an instance before of so unanimous an opinion of the people, and that through every state in the Union," concluded Thomas Jefferson. Veteran congressman Richard Johnson of Kentucky contended that the Compensation Bill had aroused more opposition than any other measure since George

Washington first took office, including "the alien or sedition laws, the quasi war with France, the internal taxes of 1798, the embargo, the late war with Great Britain, the Treaty of Ghent, or any other one measure of the Government." Critics issued dire warnings that the United States was headed down the same path of corruption and extravagance that had destroyed republican Rome. In a portent of things to come, early congressional elections held during the summer in New York State resulted in the defeat of nearly all the incumbents who ran for reelection.

No one expected similar excitement in the presidential election campaign of 1816. Each party chose its presidential candidate through a caucus of its congressional representatives; although the caucus system was increasingly viewed as a relic of an age of gentleman politicians, the first national nominating convention lay eight years in the future. The Federalists, nearly extinct outside of their New England base, selected (without noticeable enthusiasm) Senator Rufus King of New York to carry their banner. King, who had served in the Constitutional Convention and filled a variety of political and diplomatic positions with distinction, had no desire to be president, and grudgingly agreed to run only after several weeks of soul-searching. The Democratic-Republican caucus turned into a more contentious affair, as supporters of Secretary of War William Harris Crawford of Georgia attempted to pry the nomination from the heir apparent of the Virginia dynasty, Secretary of State James Monroe. President Madison, as titular head of the party, refused to publicly endorse either candidate. Eventually Monroe triumphed by the unexpectedly narrow margin of eleven votes.

James Monroe evoked a variety of reactions within his party, not all of them positive. He certainly looked the part of a president, especially compared to Madison. While Madison was short, slight, prim, and bald, Monroe was six feet tall, with broad shoulders and a rugged physique. Those who met him got the impression of great physical strength and endurance. Like Madison,

Monroe was born along the Rappahannock in central Virginia; both were members of the Revolutionary generation; and both swore allegiance to Jeffersonian political principles. But even Madison's opponents acknowledged the depth of the president's intellect, while Monroe seemed "awkward and diffident; and without grace either in manner or appearance."

"A mind neither rapid nor rich," wrote Virginia attorney William Wirt of Monroe (an interesting characterization, considering that Monroe would appoint Wirt attorney general in 1817). "Madison is quick, temperate and clear," noted a prominent New York politician. "Monroe slow, passionate and dull. Madison's word may always be relied on . . . I am sorry to say I cannot bear the same testimony to Monroe." Aaron Burr, living in exile in Europe, dismissed Monroe as "stupid and illiterate . . . improper, hypocritical, and indecisive." To some critics, Monroe seemed a complete nonentity. One contemptuous Federalist journal expressed amazement that the Democratic-Republican party would nominate "this ridiculous man of straw—this thing—this nothing, as a suitable candidate, by way of insult to their fellow citizens, as if such a compound of negatives in their hands could stand up [as] the future President of this country."

So the presidential campaign began.

BEGINNING in late July, clerics in English churches offered public prayers for a change in the weather. Clearly something had gone terribly wrong somewhere; the persistent rain and cold could not be explained by the normal pattern of weather variation. "A belief begins to prevail among the many in all countries that there is something more than natural in the present state of the weather," noted the seventy-three-year-old British politician Lord Glenbervie during a tour of France in the first week of August.

New spots had appeared on the sun, reviving speculation about their responsibility for the disastrous weather. A physician in Lyon claimed to have evidence that the sun was ill and the moon was dying. On the other hand, the *London Chronicle* argued that the sun's influence was waning (as evidenced by the dark spots) while the moon's was waxing; the confluence of these developments, the editors argued, "are the conceived cause of the backwardness of the season, from its accustomed heat and vegetation; as also of continued rains, with an unusual swelling of rivers." A writer in the *Gentleman's Magazine* suggested that the sunspots were actually small objects hovering between the sun and Earth. Although these objects presumably would cast a shadow of "a kind of cone of a certain length, according to the diameter of the obstructing body, and its distance from the luminary [i.e., the sun]," he claimed that they had little effect on Earth's temperature. Since the obstruction would simply radiate whatever heat it received, instead of absorbing or consuming it, "the heat beyond, that is, toward the earth, would [still] be as great as if there were no impediment."

Never one to miss an opportunity to mock conventional opinion, British satirist William Hone blamed Napoléon Bonaparte for the weather. In his poem, "Napoléon and the Spots in the Sun; or, The Regent's Waltz . . ." Hone claimed that the former emperor had escaped from Saint Helena and invaded the sun; the spots were simply the different parts of his body. As revenge for his defeat at Waterloo, Napoléon "has occasion'd this change in the weather, / Stopp'd the sun-shine and drench'd us with rain, / And made hot and cold come together! / It is he that kept backward the Spring, / And turn'd Summer into November." Hone proposed to thwart the plot by catapulting the Prince Regent sunward into space so he could defeat Napoléon in hand-to-hand combat.

At the end of July, the price of wheat rose sharply on London markets. A British businessmen who toured the counties of Devon and Somerset to ascertain the state of the crops reported that "the wheat crop has suffered a little from the late frosts," but he felt confident it would recover, given good weather for the remainder of the summer. "The hay crop," on the other hand, "has certainly been greatly injured by the rain, not only that which has been cut, but that which is growing also." Merchants and speculators, he concluded, were driving up the price of wheat by buying all the high-quality grain—both domestic and foreign—they could obtain, in expectation of an inferior harvest.

"Have you been apprehensive of a second Flood?" Lady Noel, Byron's mother-in-law, asked her daughter, Annabella, in a letter on July 21. "Hay spoilt, Corn laid, and all the cc & cs of farming distresses." Several days later, another severe storm lashed crops in Norfolk. "The rain descended in such torrents, accompanied by large hailstones, after a few peals of thunder, as to prostrate the heavy crops of wheat and barley in many places of this county," reported one observer. "In some villages the ditches and lanes were so full of water, that boats might have been rowed in them." Elsewhere in northern Britain, thunderstorms and hail produced landslides and floods that washed away more crops—at least one worker was reported killed trying to protect his hay—and left water four feet deep in the streets.

Britons who traveled to the Continent found conditions even worse there. "I thought I was to leave all grumbling behind me in England," noted a British tourist in Amsterdam, "but here the good folks are ten times worse, for nobody is pleased: it is quite shocking—poverty prevailing, and the country drowning: rains have been dreadful; in short, we have not had one day without rain since our arrival." In Burgundy, the rain and cold had left the vineyards "in such a state, that the vintage is expected to be wholly unproductive." In the wine-making region of northwest Switzerland, Lake Bienne overflowed its banks, inundating a vast tract of countryside. Much of the Bernese Oberland remained under snow, forcing cattle to remain in their stables (at considerable expense to the farmers) instead of grazing in the pastures. The Rems River in southwestern Germany flooded on more than a dozen separate occasions, ruining the crops of grain and hay in the surrounding fields.

In late July, a procession of eighty young women paraded through the streets of Paris, holding lighted candles and praying to St. Genevieve—the patron saint of the city—for drier weather, but the rain did not stop. By the end of the month, the rainfall totals for July for most of France, parts of Belgium, Holland, and western Germany, southern Ireland, and southwestern England were more than three times normal.

Incessant rain and gloomy skies confined Parisians to their homes and indoor amusements. Their mood darkened further with the flocks of British visitors who swarmed into the city that summer. It was the first summer in nearly a decade that Britain and France had not been at war, and English sightseers took full advantage of the opportunity to cross the Channel; one journalist estimated there were twenty-nine thousand Englishmen in Paris in midsummer. Even though their French hosts appreciated the British willingness to spend considerable sums during their stay, a national resentment over the presence of Allied occupation troops occasionally surfaced as insults or attacks on British tourists. Parisians did enjoy an opportunity to participate in the festivities surrounding the marriage of the king's nephew, the Duc de Berry, to Princess Caroline of Naples and Sicily, a direct descendant of Philip V of Spain, the grandson of Louis XIV. Unfortunately for the princess, married life did little to domesticate the duke, who was notorious for both his philandering and his hot temper.

King Louis XVIII spent much of the summer deciding what to do about the intractable Ultra-Royalist legislature—the *Chambre introuvable*—which had not met since the end of April. Allied representatives in Paris, notably the Duke of Wellington, favored a dissolution of the chamber followed by new elections, and hopefully a more moderate assembly. The Allies suspected that the current deputies would never vote enough new taxes to pay France's war indemnities to their governments, the first installment of which was due in November 1816. They also feared that the continued heavy-handed repression of antimonarchist elements would invite

a popular backlash and lead to a new round of civil strife. Louis'
minister of police, Élie Decazes, a moderate royalist, joined the Allies' campaign to persuade the king to dismiss the legislature, in
part because he felt a more conciliatory chamber would convince
the Allies to end their occupation earlier. Since the restoration,
Louis had grown quite dependent upon Decazes (whom he referred to as "my dear boy") both to handle the daily administrative
details of domestic policy and to keep him entertained with sala-
cious gossip about well-known figures in Paris, which Decazes obtained through an extensive network of spies and informers. By the
middle of August, Wellington and Decazes had worn down the
king's resistance, and Louis agreed to dissolve the chamber.

That solved only one of the French government's problems. The
nation's finances remained in a desperate state. Like the rest of
Europe, the French economy remained primarily agricultural, and
by the end of July 1816 it seemed clear that the coming harvest
would be a disaster. That meant Louis' government would be hard-
pressed to collect its normal tax revenues, much less impose new
taxes, and that spending on emergency relief measures would almost
certainly soar. Since the national budget already was badly out of
balance, the government could meet its obligations only by assuming
a new foreign loan.

And the price of bread continued to climb. In late July, textile
workers in the town of Castres, in southern France, rioted to demand cheaper bread. The mayor called out the national guard to
suppress the demonstrations, but when many members of the
guard decided to support the rioters, the authorities had no choice
but to grant the workers' demands. To prevent further outbursts of
violence, King Louis issued an ordinance stating that "grain, meal
of every kind, bread, and sea biscuit, may be imported free of duty,
either by sea or land, till otherwise ordered."

More than a year after Napoléon's defeat at Waterloo, the
French economy was still struggling to recover from the lengthy
wars. Nearly two decades of conflict had disarranged commerce,

increased taxation, and consumed vast amounts of manpower. Resources that might have been used in productive enterprises had vanished on battlefields from Spain to Moscow. Nor could the French economy transform itself overnight from a wartime footing to peacetime production; the transition would need time, as businesses reallocated capital to the manufacture of civilian goods. "And the necessary consequence," noted one contemporary observer, "is that many of the labourers, to whom these capitals had given employment [during wartime], are thrown out of work, and wander idle in our streets, because no man hath hired them."

French ports that had been crippled by the British blockade sank into depression. French manufactures—which had flourished during the war in the absence of British competition—could not survive the flood of cheap British imports once peace returned. The French linen industry, a major supplement to the income of farm families who spun the flax and wove the fabric in their homes, collapsed under a wave of inexpensive Irish linens and British cotton goods. (In 1810, Napoléon reportedly had offered a reward of a million francs to anyone who could invent a mechanical loom to produce linen, but no one did.)

Belgium, the German states, Switzerland, and the Netherlands faced similar difficulties. Both the Belgian cotton industry, based in Ghent, and its Swiss counterpart succumbed to British textile imports woven on machines that reduced production costs far below those of their continental competitors. As European textile firms laid off workers, demand for manufactured goods declined further. The rising price of bread added to the distress, especially among working families who spent half their income on bread in normal times. No wonder a crowd of Belgian workingmen made a public display of burning a mountain of English textiles, particularly shawls and handkerchiefs, at the corn market in Ghent in late July.

Even though the importation of inexpensive British goods exacerbated the unemployment problem on the Continent, the British economy was suffering its own travails in the summer of 1816. The resumption of trade between Britain and the Continent in 1815 led British manufacturers to produce more than European consumers—impoverished by war and taxation—could purchase, and so a glut of British goods sat on the docks for months. They were sold only at a substantial loss; so while they undercut continental manufactures, and forced layoffs in the French and German textile industries, they brought no profit to British firms and led those employers, too, to reduce their workforce.

In short, Britain had too many workers and not enough work. "Instead of crowding our ports with ships and goods, and filling our streets with the bustle of trade," noted one perceptive observer, peace had produced "a calm, a stillness, as to trade, truly gloomy." The Bank of England's decision to sharply contract the amount of money in circulation only deepened the slump in trade. By the summer of 1816, employment on the London docks had fallen from 1,500 men to a mere 500 as commerce slowed to a trickle. On one particularly quiet day, the Customs House recorded no entry for either import or export, "a circumstance without parallel in the annals of that extensive establishment."

Iron prices plunged by more than half; artisans sold their tools to buy bread. Up to 10,000 servants reportedly lacked employment. For months, members of the opposition had been complaining in Parliament about the numbers of beggars tramping throughout Britain—over 30,000 in London alone. "Scarcely a day passes without bringing one, and generally more, beggars to my door," declared William Cobbett, a leading advocate of parliamentary reform. "They swarm over the country like vermin upon their own bodies; and are produced by causes nearly similar."

Small wonder that investors displayed a marked lack of enthusiasm to buy British government securities, but *The Times* of London feared "something peculiar" was at work in the financial markets. "When no other sufficient cause can be assigned for low spirits in individuals," *The Times* noted, "it is generally thought to be unpleasant weather that produces them: but . . . we apprehend it is the low spirits of the nation that occasion the depressed state of the funds." Or perhaps the unpleasant weather played upon the spirits of investors, as well.

Aside from a few minor disturbances in the Midlands and northern England, workers still hesitated to engage in violent protest. But the ruling class could see trouble ahead. On July 29, a distinguished company gathered at the City of London Tavern for a public meeting to revive the Association for the Relief of the Manufacturing and Labouring Poor, a society originally founded in 1812 by a group of philanthropists including William Wilberforce, the evangelical politician best known for his campaign to end Britain's participation in the international slave trade. The July 29 meeting was chaired by the Duke of York, the king's fourth son and commander in chief of the British army; others present included two of York's younger brothers, the Duke of Kent and the Duke of Cambridge, the Chancellor of the Exchequer, the Archbishop of Canterbury, and the Bishop of London.

The purpose of the association was to encourage "conservative philanthropy"—private donations to alleviate the plight of the poor while rejecting any government responsibility for their condition. The organizers planned to spend the evening in a dignified discussion of "the present distressed state of the lower classes, and the most effectual means of extending relief to them," but almost as soon as the meeting commenced, radicals among the audience (led by Lord Cochrane, a famous British admiral and vocal proponent of parliamentary reform) began calling for stronger measures by the government. York could not maintain order long enough to conclude a rational discussion of the issues, and the meeting soon deteriorated into disorganized squabbling. "No newspaper can describe the meeting at the City of London Tavern last Monday," wrote reformer Francis Place to a friend. "Many years have passed since I witnessed anything so exhilirating." As York slipped out of the tavern under a shower of catcalls, the group concluded its business by proclaiming that while "it be impossible for any Association to attempt the general relief of such difficulties"—nor would the government attempt to do so—it expected that "those who are able to afford the means of relief will contribute their utmost endeavours to alleviate these sufferings."

It would be a daunting task, especially as the cold, wet weather threw more agricultural laborers out of work. In the town of Barnet, just north of London, scores of unemployed haymakers gathered day after day in the marketplace. "It is impossible to conceive the distress in which these poor people (a majority of them itinerant strangers) have been reduced by the late incessant rains," wrote one witness; many of them were "literally starving." When a passing gentleman saw about 140 of the desperate men standing together, he ordered them all to be supplied with bread, and told them to come back tomorrow for more. The next day, more than three hundred appeared, all of whom he fed. The third day there were nearly eight hundred; they, too, received bread, and a quarter pound of cheese from the parish.

Londoners who assembled outside St. James's Palace on the evening of July 23 received cake instead. In the season's second royal wedding, William Frederick, the Duke of Gloucester, a nephew of the king, married his cousin Princess Mary, one of the king's daughters. (Contemporaries noted that it seemed a suitable union, since both parties had been born in the same year—1776.) King George did not attend his daughter's wedding, of course, although Queen Charlotte appeared near the end of the festivities. The ceremony featured an altar adorned with a spectacular display of gold plate, including chalices made of solid gold. After the bride and groom rode away in a carriage, the crowd—according to custom—was treated to pieces of wedding cake.

The wedding may have cheered Englishmen still saddened by the death on July 7 of Richard Brinsley Sheridan, the greatest playwright of his age. While still in his twenties, Sheridan authored two brilliant comedies, *The Rivals* and *The School for Scandal*, and then wrote very little for the rest of his life, perhaps fearful he could not replicate his early success. He served in Parliament as a leading member of the Whig Party, earning a reputation as a remarkably persuasive speaker and an incorruptible politician (although his private moral standards were not as strict). Sheridan also managed and owned London's most famous playhouse, the Drury Lane Theatre, until it was destroyed in 1809 by fire, despite a curtain made of iron and a large reservoir of water on the roof for just such emergencies. Sheridan, who calmly watched his theater burn ("A man may surely be allowed to take a glass of wine by his own fireside," he reportedly remarked to a bystander), never recovered from the financial loss. He subsequently quarreled with his patron and longtime crony, the Prince Regent, began drinking heavily, and died deeply in debt.

Wrote Byron:

> *A mighty Spirit is eclipsed—a Power*
> *Hath pass'd from day to darkness—to whose hour*
> *Of light no likeness is bequeath'd—no name,*
> *Focus at once of all the rays of Fame!*
> *The flash of Wit—the bright Intelligence,*
> *The beam of Song,—the blaze of Eloquence,*
> *Set with their Sun—but still have left behind*
> *The enduring produce of immortal Mind . . .*

7.

POVERTY AND MISERY

"These are bad times for getting on . . ."

IN THE AUGUST 10 issue of *Niles' Weekly Register*, editor Hezekiah Niles, a highly respected journalist, surveyed the state of agriculture in the Eastern United States and decided that prospects for a plentiful harvest of grains remained surprisingly encouraging. Due to nearly four weeks of steady warm weather, "the crops of wheat and rye are reported to be as good as usual" in many states, although there remained problem areas. Western Pennsylvania, for instance, promised "very little grain and very little fruit." Even in eastern Pennsylvania, "we understand that the crops are thin." Hay was a disaster just about everywhere, and corn—well, corn could still go either way. As far as apples and peaches were concerned, "we believe there is little fruit to the northward of Pennsylvania."

But Niles' concern in August 1816 stretched beyond a single season's harvest. In a lengthy front-page article in his *Register*, the first weekly news magazine in America, Niles argued that the United States' climate was changing, and not for the better. "It has been observed by the most careless observer, that since 1812, the seasons have been very unlike what they had formerly been," he wrote. The present summer, Niles continued, "has hitherto been extremely cold, with the exception of a very few days that were extremely warm." He believed that the cooler temperatures were responsible for the drought, since "the chillness . . . has retarded nature's great process of evaporation, and depressed the range of the clouds."

After providing his readers with a summary of the unusual weather events of June and July, Niles skirted the issue of causation. He briefly considered the sunspot theory, but found little evidence to support it. Instead, Niles suspected that the series of earthquakes earlier in the decade might bear at least part of the responsibility for the altered climate.

Niles was more concerned with the effects of climate change on public health. As American weather grew colder and increasingly damp, Niles claimed to detect a rise in cases of what he called "typhus mitior," or "the low nervous fever," or simply "typhus fever." This disease, which Niles claimed was virtually unknown previously in the United States, allegedly attacked the nervous and vascular systems, causing chills, headaches, nausea, and depression. Niles believed that it first appeared in New England, "in the course of a long period of unusually cold damp weather," then extended itself through New York State, and finally pervaded all of North America. It had become so common by the summer of 1816, according to Niles, that "almost every disease is now liable to assume a typhus cast—a depression of pulse and prostration of power often taking place in cases that had never heretofore been thought liable to such symptoms." Niles optimistically predicted that Americans' bodies eventually would adjust to the changes in climate, just as vegetables did when transplanted to unfamiliar environments.

New England farmers remained optimistic as well. On sunny days in early August, they continued to plant new crops in sheltered areas, hopeful that the growing season—so slow to get started—might compensate by extending a bit beyond the usual first frost in October. Newspapers reminded them to replant fodder crops to keep their animals fed through the winter. When morning temperatures in Maine dipped into the 30s at the end of the first week of August, farmers wrapped old shawls or rags around the seedlings for protection.

Throughout the month, winds remained unusually steady from the north and west, keeping the air drier than normal. The first hint of disaster occurred on August 13, as a cold wave passing through northern New England brought frost that damaged corn in the fields north of Concord, New Hampshire. Temperatures dipped below freezing again the following evening, causing frost damage in western Massachusetts, then rose and remained warm for nearly a week. On August 18, Middlebury, Connecticut, recorded a high of 92 degrees, and a local pastor led a special prayer for rain to end the troubling drought.

Around noon on August 20, "a very violent storm of rain and wind" struck Amherst, New Hampshire. "It came up very suddenly and was of short duration," reported a local newspaper, "but it rained and blew tremendously accompanied by heavy thunder." The storm signaled the arrival of a powerful cold front. Temperatures plunged 30 degrees in the next few hours. Residents of Keene, New Hampshire, claimed that they had never witnessed such a sharp change in temperature; in the town of Warren, a hundred miles to the north, some residents observed snow on a nearby mountaintop. New Hampshire's governor, William Plumer, was riding from Concord to Hanover that day, and as he neared Hanover, he noticed that the combination of drought and cold had essentially ruined the crop of Indian corn.

In Albany, the storm arrived late in the morning. After a warm dawn, "all of a sudden, the fine flying clouds which were driven by the S. wind, were suddenly driven back by a strong, cold blast from the N. and the temperature changed very rapidly," wrote a local resident. "A cold wind from the N.W. set in, & blew with great violence for about 24 hours." That evening, frost was reported all the way from East Windsor, Connecticut, to Portland, Maine.

Freezing temperatures returned on August 21, striking a far wider area, extending as far south as Kentucky and west to Ohio. The frost killed or damaged crops—particularly corn—throughout Maine and New Hampshire, reaching into Massachusetts from Stockbridge to Boston, and in low-lying areas in upstate New York. "Indeed we have the air of October rather than that of August," claimed one New Yorker whose plants looked dry and stiffened, "as we see them late in autumn." At this point, some New England farmers abandoned all hopes of a profitable crop of corn and cut the stalks for fodder, but it spoiled nonetheless.

Towns in central Pennsylvania experienced severe frost, and "a temperature, such as is generally experienced in the latter end of October, making thin clothes uncomfortably cool." Cincinnati also suffered heavy frosts, and the town of Washington, Kentucky, reported "frost so severe, as in some instances to kill vines in exposed situations." Snow covered mountaintops across Vermont. In Hanover, Governor Plumer witnessed "a hard frost, that in many places of vast extent killed Indian corn (particularly in pine lands), potatoe [sic] vines, pumpkins, cucumbers, etc. We shall have but a small crop of corn—that which is not killed is chilled."

Plumer already had enough problems on his hands. The state of New Hampshire was nearly insolvent, at least in the short run. Upon taking office in March, Plumer—a former United States senator who also had previously served one term as governor, in 1812–13—learned that the state treasury had less than a hundred dollars in cash, and a daunting stack of unpaid bills. The governor asked every bank in Portsmouth for a loan until tax payments arrived in the autumn, but they all turned him down. Plumer then persuaded the state legislature to reduce the salaries of a number of state officials (including himself), but those savings were a mere drop in the bucket. Only the federal government's generosity in advancing funds due New Hampshire for the use of its militia during the recent war kept the state afloat. (Despite the state's financial embarrassment, the legislature approved the construction of a new statehouse in Concord. Plumer managed to curtail costs, however, by using inmates from the nearby state prison to cut and shape blocks of granite for the capitol.)

A more vexing problem—and the main reason Plumer was in Hanover in August—stemmed from the controversy surrounding Dartmouth College and the conflict between the college's president and its board of trustees. Dartmouth originally grew out of an Indian mission school known as Moor's Charity School, founded by Eleazar Wheelock in 1754 in Lebanon, Connecticut. In 1769, Wheelock moved his school to Hanover, in southwestern New Hampshire, and obtained a royal charter to turn it into a college "for the education and instruction of Youth of the Indian Tribes in this Land—and also of English Youth and any others."

Wheelock served as president of Dartmouth College until his death in 1779, whereupon his son, John, assumed the presidency. By 1816, John Wheelock and the trustees of the college were locked in a struggle over the future direction of the school. A majority of the board of trustees—a self-perpetuating body—were staunch Federalists who supported strict, orthodox Calvinist doctrine and the Congregationalist Church, which still received state tax funds as New Hampshire's established church. Wheelock took a slightly more liberal theological stance than the trustees, but the minor doctrinal differences between himself and the board were exacerbated by a multitude of personal and, to an outsider, frankly trivial disagreements. In 1815, the disputatious Wheelock turned the simmering dispute into a full-fledged political controversy by inviting the state legislature to investigate conditions at Dartmouth. The equally stubborn trustees responded by firing Wheelock, who then appealed to the public for support against the board. He framed the issue in terms of freedom of conscience, arguing that the trustees "had perverted the college into an agency . . . to establish a politico-religious hierarchy in New England."

A longtime defender of religious tolerance, Plumer took up Wheelock's cause and persuaded the state legislature—now solidly Democratic-Republican—to pass a measure at the end of June 1816 permitting the governor to appoint nine additional trustees to the board, and to establish a board of overseers (also appointed by the governor) with veto power over the trustees. The bill also re-named the school as Dartmouth University, and provided for free-dom of religious opinion for its students and officers.

Coverage of the Dartmouth controversy dominated state news-papers during the summer of 1816. To the extent that they fol-lowed state political affairs—and interest was increasing, although fewer than twenty percent of eligible voters cast ballots in the 1816 gubernatorial election—New Hampshire voters supported Plumer and the legislature in the Dartmouth College controversy. So did Thomas Jefferson, in a well-publicized congratulatory letter to the governor. The long-standing tradition of deference to established social and religious authority—a legacy of the colonial era—was disintegrating, and both the Federalist Party and the special privi-leges of the Congregational Church would expire in the next few years.

A sizable percentage of New Hampshire residents undoubt-edly had more pressing concerns that summer than the quarrel over Dartmouth's future. The arduous life of a farmer in the rugged interior of New Hampshire was about to get even harder. Over 80 percent of the state's 70,000 residents lived and worked in rural areas, nearly all engaged in subsistence agriculture. The Merri-mack and Connecticut river valleys provided fertile soil for the production of corn and grain (wheat, barley, and rye), but it was a challenge to survive on barely marginal lands in the hill country. To supplement their income, New Hampshire farmers increas-ingly were raising cattle, which meant they needed to grow more hay, corn, and grain for fodder. Daughters also contributed by do-ing piecework for the nascent textile industry.

But the state's economy offered few opportunities to diversify.

Transportation remained primitive; it took a week to go overland from New York City to New Hampshire. Communication and news of current events lagged: Newspapers and books were rare, and there were no free public libraries anywhere in the state. While textile manufacturing had gained a foothold, the power looms and shoe factories that would provide thousands of jobs lay in the future. And Dartmouth was the only institution of higher education in New Hampshire, which did not bode well for the state's store of human capital.

On August 28, Dartmouth College celebrated Commencement Day. The conflict had grown even more complicated over the past two months. The new state-appointed board of trustees dismissed all five of Dartmouth's faculty members; undaunted, the faculty retired to private homes to conduct their classes, and most of the school's students (approximately 160 young men) followed them. With an eye to the grand gesture, the college's pre-Plumer board of trustees chose Commencement Day to announce its defiance of the state legislature's reform bill.

While Dartmouth's graduates celebrated their commencement, another cold front passed through New England. In much of New Hampshire, whatever remained of the corn crop—the staple upon which the state's farmers depended most of all—perished. Entire fields were cut up and used for fodder. As Plumer rode back to Concord, he confirmed that New Hampshire's corn harvest had perished, although he still held out hope for the grains.

Maine suffered worse damage. "August proved to be the worst month of all," noted one diarist. Farmers saved less than half the crop of hay, and less than 10 percent of the corn—and even that was inferior quality. Like New Hampshire, Maine's economy centered around subsistence farming, with corn the most critical crop. In years of normal weather, some farmers sold hay and timber to Boston merchants, while others provided food—wheat, barley, rye, or buckwheat—to workers in the local lumber industry. But there would be no surplus in 1816. A recent study of Maine agriculture by a team of scientists led by David C. Smith revealed that in the century from 1785–1885, there were nine years in which Maine suffered severe frosts in June, and four years with severe frosts in August. Yet only one year appeared on both lists: 1816.

In Vermont, farmers gathered what little hay they had saved and burned it in a desperate attempt to keep their corn from freezing. Some farmers in eastern Massachusetts tried a different strategy by cutting up their cornstalks by the roots and placing them upright, where they purportedly continued to ripen. But most New Englanders agreed with the *Connecticut Courant*'s verdict that "August was more cheerless, if possible, than the Summer months already past."

From below the Mason-Dixon line came reports of heavy frost in South Carolina on August 29. A correspondent in Danville, North Carolina, noted that his meadow "was white with frost" on the same day, and again on August 30. With a touch of grim humor, he added that the frost "killed nothing, as all was dead before" from the continuing drought. He had recently returned from Mecklenburg, and reported that "in the country thro' which I past [sic], and as far southward as the Savannah river, there will be the greatest scarcity of provisions ever known in my traveling." The combination of drought and cold had left fields "that would not make one grain of corn. . . . What the inhabitants are to do for support time must discover."

"The crops will be extremely short in all the upper districts of South Carolina—they are said to be worse than they have ever been known to be," observed another traveler. "The people seem to be alarmed about their situation, and considerable emigration is likely to take place." The frost on the morning of August 29 in that state was sufficiently severe "as to singe pumpkin and potato leaves; and I was informed by a respectable gentleman, that he saw the dew collected on a blade of corn, congealed into ice."

Frost also struck fields around Petersburg, Virginia, "a circumstance unparalleled in this part of the country," claimed one observer, "and what is equally extraordinary, we have had frost every month during the year." The Richmond area, too, sustained frost, leading the *Richmond Enquirer* to sound the now-familiar refrain that "the oldest inhabitants have no recollection of such a prodigy."

Thomas Jefferson confirmed that the same late-August cold wave "killed much corn over the mountains," in western Virginia. "We have had the most extraordinary year of drought and cold ever known in the history of America," Jefferson wrote to Albert Gallatin, his Swiss-born former secretary of the treasury. In August, the meticulously observant Jefferson measured only 0.8 inches of rain at Monticello, as opposed to the monthly average of 9.2 inches. And still the drought continued. "The summer, too, has been as cold as a moderate winter," Jefferson informed his friend. "The crop of corn through the Atlantic States will probably be less than one-third of an ordinary one, that of tobacco still less, and of mean quality." Wheat was "middling in quantity, but excellent in quality." Most of all, Jefferson feared the specter of famine in Virginia, especially since he could recall the deaths that followed the devastating drought of 1755. "Every species of bread grain taken together will not be sufficient for the subsistence of the inhabitants," he warned, "and the exportation of flour, already begun by the indebted and the improvident, to whatsoever degree it may be carried, will be exactly so much taken from the mouths of our own citizens."

"OH! It rains again; it beats against the window," wrote Jane Austen at her home in Chawton, about eighty miles east of Bath in southwestern England. "Such weather," she told her nephew, Edward, "gives one little temptation to be out. It is really too bad, & has been for a long time, much worse than anybody can bear, & I begin to think it will never be fine again."

Austen spent the summer of 1816 finishing a novel tentatively titled *The Elliots*, which she had been writing for the past year. She initially thought she had completed the manuscript on July 18; dissatisfied with the ending, she rewrote the final two chapters and finally brought the novel to a close on August 6. Along the way, Austen changed the title as well, to *Persuasion*.

Her previous novel, *Emma*, had been published in December 1815 and gathered respectable reviews. "Whoever is fond of an amusing, inoffensive, and well-principled novel, will be well pleased with the perusal of *Emma*," concluded the *British Critic* in a typical reaction. Austen's publisher sent a specially bound copy to the Prince Regent several days prior to publication, and His Royal Highness had kind if uninspired words for the novel. There was, he wrote, "so much nature . . . and excellent description of character." His librarian invited Austen to the Prince Regent's residence, Carlton House, and informed her that she had permission to dedicate her next novel to the prince.

Sales of *Emma* disappointed Austen's hopes—unfortunately, because her family could have used the money. In March, Jane's brother Henry was forced to declare bankruptcy when his bank failed, a misfortune that also wiped out the investments of several other family members. The collapse was precipitated in part by the failure of one of Henry's partners, a merchant whose trade suffered when the government slashed its orders for food, uniforms, and other supplies once peace returned. Another brother, Frank, a naval officer, was forced to live on half pay since the end of the war. A third brother, Charles, also a ship's captain, lost his command and his fortune when his ship was wrecked in the Mediterranean in February 1816; he returned to England impoverished. Austen had invested the royalties from her previous novels (about 600 pounds sterling) in Navy stock, but the 5 percent interest she received on that sum provided only minimal support for her family. As Admiral Croft declared in *Persuasion*, "These are bad times for getting on."

An acquaintance suggested Austen might sell more books if she wrote historical romances instead, but she refused. "I could no more write a romance than an epic poem," Austen admitted. "And if it were indispensable for me to keep it up and never relax into laughing at myself or other people, I am sure I should be hung before I had finished the first chapter. No, I must keep to my own style and go on in my own way, though I may never succeed again in that. I am convinced that I should totally fail in any other."

With money scarce, Austen rarely ventured far from Chawton. She shared her cottage with her mother (who was chronically ill), and various nephews and nieces, whom she babysat for weeks at a time. One of her favorite charges was Frank's nine-year-old daughter Mary Jane, who spent much of July 1816 at Chawton. Fortunately, Mary Jane proved good company, because the soggy weather kept them indoors most of the time. One day they set off in a donkey carriage to see a farmer, Mr. Woolls, in a nearby town who wanted to show off the improvements to his property. They did not get far. "We were obliged to turn back before we got there," wrote Austen, "but not soon enough to avoid a Pelter all the way home." When Austen finally sat down with Woolls, she talked of "it's being bad weather for the Hay—& he returned me the comfort of it's being much worse for the Wheat."

Austen had an ulterior motive in discussing the weather in her correspondence: "I have often observed that if one writes about the weather, it is generally completely changed before the Letter is read." She yearned for a change from the cold and the damp, because she had been suffering back pains since early in the year. Perhaps it was rheumatism; perhaps she spent too much time bent over her writing desk; perhaps it was a natural part of middle age, since Austen had turned forty the previous December. Her sister, Cassandra, had taken Jane to the spa town of Cheltenham in the spring, but the treatments did not help. The pains grew worse.

At the end of the summer, Jane received a note from a friend who had recently returned from a visit to the Continent. "She speaks of France as a scene of general Poverty & Misery," Austen told Cassandra. "No money, no Trade—nothing to be got but by the Innkeepers." And at Chawton, "likewise more rain again, by the look & sound of things. . . . We hear now there is to be no Honey this year."

NEARLY three hundred miles away, Britain's most famous landscape artist was in the midst of a working tour of Yorkshire and the surrounding area, sketching subjects for a proposed history of the county of York. "Weather miserably wet," complained Joseph Mallord William Turner from Richmond. "I shall be web-footed like a drake . . . but I must proceed northwards."

Forty-one years old in the summer of 1816, William Turner had been elected a full member of the Royal Academy at the age of twenty-six; five years later, the academy named him Professor of Perspective. Equally proficient in the use of watercolors and oils, Turner had built his reputation on a remarkable ability to move beyond the literal reproduction of a landscape and portray its essence—one admirer claimed that his dark and threatening 1796 painting of *Fishermen at Sea* was "a summary of all that had been said about the sea by the artists of the eighteenth century."

Although the incessant rains of July and August 1816 hindered Turner's progress as he and a close friend, Walter Fawkes, traveled through northern England, he was amply compensated for his discomfort. Turner's fee for providing 120 watercolors for the history of York reportedly was the princely sum of 3,150 pounds sterling (the equivalent of approximately 150,000 pounds in 2011), the highest fee ever paid to a British artist at the time.

In the rare intervals between storms and showers, Turner managed to complete a series of pencil sketches of numerous landscapes, castles, and local inhabitants in Yorkshire and Lancashire that he would subsequently turn into accomplished watercolor paintings. Few of these works, however, reveal the unique weather conditions of the summer of 1816; as one biographer has pointed out, Turner wished the finished works to "reflect the form and essence of the North of England as it had been for centuries," rather than to serve "as a diary of 1816."

One startling scene proved the exception. In *Lancaster Sands*, a portrayal of horsemen and a carriage crossing Morecambe Bay at low tide between Arnside and Kents Bank, Turner eloquently conveyed the misery of that summer. The crossing itself was notoriously dangerous—hundreds of unwary travelers had perished when they lost their way in the darkness or mists, or when the rising tide cut off the passage. In Turner's vision, the small band bunches together for safety under a driving rain, hastening across the sands with red-tinged clouds reflected in the low-lying water, heading toward a distant goal that remains indistinct under an angry sky. There was no assurance of a safe arrival.

LADY Shelley arrived at Lausanne in a dark mood. Heavy rains in late July forced her and her husband to take a detour six miles out of their way to get to the city, since the customary route was under water. Lady Shelley found the countryside between Lausanne and Geneva "flat and tame." Lausanne itself was "decidedly picturesque," but not in a positive sense: "Its antiquity is only too apparent from the condition of its dwellings, which look wretched . . . The streets are narrow, steep, and dirty." In the distance she could see mountaintops covered with snow, which, according to a local source, was "unusual at this time of the year."

Navigating through the low-lying areas of Switzerland in the summer of 1816 tested the nerves of even experienced travelers. En route to Lausanne, Lady Shelley passed the town of Yverdon, famous for its thermal springs, and marshy at the best of times. But the rains had washed out one section of road completely, and the lake "was violently lashing its waves upon our carriage wheels as we crawled along its marge." Yverdon, Lady Shelley noted, "wore a wintry aspect, the surrounding lands being under water, and the harvest destroyed." Facing a massive shortage of food, local authorities had prohibited the baking of white bread; violators were fined eight *louis d'or*.

Among the Englishmen Lady Shelley encountered in Lausanne—she claimed there were more than a thousand visiting the area—was Henry Brougham, a rising young Whig politician. Brougham frequently visited Madame de Staël's salon at Coppet and found it entertaining, but he dismissed the rest of Switzerland as unconscionably boring. "It is a country to be in for two hours," he wrote a friend. "Ennui comes on the third hour, and suicide attacks you before night. There is no resource whatever for passing the time, except looking at lakes and hills, which is over immediately."

Or one might stare at Lord Byron. Although Lady Shelley and Byron resided on opposite shores of Lake Geneva, she recognized the poet when he arrived at a party overflowing with English tourists. "Lord Byron looked in for a moment," she wrote in her diary, "but on seeing so many people he went away without speaking to anyone. He was evidently very much put out about something; and the expression on his face was somewhat demoniacal. What a strange person!"

Day after day, Lady Shelley planned excursions through the Swiss countryside, only to postpone the outings when the rains returned. Local residents noted that the ground was so thoroughly soaked that fountains came bubbling through the ground, and new streams formed where none had previously existed. On July 29, Lord and Lady Shelley set out after a morning of heavy rains to travel along the Arve River, on the west side of Geneva, but the river "had washed away so much of the bank, which had been raised at least twenty feet above the normal flow of the stream, that a boat would have been very useful at times." The following day the weather turned even worse. "Alas! All our hopes of fine weather are destroyed. Snow has fallen on the mountains during the night, and the rain is so persistent, that we were compelled to abandon our excursion."

It rained again on July 31, and on the first day of August. When the skies finally cleared to allow her to visit the Castle of Chillon, Lady Shelley encountered a dismal scene along the shores of Lake Geneva: "The inundations have had grievous results. All the gardens bordering on the lake are completely under water. We saw women hard at work trying to rescue their vegetables, while the men were bringing the hay home in boats."

Mary Godwin spent most of August indoors at her château in Chapuis, reading the Roman historian Curtius and a life of Montaigne, and writing the story that eventually became *Frankenstein*. Two years had passed since Percy Shelley and Mary ran away to France; apparently they did not celebrate the anniversary at Chapuis, although Mary did venture into Geneva to buy Shelley a telescope for his twenty-fourth birthday (August 4).

Occasionally Percy Shelley would take the time to discuss Mary's story with her, but he spent most of his time writing, reading history (Tacitus, Plutarch), or chatting with Byron. At least for the next several weeks, Shelley clearly preferred Byron's company to Mary's. The two men sailed on the lake nearly every day the weather allowed, dodging the storms—sometimes in the morning, sometimes after dinner, and occasionally both. On the evenings they remained ashore, Shelley typically visited Byron at Diodati.

They were joined for a week in mid-August by Matthew Gregory "Monk" Lewis, an English gothic-horror novelist who had inherited a plantation in the West Indies. On the evening of August 14, Lewis, Byron, Shelley, and Mary Godwin gathered to speak again of ghosts and Goethe's *Faust*. Lewis recited a poem which the Princess of Wales had asked him to compose; the princess, said Lewis, "was not only a believer in ghosts, but in magic & witchcraft, & asserted that prophecies made in her youth had been accomplished since." Lewis then regaled his hosts with a series of ghost stories which Mary later summarized at length in her journal. Twelve nights later, Coleridge's "Christabel" again graced a gathering; this time Shelley read the poem aloud, and Mary experienced a vision of a horrifying yet pathetic creature, which she filed away in her memory.

Shelley had elbowed Dr. Polidori out of Byron's company; wounded, the aspiring novelist assuaged the snub by visiting Madame de Staël's salon at Coppet. He, too, spent much of August writing of fantastic characters, completing the story *The Vampyre*, which subsequently served as the inspiration for Bram Stoker's *Dracula*.

Claire Clairmont, now visibly pregnant with Byron's child, continued to beg Byron for attention, but he refused to meet with her alone. "A foolish girl," he called her, and told his half sister Augusta that "I could not help this [affair], that I did all I could to prevent it, and have at last put an end to it. I was not in love, nor have any love left for any." Banished from Byron's bed, Claire settled for serving as his amanuensis, copying his drafts of "The Prisoner of Chillon" and the third canto of "Childe Harold's Pilgrimage" into legible versions for his publisher in England. Shelley attempted a reconciliation between the pair, but Byron would concede nothing more than a promise to let Claire raise their child (assuming, he said, it *was* his child) until he should decide to send for it.

Their summer ended abruptly after Shelley received a message from his father, whom he had asked for an increase in his allowance. His father consented, providing Shelley returned to England. Unable to live on their own meager income, Shelley and Mary (accompanied by Claire) began packing for the journey home; on the evening of August 28, Shelley visited Diodati for the last time. Besides their own belongings, they packed the manuscripts of "The Prisoner of Chillon" and the third canto of "Childe Harold's Pilgrimage," which Shelley promised to deliver to Byron's publisher.

At some point between July 21 and August 25, Byron completed the poem, "Darkness," the literary work most closely associated with the summer of 1816. After leaving Switzerland, he told a friend that he had composed the poem "at Geneva, where there was a celebrated dark day, on which the fowls went to roost at noon, and the candles were lighted as at midnight." There was no shortage of candidates for such a day. "Darkness" captured the summer's sense of impending apocalypse, the fears of a dying sun, the frigid atmosphere, the approaching and inevitable famine, and the desolation and mockery of faith as prayers went unanswered:

> I had a dream, which was not all a dream.
> The bright sun was extinguish'd, and the stars
> Did wander darkling in the eternal space,
> Rayless, and pathless, and the icy earth
> Swung blind and blackening in the moonless air;
> Morn came and went—and came, and brought no day,
> And men forgot their passions in the dread
> Of this their desolation; and all hearts
> Were chill'd into a selfish prayer for light:
> And they did live by watchfires—and the thrones,
> The palaces of crowned kings—the huts,
> The habitations of all things which dwell,
> Were burnt for beacons; cities were consumed,
> And men were gathered round their blazing homes
> To look once more into each other's face;
> Happy were those who dwelt within the eye
> Of the volcanoes, and their mountain-torch:
> A fearful hope was all the world contain'd;
> Forests were set on fire—but hour by hour
> They fell and faded—and the crackling trunks
> Extinguish'd with a crash—and all was black . . . .

8.

THE PRICE OF BREAD

*"There has not been this whole summer one day of
steady sunshine, not one day of heat, nor one night
when a coverlet and blanket could have been thrown
off with comfort . . . "*

GHENT, AUGUST 3: "The waters are excessively high, and
have not subsided for these three days. The Scheldt is at the
height of 16 feet at Oudenarde. Our rich and beautiful meadows
are partly inundated. The grass which is not mown will rot in the
water, and that which was already mown has been carried off
by the current. Hay has risen 100 per cent." Outside of Antwerp,
a severe hailstorm ruined crops waiting to be harvested.

In Württemberg in southwestern Germany, the sun seldom
shone for more than a small part of the day. "Thunderstorms
brought forth the worst weather, so that one could say a quarter or
even a third of the grain was ruined throughout the state," wrote
the mayor of Geradstetten. "The weather also caused the potatoes
to rot in the ground, and in many towns you could not harvest
as many potatoes as you planted. Similarly it went in the vineyards,

where the grapes did not ripen. The same fate befell the high hills as well as the high meadow." From all parts of Denmark came complaints of constant storms; in Copenhagen it rained nearly every day for five weeks.

Reports of devastating storms and floods throughout France poured into London in the first week of August. "The weather continues as ungenial in that country as with us," noted *The Times*. In Burgundy, rain and cold "have ruined the finer sort of vines," and threatened to wipe out the common ones as well. At Chambray, just south of Geneva, snow fell on the mountains outside of town. Residents of Grenoble, in southeastern France, were trapped between two flooding rivers. The Isère overflowed its banks, sending water cascading through the entire valley. Meanwhile the Drec "burst its dikes . . . and in consequence three or four villages, together with the suburbs of Grenoble, were inundated."

On August 5, storms struck the department of Haute-Marne to the north. "The increase of waters has every where been greater than was ever before known," reported one correspondent, "and what yet remained in the meadows has been swept away and destroyed. Independent of the loss of hay, more than 15 communes have had their crops completely destroyed." The same storm struck Nancy, where "the harvest is completely destroyed: wheat, barley, oats, vegetables, vines, and even trees . . ."

In Paris, the Seine continued to rise. On August 4, church authorities ordered additional prayers for nine days in all the city's churches for better weather; the following day, the churches were filled "with an immense concourse of the faithful." For a moment, it seemed as if their prayers were answered. By August 9, the rain ceased and warm temperatures returned. An unofficial survey of the state of French crops concluded that "the first crop of hay has been almost universally destroyed or spoiled; and though the rains will have rendered the second crop more productive, that will not be sufficient: the rye likewise turns out bad in quality, and not abundant. The wine probably will be scarce and bad."

Anticipating poor harvests in France, Holland, Belgium, Switzerland, and the German states, merchants bid up the price of grain. Popular anxiety intensified, and governments strengthened their efforts to forestall panic. The city of Mainz, considered a vital link in the Prussian and Austrian defenses against France, received gifts from both those nations to help allay its residents' fears about the rising price of bread. Austrian officials gave the city 300,000 pounds of flour, while Prussian authorities pledged an equal amount of wheat, to be delivered after the harvest.

Lord Liverpool's government preferred to leave relief efforts to private charities and local parishes. In early August, pressure mounted on the Prince Regent to recall Parliament to deal with the rising distress in Britain, but conventional Tory opinion firmly opposed the idea. New taxes appeared out of the question at a time when the existing rates were, in *The Times'* words, "laid on with a sufficiently heavy hand already." Besides, reasoned *The Times*, it would be a mistake to bring members of Parliament to London so near to harvest season; far better to allow them to remain in their home districts, where they could direct charitable relief efforts if necessary. "It would, in fact, be as rational to call Parliament together for the wet weather, or the spots in the Sun," sniffed *The Times*, "as for the want of work and consequent distress in particular districts."

In any event, the Prince Regent was in no condition to participate in any political concourse in August 1816. His inveterate habit of overindulgence and gluttony left him extremely ill with a condition known delicately as an "inflammation of the bowels." The cure prescribed by his physicians, according to Ambassador John Quincy Adams, involved "a girdle of thirty-six leeches round his waist, and, when they dropped off, [he] was put into a warm bath to continue the bleeding." Before his doctors were done, they reportedly took eighty ounces of blood from the Prince Regent. He recovered nonetheless.

Adams met frequently with Lord Castlereagh during August

to discuss a new commercial treaty between the United States and the United Kingdom. Castlereagh typically began their conversations by discussing the weather, and to Adams' surprise, the foreign secretary seemed remarkably sanguine about the prospects for the forthcoming harvest. "He said that he hoped we should now have a month or six weeks of fine weather," Adams noted in his diary on August 21, "and if so, from the accounts he had from the different parts of the country, there would be a fine harvest." Adams found this optimism quite surprising, "as all the appearances of the harvest in our neighborhood are unfavorable; as there have been now for a full month public prayers in the churches for a change of weather; and as the average price of flour and wheat throughout England and Wales has been gradually rising at the moment when the harvest season is arrived."

English newspapers echoed Castlereagh's confident rhetoric, at least from mid-August on. In the early part of the month, they acknowledged that weeks of cold and rain had produced much "fire-blast" (a fungus) and mold—not to mention an explosion in the population of vermin—among crops in Kent and Sussex, and that a great deal of hay already had rotted in various districts. Starting around August 10, however, press reports suddenly turned stoutly optimistic. "The wheats everywhere present a bold, heavy, and well set ear," ran one article. "The late rains have done more good than harm," claimed another. "The corn generally looks very thriving, and promises a more than average crop." "The weather continues fine," observed *The Times* on August 20, "and the crop of wheat will be very abundant. You can form no idea of the uneasiness which pervaded all ranks on this subject before the change of weather."

But some opposition leaders believed these optimistic news stories were nothing more than a clumsy government ruse. William Cobbett and Henry Hunt, two of the leading radical reformers in Britain, suspected that the Liverpool ministry and moderate Whig leaders were trying to lull the public into a false sense of security—and thereby dampen enthusiasm for reform—by encouraging the press to publish misleading articles about the state of the approaching harvest. So the weather and its effects turned into a political controversy, as Cobbett and Hunt spent much of August telling their audiences to expect widespread crop failures. When the *Morning Chronicle*, a Whig journal, printed an article on August 21 asserting that, "notwithstanding the lateness of the season, there would be this year an uncommon fine harvest," Hunt publicly contradicted the newspaper and "pledged his honor" as a gentleman that England's crops would fail miserably. The *Morning Chronicle*'s editor insisted that his information indicated an excellent harvest, and Castlereagh supported him. "It is strange that such a thing should be made a party question," mused John Quincy Adams, "but it is."

AMERICANS could not generate any enthusiasm about the presidential election campaign of 1816. The election of James Monroe seemed a foregone conclusion—not because of any overwhelming groundswell of support for his candidacy, although most voters had no serious objection to him, save for a parochial objection to yet another president (four out of five) from Virginia. Rather, it resulted partly from the Federalist Party's inability to nominate a slate of electors in nearly half of the eighteen states, and partly from the almost total indifference of the Federalist nominee. "So certain is the result," wrote Rufus King of his own impending defeat, "that no pains are taken to excite the community on the subject." Ten states allowed voters to choose presidential electors directly; the others still allowed state legislatures to select electors. And each state chose its own election day, so voting was staggered throughout the summer and autumn.

Elections on the state level were more hotly contested. As Virginia's acerbic congressman John Randolph pointed out, "There was no election for Burgesses to the General Assembly which had not caused ten times the excitement that had been caused by the election of the President of the United States." Incumbent congressmen continued to suffer unremitting abuse for their support of the Compensation Bill. In one state after another, they went down to defeat; in New York, only one-fourth of the incumbent congressional representatives won reelection.

On the first Monday in September, Maine held a special election to vote on its separation from Massachusetts. A referendum in March had produced a slight majority in favor of statehood, but Massachusetts law required a majority of more than 60 percent before Maine could obtain its independence. Agitation for separation came primarily from the interior, from small farmers who wanted more equitable taxation and lower government expenses. Merchants and businessmen in coastal areas generally were content to remain safely and profitably within Boston's commercial orbit. In September, the Massachusetts General Court dropped the statehood requirement to a five-ninths majority, but again the advocates of separation fell slightly short of victory.

Temperatures in early September recovered to slightly above normal levels over most of the Eastern United States, but the drought dragged on. In Philadelphia, the Schuylkill River fell to a lower level than anyone could remember—"it may be crossed on foot at the Falls, without wetting the feet," claimed the *Farmer's Cabinet*—endangering the crops in the surrounding counties.

The *Richmond Enquirer* warned that "never has there been in America, especially in Virginia, so gloomy a prospect. It appears, that it is more than probable that there will be very short crops of Corn, on account of which, people in general are very much alarmed." The newspaper urged its readers to keep their grain and flour within the state, rather than selling to merchants who might send it out of Virginia. "Although it is true, that if any were like to starve, and we could assist them, we ought to do so," reasoned the *Enquirer*, "but to use a scripture phrase, 'he that provides not for his own, especially those of his own household, hath denied the faith, and is worse than an infidel.'" A letter writer to the *Enquirer* who signed himself "A Starving People" suggested that Governor Wilson Cary Nicholas ask the General Assembly to reduce taxes until the crisis abated.

Relief arrived in Virginia on September 6 in the form of a heavy rainstorm—possibly the residue of a hurricane—that traveled slowly up the coast, reaching Philadelphia and New York on September 8, and Boston shortly thereafter. Farmers did not rejoice for long. Accompanied by high winds that wrought considerable damage to shipping in coastal areas, the rain continued for a week, drenching fields in low-lying areas, particularly in the South. Petersburg, Virginia, reported that "every part of the town and the adjacent country was under water," with streams overflowing their banks to create a scene "grand, awful and devastating."

While the storm battered coastal areas, it left inland areas of New England virtually untouched. Much of Vermont received no rain at all; indeed, in some areas of the state there had been no measurable precipitation other than snow for more than three months. "A failure of the crops generally was therefore certain," concluded the *American Advocate*. At Brunswick, Maine, an observer measured less than half an inch of rain for all of September. Not surprisingly, a number of forest fires ravaged the parched woodlands of northern New England, blackening the skies with thick acrid smoke.

Then a cold wave struck on the evening of September 10, bringing frost followed by snow that covered mountaintops in northern Vermont. Farmers hurried to harvest whatever potatoes survived, even if they had not yet ripened. In Sutton, New Hampshire, "corn froze to the centre of the cob, and apples froze upon the trees." The same cold front brought frost to Concord, New Hampshire, and left two to three inches of snow on the ground at Springfield, Massachusetts. "It is believed," reported one Boston newspaper, "that no person can recollect a summer so inconsistant [sic] and fluctuating."

Across the border, Quebec inched closer to famine. Hard-pressed by a short growing season in the best of times, Canadian farmers found their last hopes for a decent harvest—crops planted belatedly after the June snows—shattered by sharp frosts in September. Some cut their wheat before it was ripe, to save it from freezing. Others gambled that the warmer temperatures of late July and August would persist, and lost. Between two-thirds and four-fifths of the hay crop was ruined; "the corn is said to be cut off; and the wheat to be much injured, even in that most Southern district of the two Canadian provinces." Farmers sold their milch cows to buy bread; instead of their usual summertime diet of bread and milk, some reportedly subsisted on wild herbs.

"JULY of 1816 was a particularly unusual month concerning both rainfall and temperature," wrote José Manuel da Silva Tedim, a lawyer and priest in Braga, Portugal. "I am 78 years old and I have never seen so much rain and cold, not even in winter months." August in Portugal was only slightly warmer and drier. In Barcelona, the Baron of Malda decided that summer seemed more like spring. On August 18, he noted in his diary that the cool air reminded him of May; but then August 22 turned even colder, resembling the weather of April. (The baron ascribed the drop in temperature in Barcelona to a recent snowfall—it may actually have been a hailstorm—in central Spain.)

Conditions on the Iberian peninsula that season varied little from those in France, Germany, or Britain. While the decade of 1811–1820 as a whole was wet and cool in Spain and Portugal, the summer of 1816—notably July and August—was especially cold, with an average temperature two to three degrees Celsius below normal. Precipitation totals for July and August 1816 also were considerably higher than usual. In fact, summer rain typically is so scant in both countries that several successive rainy days in August 1816 struck observers as quite remarkable.

Perhaps not as remarkable, though, as a monarchy without a monarch. Portugal's royal family had fled the country when Napoléon invaded in 1807, and spent the rest of the war years in Brazil. Like Britain, its close ally, Portugal was officially ruled by a regent in 1816; Queen Maria had been declared incurably mad in 1799— she was, in fact, treated by Dr. Francis Willis, one of the physicians who had attended King George III during his episode of madness in 1788–89—and her son, John, ruled in her stead. Upon learning of Napoléon's surrender in 1814, John had made plans to return to Portugal, but he reconsidered when he heard that Napoléon had returned from Elba. Even after Maria died on March 20, 1816, and the regent was crowned as King John VI, he decided to remain comfortably ensconced in Brazil. In his absence, British officials carried out much of the day-to-day administration of Portugal.

That arrangement provided Portugal with a considerably more competent government than Spain, where King Fernando VII held sway. In the words of one historian, Fernando was "in many ways the basest king in Spanish history"; among other traits, he appeared "cowardly, selfish, grasping, suspicious, and vengeful." In 1808, Napoléon replaced Fernando on the Spanish throne with the emperor's brother, Joseph Bonaparte, disdainfully nicknamed "Pepe Botellas"—"Joe Bottles"—by Spaniards for his fondness for drink. For the next five years, Fernando remained under guard in a French château while British soldiers and Spanish irregulars battled Napoléon's troops in a savage cycle of guerilla attacks and reprisals.

Meanwhile, the Bonapartist government launched a series of legal and administrative reforms of Spanish society, including the abolition of monasteries and distribution of their property. Recognizing that the fluid political situation provided them with an opportunity to carry out even more radical reforms, Spanish liberals convened a legislative assembly in the southern port of Cadiz, under the protection of the British Navy, and drafted a new constitution in 1812 that stripped the monarchy of most of its powers and finally brought a formal end to the Inquisition. The new regime did not last long. Upon his return to Spain in 1814, Don Fernando supported an army coup that rescinded the new constitution, thereby turning back the clock to 1808 and leaving Spain deeply divided into hostile political camps.

A decade of political turbulence and military conflict, exacerbated by the incompetence and corruption of Don Fernando's government, severely dislocated the Spanish economy. Ongoing rebellions in Spain's colonies in the Western Hemisphere—Argentina was the latest to declare its independence, in July 1816—aggravated the difficulties by depriving Spain of vital markets and materials. The last thing Spaniards needed in the summer of 1816 was a widespread failure of the harvest.

Reliable evidence of weather phenomena in the summer of 1816 is scarcer for Spain and Portugal than for other countries in Western Europe. Nevertheless, military and medical personnel recently had started to gather and publish data, for much the same reason as their counterparts in other European nations and the United States. In December 1815, a Portuguese scientist, politician, and naval officer named Marino Miguel Franzini began to regularly record meteorological observations from his station at Lisbon, initially to provide a local doctor with data to evaluate the relationship between changes in the weather and the state of public health. In Madrid, a group of scientists and medical officials maintained similar records, taking three temperature readings per day; additional observations (albeit on a less consistent basis) were made at the Observatory of the Spanish Navy in Cadiz, and at Barcelona. Private individuals such as da Silva Tedim, of course, supplemented these records with their own informal evidence.

No one disagreed that the summer of 1816 brought exceptionally cold, wet weather that damaged crops across the Iberian peninsula. Tedim noted that "July had only three clear days," and the highest temperature in Braga that month was only 77 degrees—eight degrees lower than the high temperature in July 1814. August provided only ten clear days, with the mercury never advancing beyond 79 degrees.

Frigid temperatures killed some fruit on the trees and ruined much of the rest. In central Portugal, "the unusual cool weather in summer had evil consequences on fruit, that was unpleasant to taste," noted Senhor Franzini. "Grapes have suffered for the same reason and never got ripe and as a consequence the wine was of inferior quality." In Spanish vineyards, too, only a small percentage of grapes ever matured, producing a scant and unpalatable harvest. Olive trees, always sensitive to cold, lacked the heat to produce quality fruit.

In the wheat fields of Spain, the harvest commenced much later than usual. "I note here as something strange and worthy of comment that throughout the months of June and July it was not at all hot," noted one resident of Arenys de Mar, just outside of Barcelona. "If anything it was cold, because of the excessively cool sea air caused by the hail that fell in Mallorca and other places. This delayed the wheat harvest . . . which meant that threshing was also late, because there was no sun and it was misty all day and clear all night, quite the opposite of what was needed." Workers painstakingly separated ripe, dry grain from immature green seeds, a process that required significantly more labor and drove up the price of bread.

FROM a meteorological diary in Paris, August 31: At five o'clock in the morning, cloudy with rain; at noon, rain; at three o'clock in the afternoon, rain with thunder. "A cold and humid temperature has succeeded the too few days we have had of fine weather," reported a French correspondent in the first week of September. "The thermometer has fallen from 16 and 20 degrees [Celsius] to 8 and 9; and it is said that one of these nights there was frost in the country."

As the temperature declined, concerns for the harvest rose

along with the price of bread. A loaf that cost sixteen sous in the springtime cost thirty or thirty-two sous in August. Fruit of any kind grew scarce. In the Norman town of Dieppe, the poor already were in such distress that the police requisitioned bread to distribute among them. And still the rain continued to pour down, especially in the northern departments. "The state of the weather is now almost as interesting a political topic as can well occur," remarked *The Times* of London, "considering the effect which it must have upon the contentment and tranquility of States for a year to come."

Against this ominous and sodden backdrop, King Louis formally signed the ordinance dissolving the Chamber of Deputies on September 5. In its brief existence, the *Chambre introuvable* had solved none of France's critical difficulties; instead, it had tried to restore aristocratic and religious privileges inimical to the interests of the nation's masses. "Such a set of venal, merciless, and ignorant bigots and blockheads never were collected in any assembly," concluded a British visitor in Paris. The French public appears to have greeted the call for new elections with relief; certainly the Allied governments welcomed it. The Duke of Wellington responded by reducing (slightly) the size of the army of occupation, partly to relieve pressure on the French treasury, but also to ease tensions at a time when reports of Gallic insults to English tourists appeared in newspapers nearly every day. Wellington also agreed to postpone the autumn maneuvers of the Allied occupation force— ostensibly because of the shortage of food in the most hard-pressed departments, but also to avoid arousing antigovernment sentiment during the election campaign.

Ultra-Royalists and moderate monarchists alike spent September canvassing the countryside. Although France's electoral qualifications had not changed, the government clearly hoped that voters who had abstained from the previous election would exercise their franchise this time. Government officials in the provinces received orders from Paris to encourage voters to reject extremists (i.e., Ultras) and support only "pure but moderate" candidates "who do not believe that loving the king and serving him well exempts them from obeying the laws." Local officials who supported the Ultras exerted their own pressure on voters to return the incumbent deputies. With the king firmly aligned with the moderates, erstwhile revolutionaries were heard shouting "Vive le Roi!" as they passed Ultras in the street.

Rain, elections, cold, the rising price of bread—and then sunspots returned in the middle of September. "They are more considerable, and in greater numbers, than were remarked during the month of July," noted the *Gazette de France*. This time they resembled two strings of beads: the first dominated by spots that looked like two large cherries, with a dozen other spots between them; the second consisting of seven or eight smaller spots strung together. To an English commentator, the accompanying diagram in the *Gazette* of the sun "with its cheeks all covered with spots" resembled caricatures of "the patches on a fashionable English lady one hundred years ago."

"THERE has not been this whole summer one day of steady sunshine, not one day of heat, nor one night when a coverlet and blanket could have been thrown off with comfort," wrote an exasperated John Quincy Adams in his diary in London on Wednesday, August 28. "There was not one of the forty days from St. Swithin's [July 15], to a certainty, without rain, so that the old prediction"—if it rained on St. Swithin's Day, it would rain for the next forty days—"seems to have been this year made good." Adams recently had managed to get through one night without his flannel waistcoat, but was obliged to don it again the next day. The 28th actually turned out to be "warm and fine," Adams noted, the day "most like summer" all season, despite a frost the previous evening. But Adams feared for the British harvest, whose prospects he termed "precarious."

Two days later, another powerful storm struck Britain. One report from Kent, in southeast England, described it as "one of the most violent storms of wind and rain . . . that has occurred at this period of the year within recollection." Brutal winds tore up trees and broke them into pieces, leveled poles of hops, and left shocks of corn strewn over the ground. "In the orchards and gardens," noted an observer, "the far greater portion of the fruit has been stripped from the trees." Snow fell in Barnet, about forty miles north of London, and in the Sussex town of Lewes. "Snow in harvest is no common occurrence," noted the Lewes Journal, "but it is a fact that it occurred here yesterday, as witnessed by several persons in the town."

When the gale reached Bury, outside of Manchester, it shattered trees and flattened fields of wheat and oats. The region around Newcastle suffered similar damage. In Cambridge and Huntingdonshire, "a considerable fall of snow" accompanied by a severe frost destroyed the area's extensive market vegetable crops of French beans and cucumbers. A local newspaper in Essex reported that a combination of snow, a hailstorm, and the "somewhat extraordinary" appearance of ice four inches thick threatened to completely ruin the second crop of hay. Even from Edinburgh, known for its sudden shocks of cold, wind, and rain, came complaints that "the weather here, for these eight days past, has been excessively cold and rainy; and this unfavourable change has considerably damped those hopes which the genial weather of the preceding fortnight had excited." The price of grain in the city's markets rose dramatically.

"Indeed, the whole country is in a very disastrous state," reported *The Times* of London, "as the little corn yet reaped is too green to be carried, and without more warmth and sunshine than we have at present, can never be completely ripened, and must prove of bad sample." Unless the weather drastically improved, farmers feared their wheat would never ripen; "and still the weather is very cold and unseasonable."

"The gale has abated," noted Adams on the evening of September 2, "and the weather this day was part of the day, fair, but with the decided character of autumn, and so cold that we had a fire again in the evening." All the hopes for a good, albeit late harvest had vanished, Adams wrote. "They are now desperate."

Reports from across England confirmed Adams' assessment. In Worcester, the cold nights had ruined the hops, and prices already had increased by nearly a third. At Chelmsford in Essex, potatoes, beans, peas, barley, and grapes were severely damaged by the "extraordinary visitation" of snow and ice, which "already remind us of the approaching winter." The Hereford *Journal* reported substantial damage to the wheat from the continuous rains; and "the hops have been nearly destroyed in the course of the last week by the inclement season." The cold nights left farmers in Worcestershire so little to harvest that they wondered if the profit would outweigh the expense of picking. The oat crop suffered significantly from the recent evening frosts, and hay already was scarce. And in Littleham, Exeter, a seventy-three-year-old farmer who had reaped wheat every summer for fifty-three years declared that "the present harvest is one month later than any year he has known."

A week of fair weather provided a window for farmers to harvest any remaining crops that were even close to maturing, but when rain returned on September 9, they could only watch helplessly as the downpour pounded their fields. Two days later southeastern England suffered another violent storm that brought rain, hail, and snow. Outside of Maidstone, in Kent, hailstones "as large as nuts" severely damaged both wheat and barley. "Snow fell once or twice in the neighbourhood during the week," reported *The Times*, "and more than once ice of the thickness of half-a-crown was found in the morning." Hops farmers in Canterbury suffered losses worth thousands of pounds sterling from storm damage.

Surveying the devastation, *The Times* of London clung to its assertion that despite "the late and wet season," the wheat harvest "has proved propitious as the husbandman could desire." It acknowledged, however, that the quality of wheat varied widely among different regions, especially since many farmers cut their grain too early or when it was damp. With so much wheat spoiled, seed for the following season would be in short supply. Even optimistic observers acknowledged that more than 75 percent of the hops harvest was lost. A considerable quantity of barley had been harvested, but most of it was of inferior quality. Although peas and beans from the east were plentiful, in the home counties "they have run too much to straw."

From Gatcombe Park, David Ricardo reported that "the continuance of the cold and wet weather does not afford us a very good propect for the harvest, and I am very much afraid that the poor will have much to suffer during the next winter." Malthus agreed. The harvest in Hertfordshire, Malthus informed his friend in a letter of September 8, "has begun about us at last and seems as if it would be pretty good if it could be got in, but there has hardly ever been known so late a year, and in the backward parts of the country, a late year is always a bad one."

As real and anticipated shortages sent commodity prices higher, the peculiar operation of the Corn Laws delayed the importation of foreign grain. The legislation compelled the government to close or open the ports to grain imports for three months at a time, based upon the average price of wheat over a six-week period. The implementation of the law therefore always lagged behind the actual movement of prices. By the end of September 1816, wheat was selling well above the eighty shillings per quarter threshold established by the Corn Laws. Given the dismal failure of the harvest on much of the Continent, there seemed little chance the price of wheat would fall below the threshold anytime soon.

Lord Liverpool's ministry inadvertently contributed to public anxiety over the prospect of sharply higher food prices when it attempted to suppress the quarterly Report on the Agricultural State of the Kingdom for March, April, and May. The report was a routine gathering of information from farmers throughout

Britain about the condition of their crops and livestock, but the government found the farmers' responses so alarming that it printed only twenty-two copies of the report and tried to restrict access to it. Even *The Times* deemed this foolish: "Secrecy is looked upon as a sign of extreme and imminent danger; and what is kept back from knowledge acts far more terribly than what is known."

Nevertheless, public demonstrations against the government remained rare, save for isolated outbursts in Preston and Glasgow. Yet it seemed likely that widespread protests wanted only deepening distress and the coordination of discontent by parliamentary reformers. Following the end of the war against France, radicals led by Major Cartwright and Sir Francis Burdett had helped to establish local reform clubs—usually known as Hampden clubs—in numerous English counties. Unlike previous reform efforts, which sought to mobilize only the middle and upper classes, this campaign attempted to mobilize as many Englishmen as possible behind a platform of annual elections, equal parliamentary constituencies, and the extension of the franchise to all taxpayers, and eventually to all adult males. William Cobbett contributed ammunition on a weekly basis through his "Two-Penny Trash," an inexpensive, pamphlet version (which avoided the newspaper tax) of his more staid *Political Register*; by the summer of 1816, Cobbett's pamphlets were the primary printed source of news for Britain's working class, with a circulation that often exceeded 50,000.

In open-air meetings and gatherings in taverns and guild halls, speakers informed factory hands and farm laborers that their current distress stemmed in large measure from a corrupt and uncaring political system, and that their only remedy lay in a reformed Parliament. In late August, a meeting of eight thousand angry liverymen—members of London's trade and craft organizations—unanimously demanded lower taxes and legislative reform. When John Quincy Adams asked the Lord Mayor of London how such resolutions could have been carried without even a murmur of dissent, the Lord Mayor replied that "the friends of the Government had not dared to make any opposition." At another meeting on September 5 in Westminster, speakers denounced the government's attempted suppression of the Board of Agriculture's report, and insisted that "the distresses of the country were without parallel." Shortly thereafter, a self-styled "Committee of Public Safety"—a charged term, given the government's paranoia about any movement recalling the French Revolution—launched a campaign to obtain thousands of signatures on petitions demanding reform, to be presented to Parliament when it reconvened in early 1817.

Tory journals insisted the government's policies bore little, if any, responsibility for the nation's economic troubles. "Of distresses, such as now pervade the mass of the community," noted the *Quarterly Review*, "small indeed is the part which parliaments or governments either create or cure." Certainly Liverpool's ministers and individual members of the royal family could encourage more affluent Englishmen to contribute to charitable causes, while the government cut spending and reduced taxes, in hopes of stimulating business activity. "Every expedient should be used to reduce the expenses of Government, and lessen the burdens of the people," urged the editors of *The Times* of London, "in order that they may be put in good humour . . . The diminution of the public burdens must and ought at all events to take place, whatever other measure may ensue."

Across the Atlantic, the American press foresaw trouble for Britain if the harvest failed. In a September 10 editorial, the *Daily National Intelligencer* informed its readers that as bad as the summer had been for American farmers, "the season has been even more unfavorable to agriculture in Europe than in this country." And if the poorer classes of Britain were stalked by hunger, at a time when the rest of British society lived in relative comfort, "the consequences of a scarcity will be terrible indeed."

James Mill, the utilitarian political philosopher and economist, painted his own grim picture of Britain's future. In a letter to David Ricardo, Mill wrote from Ford Abbey in Dorset that "the corn here is absolutely green, nothing whatsoever in the ear; and a perfect continuance of rain and cold. There must now be of necessity a very deficient crop, and very high prices—and these with an unexampled scarcity of work will produce a degree of misery, the thought of which makes the flesh creep on ones [sic] bones— one third of the people must die—it would be a blessing to take them into the streets and highways, and cut their throats as we do with pigs."

PERCY Shelley arrived in England shortly before the harvest began. After leaving Geneva on the morning of August 29, Shelley, Mary Godwin, and Claire Clairmont made their way back over the Jura Mountains ("The Swiss are very slow drivers," complained an impatient Mary) and then through France in the same stormy weather that had crushed British crops in the last days of August. When the sun finally broke through, they stopped to visit the palaces and gardens at Fontainebleau and Versailles, which Mary found disappointing. "In all that essentially belongs to a garden they are extraordinarily deficient," she noted in her journal. "The orangery is a stupid piece of expense."

Contrary winds delayed the party at Le Havre for several days, but they finally crossed the Channel through heavy seas and arrived in Portsmouth on September 8. ("Our passage from Havre hither was wretched—26 hours," grumbled Shelley.) It took longer than expected to pass through customs when an officious clerk— "greasy," Shelley called him—decided to leaf laboriously through the manuscript of Byron's third canto of "Childe Harold's Pilgrimage" to make sure Shelley was not smuggling Belgian lace between its pages. Bureaucratic curiosity satisfied, Shelley headed for London to deliver Byron's manuscripts to his publisher and settle some personal financial matters, before heading to Marlow, a town between the city and Oxford, to look for a new house.

Since Claire did not want the Godwins to learn about her

188 ∿ THE YEAR WITHOUT SUMMER

pregnancy, she and Mary told them Claire felt ill, and that she would stay in Bath until she recovered. Mary agreed to help Claire get settled; they found lodgings next to the Pump Room, the fashionable meeting hall frequented by Jane Austen's characters in *Northanger Abbey*. Mary spent the next week reading, working on the manuscript of her novel, and attending scientific lectures at the Literary and Philosophical Society. Several blocks away, at the spacious and elegantly decorated Theatre Royale (which opened in its new location on the south side of Beauford Square in 1805), the company was posthumously honoring the late Richard Brinsley Sheridan—a friend of William Godwin—with its productions of *The School for Scandal* and *The Rivals*.

Shelley sent for Mary on September 18; she left Bath and Claire with alacrity. Meanwhile, Shelley drafted a letter to Byron to update him on events in England. "The harvest is not yet cut," he told his friend. "There are, however, as yet no very glaring symptoms of disaffection, though the distress is said to be severe. But winter is the season when the burthen will be felt. Most earnestly I do hope that despair will not drive the people to premature and useless struggles."

"EVEN now we have suffered much from the Cold and the dreadful storms of Wind & Thunder," wrote Lady Caroline Capel from Lausanne in early September. From April through August, Switzerland had received measurable rainfall for 130 out of 152 days. The harvest of 1816 was the worst in years—twice as bad as the dismal harvest of 1815. Grain was almost completely ruined, as was much of the hay crop, and the grape harvest failed altogether. Fodder for cattle grew scarce. The price of bread more than doubled; hostesses asked their guests to bring their own loaves to dinner parties.

For the first two weeks of September, Byron divided his time between Coppet and Diodati, where he welcomed John Hobhouse, a friend from Trinity College days. Accompanied by Polidori, Byron and Hobhouse visited Madame de Staël on September 12 despite a hard, driving rain; their dinner conversation turned to Richard Sheridan and the book Madame de Staël was writing about Napoléon. Several days later, Byron dismissed Polidori. To Hobhouse—who had known the Italian physician for a brief time only—it seemed that Polidori, with his literary aspirations, "does not answer to Madame de Staël's definition of a happy man, whose capacities are squared with his inclinations. . . . He is anything but an amiable man, and has a most unmeasured ambition, as well as inordinate vanity. The true ingredients of misery . . ."

On September 17, Byron and Hobhouse embarked on another tour of the Alps. This time the weather cooperated; it rained for only four hours in eight days. As they traveled, Hobhouse noticed the backward state of Swiss vineyards: "Grapes appeared many, but little hopes of ripening." Passing through Yverdon, they saw more crops that would never mature. By the time Byron and Hobhouse returned to Diodati on September 29, the Grand Council of Geneva had approved an emergency expenditure of 800,000 francs to purchase food for the inhabitants of the canton. The council subsequently doubled that amount.

Rain continued to pelt the crops around Brussels through September. One local observer deemed the season "the most inclement within the memory of man." Grain already was in short supply, partly because any surplus that had been stored from the previous harvest had been consumed by Allied armies earlier in the year. Newspapers called for the government to prohibit the exportation of grain. Prices rose so rapidly that "thousands of fathers of families are unable to supply the wants of their children, and can hardly give them a wretched crust of unwholesome black bread." Here, too, the grape harvest failed; fruits ripened in mid-September, much later than usual; and potatoes rotted in the soggy fields.

"How cold and triste is this vast Germany," sighed Lady Shelley as she passed through Prussia in the late summer. In Dresden, she noted that "the weather is dreadfully cold; frequent showers of rain, and very damp." In Mannheim, a violent storm on September 11 sent the Rhine flowing over its banks for the fifth time in three months—six feet above its mean height. Rain prevented farmers from harvesting the hay around Hamburg; then more rain ruined the hay still in the fields. In Württemberg, grain failed and grass took over the fields; then flooding rivers ravaged the hay as well, leaving livestock with almost nothing to eat. Potatoes decayed in the ground, and grapes failed to ripen on either hills or meadows. Losses to the crops outside of Frankfurt were deemed "incalculable." One Bavarian official deemed 1816 one of the three worst harvests since the mid-sixteenth century; the only grain that eventually ripened was almost too sodden to sell. To the east, authorities in Strasburg arrested two Jewish businessmen "of the lower class" whom they blamed for raising grain prices through their speculative activities in the local markets—*Kornjuden*, they called the accused.

As Lady Shelley crossed the Danube into Hungary, she passed through lands where stands of ruined wheat already had been cut. "This looked as dismal as anything I ever saw in Norfolk," she decided. At Vienna, she dined with royalty and wealthy landowners, one of whom—Count Francois Zichy—told her that the wheat had failed on his lands in southern Austria. "The peasants must eat rye," he concluded, and "provisions will be dear." He added that in nearby Styria, where there was barely enough food in good times, "the scarcity is great." Prospects for the following year already looked dim, since the late harvest and heavy rains made it impossible to plant more than half of the rye fields for the winter season.

As the harvest failed in one German state after another, emigration became a more attractive option. In Württemberg, an extremist Protestant sect obsessed with the New Testament Book of Revelation and the visions of Saint John suspected that the end of the world was near: first the devastation wrought by years of war, then the recent appearance of a comet, followed by the emergence of heresy within the Lutheran Church, and finally the catastrophic rains and hailstorms of the summer of 1816. Convinced that they needed to emigrate to the Holy Land to escape the coming plagues, a band of forty families departed in September, sailing down the Danube as far as Ismail in the Ukraine. There they remained, stranded, as their food ran out.

Another German writer blamed the summer's cold not on heaven or the sinfulness of man, but on the advent of peace. In a pamphlet entitled "The Effects of War upon the Seasons," the author argued that wars in the Northern Hemisphere "rendered the seasons warmer and more temperate." In normal times, he claimed, a perpetual current of cold air swept from the polar regions toward the equator. But "the concussion produced in the atmosphere by large and frequent discharges of gunpowder, obstructed this current, and often caused a current in the opposite direction." When the wars ended, therefore, the normal flow of frigid air returned, and so the statesmen of Europe bore the responsibility for the cold and wet summer.

"I recollect no period since I have had any connection with Ireland in which it has been more at rest than it is at the present moment," wrote a contented Robert Peel to Lord Sidmouth, the home secretary, on August 17. Indeed, the chief secretary for Ireland pointed out that the government in Dublin had not needed to invoke the Insurrection Act even once in 1816. Peel did not suppose that the Irish peasantry had reformed its querulous ways, nor did he believe "that the condition of the lower orders is much improved." Instead, Peel concluded that the absence of major disturbances stemmed mainly from the strong measures the government had taken the previous year to convince troublemakers "of the futility of their absurd projects to better their condition by acts of violence. We are in a much better state than we were eighteen months hence."

It is not clear whether Peel understood the disastrous state of the Irish harvest in the late summer. British officials in Dublin frequently lacked accurate and timely information about conditions outside of their immediate area, although Peel usually made a concerted effort to stay abreast of developments in even the remoter counties. But crops in Ireland certainly were suffering more from the incessant rain even than those in England. It rained for 143 days in 1816 in Ireland—a total of 34 inches, which contemporaries believed may have been a record if records had been kept—and most of the precipitation fell during the summer and autumn. Wheat and, more ominously, potatoes were rotting in the fields.

"There never was such distress and want of money known in any former times," wrote Daniel O'Connell to his wife on August 18. "Half of the gentry in the country are ruined." An attorney in Dublin, O'Connell was the rising star of Irish nationalism. The scion of a County Kerry clan that had been dispossessed of most of its lands, O'Connell was educated in France in the early 1790s, since the penal laws still precluded Roman Catholics from studying at British universities. His experiences there during the early years of the French Revolution helped turn O'Connell against the use of physical force to achieve political goals, a conviction bolstered by his subsequent reading of William Godwin's works on liberal democracy and the power of public opinion. Once O'Connell gained admission to the bar in Ireland, he became a passionate advocate for the rights of Catholic tenant farmers against their Protestant landlords.

In the summer of 1816, O'Connell's practice was growing rapidly under the pressure of hard times. "I have had an immense number of cases," he told his wife at the end of August. "The times are very distressing to the country and there is no prospect of alleviation." As the price of bread and butter rose, the prices of other Irish goods fell, because demand kept declining as the depression deepened. "Between the fall of prices and the dreadful weather," O'Connell declared on September 30, "there is nothing but rain and wretchedness."

As the summer drew to a close, emigration from Ireland to the United States increased substantially. In a single week, more than 700 Irish applied for permission to leave the country; fewer than 2,000 had left in the entire twelve months of 1815. Peel would have preferred the emigrants to have come from the southern counties, which he felt would benefit from a reduction in population, since the land clearly could not support the numbers already there. But the prospective emigrants came almost exclusively from Ulster, the northern counties, and most were Protestant. Peel was especially loath to see them go to the United States. "I think it still more unfortunate that not only Ireland should lose so many industrious and valuable inhabitants," he told Lord Liverpool, "but that the United States of America should reap the advantage." (Actually, the British government was partly responsible for the disparity in emigration figures between northern and southern Ireland. By levying higher duties on American shipping, the Liverpool administration raised the price of passage to the United States, placing it beyond the reach of most Irish Catholic peasants.)

Sometimes the arrivals brought no advantage to their new homeland. In September, a ship arrived in Philadelphia carrying emigrants from Ireland. It had left Ireland with 300 passengers, but on the journey the provisions had nearly run out. About a hundred of the most famished passengers had been put ashore at Cape May, New Jersey, "in a most miserable plight," according to one press report. "The remainder were landed at Philadelphia in a distressed situation." Many of the newcomers were "so reduced to poverty and wretchedness," continued the news story, "that they were actually dying in the streets."

9.

HARVEST

"Sleighs have been going quite brisk today . . ."

SUMMER ENDED MUCH as it began in the Eastern United States. Frost struck the Mohawk Valley in central New York State in the middle of September, ruining nearly all the corn still standing in the fields. "The whole summer has also been so cold," lamented the *Albany Gazette*, "that there will be no Indian corn in all this country." More cold air swept into the region on September 26. At sunrise that day in Hanover, New Hampshire, the temperature dipped to 23 degrees. In Rochester, New York, ice formed a quarter of an inch thick. "No prospect of crops," wrote Reverend William Fogg of Kittery, Maine, in his diary. "Crops cut short and a heavy load of taxes."

On September 27, a widespread "black" frost—which freezes the water in the tissues of plants—killed off virtually all the crops that remained north of Pennsylvania, two weeks ahead of the average date for the first killing frost. The next three days were equally cold, "the four greatest frosts known in New Hampshire at this season by the oldest man living." In Sutton, New Hampshire, apples froze on the branches, and corn in the fields froze all the way through the cob. Plymouth, Massachusetts, experienced the coldest September day in the town's record books.

There would be no more harvest in New England in 1816. "These frosts have destroyed all the corn, and the potatoes are much cut off by the drought and frost," reported the *Dartmouth Gazette.* "Frost killed almost all the corn in New England and not half of it fit to roast," wrote Enoch Little of Boscawen, New Hampshire. "On frosty ground the orchards were barren, but on warm land there was a moderate crop of apples . . . The prospects as to fodder are most alarming." In Montreal and Quebec, where stocks of grain were dwindling, the weather remained cold and very dry: "The ice on the ponds in this vicinity was sufficiently strong . . . to bear a man."

And the drought continued. "The oldest inhabitants say, that such a drowth [sic] has never been experienced here since their remembrance," wrote William Young, a teacher in Plattsburgh, New York. "The ground has not been wetted two inches deep since the month of June." The creeks were dry, wells failed, and there was no grass for cattle. Williamstown received only 1.1 inches of rain in September, less than a third of its normal precipitation. Every week, the water level in New England's rivers and Lake Champlain sank lower.

Forest fires raged out of control. Many had been set deliberately. Farmers in new settlements customarily burned woods and brush in the fall, relying upon the usual autumn rains to keep the flames under control. But the drought left the woods too dry, and the rains did not arrive to put out the flames. "The woods are every where on fire," noted Young, "and the smoke is so thick, that whilst I now write at 5 in the afternoon, though there are no clouds, the sun is not to be seen." At Williams College, Professor Dewey reported thick smoke in the atmosphere from September 24 through the 30. On some Vermont highways, travelers could see no more than ten yards in front of them. Turnpike fences burned to charcoal.

Smoke carried to the coast and beyond, impairing the visibility of ships at sea. Outside of Boston, winds blew cinders onto vessels a considerable distance from shore, and the thick smoke reportedly caused several shipwrecks.

In early October in New Hampshire, woods were burning in Alton, Gilmantown, Gildford, Farmington, Rochester, Plymouth, Barnstead, Rumney, Warren, and Wentworth. The flames burned houses, barns, and cattle. They consumed wood that farmers could have used as fuel in the winter, and endangered those foolish enough to travel through the region. "We have seen a gentleman who travelled the day before yesterday, in the vicinity of one of the fires in New Hampshire," noted a Boston newspaper, "and who for several hours was near being suffocated with the smoke." More fires burned in Maine: at Paris, Bethel, Hebron, and Albany, in Oxford County and Kennebec County, and from the Kennebec River to the New Hampshire border. Ferries on the Kennebec River needed compasses to find their way through the dense smoke. In some areas, desperate residents dug broad trenches in the earth to try to control the spread of flames.

Observers worried that the fires and smoke would aggravate the dryness of the air, and send temperatures dropping even lower. "I fear that the smoke which they produce, accumulating in the atmosphere, must intercept the rays of the sun," wrote William Young, "and deprive us of some of that genial heat of which the earth seems every where so much in want." (Smoke, like volcanic ash, does indeed reflect sunlight. Lacking a volcano's explosive power, however, the fires could send smoke only into the troposphere, where it would be removed by rain within weeks. Fires will only intensify drought if the burnt area is large enough to start the cycle of drier soils, reduced evaporation, and less rainfall.) In Britain, the *Gentleman's Magazine* attempted to explain the magnitude of the conflagrations in the North American forests to its readers: "Europeans can have little idea of extensive districts being on fire, carrying destruction for 20 and 30 miles."

From Windsor, Vermont, the editor of the *Vermont Journal* proclaimed the summer an unmitigated disaster. "Never before in this vicinity [had the weather] appeared more gloomy and cheerless than at present," he wrote. "It is extremely cold for the time of year, and the drougth [sic] was never before so severe. We have had several frosts in this county, and we believe in every county in the state, in every month during the last fourteen ones."

Contemporary records support the anecdotal evidence about the frigidity of the summer. Based on the most accurate measurements available, temperatures in New England generally ranged between two to seven degrees Fahrenheit below normal from May through September. More to the point, the sharpest declines from the norm occurred during the critical growing months of June and July.

With its stocks of grain already depleted by the two preceding poor harvests, Quebec faced the most immediate crisis. September's killing frost left the province with a minimal wheat harvest and an even smaller supply of oats. "Many parishes in Quebec must inevitably be in a state of famine before winter sets in," predicted one report. Several inches of snow fell on Quebec City on October 5–6; Kamouraska, to the north, received nearly a foot of snow, accompanied by temperatures cold enough to freeze the water on roadways hard enough to bear the weight of a horse. It seemed a fitting conclusion to the worst summer in memory. "A fall of snow on the 8th of June, and another on the 6th of October," declared a correspondent to the *Daily National Intelligencer*, "are incidents probably without example since the recollection of the oldest inhabitant of the Province."

Maine's corn harvest was virtually nonexistent. For the state's subsistence farmers, the dearth of corn was a disaster, both for their families and the livestock that depended on it for fodder; as one historian of Maine put it, "self-sufficiency and survival was a delicate balance between people & the plants and animals they raised." With no new stores from the 1816 harvest, farmers faced painful decisions on whether to consume their remaining reserves of corn, or save it as seed for next year's crop. Some towns were fortunate enough to have a few farmers who managed to harvest a small amount and shared it with (or sold it to) their neighbors. Others traveled to the nearest port to purchase a limited quantity—the price already had risen from the usual eighty or ninety cents per bushel to nearly $1.50 by the beginning of October. In Waterford, where seed corn had been scarce since the 1814 harvest and "people were in great straits for food," one farmer went to Portland and bought a bushel of corn, bringing it back on horseback. But with many roads little more than rutted trails, isolated inland towns remained very much on their own.

Vermont fared only slightly better. Much of the state's farm-land was on hillsides and rocky fields that barely provided sufficient returns in good years; hence even a minor shift in climate could have catastrophic effects. Between the late September frosts and the prolonged drought, every crop except wheat was a resounding failure in 1816. As in Maine, the shortage of corn portended calamity in the coming months. "It is not probable that enough will get ripe for seed for next year," wrote the editor of the *Journal*. "There is not sufficient hay to winter the cattle upon, and nothing with which to fatten them this fall." In some Vermont towns, including Newbury and Peacham, desperate farmers bid the price of corn up to two or three dollars a bushel in October. Even the moderate wheat harvest proved of dubious value, since the drought dried up the rivers that powered the state's flour mills. "In short," the *Journal* concluded, "we are something like the soldier, who had no allowance, and no kettle to cook it in."

New Hampshire shared Vermont's plight. "Indian corn on which a large proportion of the poor depend is cut off," remarked the *New Hampshire Patriot* on October 22. "It is believed that through New England scarcely a tenth part of the usual crop of sound corn will be gathered." To the south, Connecticut officials estimated that farmers in their state harvested only about 25 percent of the corn they had sown, and half of their hay crop. To help alleviate the shortage, two enterprising merchants from Hartford imported thirteen hundred bushels of corn "of excellent quality" from Santo Domingo at a bargain price of seventy-five cents per bushel.

In New York, a Columbia College professor of natural history declared that "there will not be half a crop of maize on Long Island, and in the southern district of this state. Further northward there will be less. The buckwheat is so scanty, that a few days ago I paid four dollars for a half bushel of the meal, for the use of my family." Most of the fruit in that region, however, appeared to have prospered (except for peaches) from the cooler weather, and in New York City, the frigid summer blessed residents with fewer mosquitoes and fleas than usual. Local populations of wild birds, unfortunately, also had declined.

As the magnitude of the harvest failure became clear, American newspapers called for farmers and merchants to display their patriotism—and make a tidy profit—by refraining from exporting any of their crops to Europe. "It would be well, in order to prevent distress here," declared the *National Register*, "to suggest to the farmers and planters the propriety of retaining their grain for the consumption of their own countrymen, from whom it is probable they will be able to get as good a price as they can any where else, and at the same time, do a service to their country." Perhaps, but American merchants already were busy selling flour to the French West Indies. By September, the failure of the harvest in France persuaded the French government—which had long reserved the grain market in its Caribbean colonies for its own exports—that it could not hope to supply the needs of Martinique or Guadeloupe, and so it opened up the trade to American shippers.

Governor Jonas Galusha of Vermont tried a more direct approach. When the state legislature convened in Montpelier on October 10, Galusha proposed a statewide campaign to encourage conservation of the existing stores of grain. "The uncommon failure of some of the most important articles of produce, on which the sustenance of man and beast depends, is so alarming," Galusha told the legislators, "that I take the liberty to recommend to you, and through you, to the people of this State, the most rigid economy in the early expenditure of those articles of provision most deficient, that by peculiar precaution we may avoid, as far as possible, the foreboded evil of this unparalleled season [i.e., famine]." Governor William Jones of Rhode Island preferred to rely on appeals for divine intervention. Citing the "coldness and dryness of the seasons, and . . . the alarming sickness with which many parts of our country have been afflicted," Jones proclaimed "a day of public Prayer, Praise, and Thanksgiving" throughout the state.

Like most of the state governors in 1816, New Jersey governor Mahlon Dickerson was a devout Jeffersonian who opposed direct government aid to individuals, and so he refused to recommend specific remedies to help his state's farmers. Nevertheless, the recently reelected Dickerson did express his pious hope that the scarcity of crops would discourage local distillers from producing their usual "poison" from corn or grain that was "intended by the bounty of Heaven to man for his nourishment." Dickerson was not the only proponent of temperance to use the shortage of grain to advance the cause. In October, a group of reform-minded citizens in Otsego County, New York, urged the state legislature to "cause such restrictions to be laid on the distilleries—as in their wisdom shall be calculated to prevent an undue monopoly of that valuable and necessary commodity." At a time when the United States supported 15,000 distilleries, and the average American consumed the equivalent of 4.5 gallons of pure grain alcohol per year, even a slight decline in the production of liquor could have paid significant dividends.

As grain prices rose, beef and pork prices dropped. During the summer, when beef prices typically spiked, farmers who foresaw shortages of fodder sent their livestock to market months ahead of their customary schedule. That pace quickened as the magnitude of the harvest disaster became clear, and more farmers realized they would never be able to feed their cattle through the winter. By October, the unusually plentiful supply sent the price of beef sharply lower, followed by a similar decline in pork prices.

Some farmers did not stop with selling their livestock; they sold their entire farm and headed west. Pressures for emigration from New England had been building: a growing population in a region where all the fertile land already was under cultivation, and where generations of wasteful agricultural practices had stripped away or exhausted even the best soil; the loss of the timber trade as forests dwindled; vanishing wildlife, fish, and game that had carried farmers through the previous years of bad harvests; a series of epidemics that swept through New England in 1813 and 1814; the deleterious economic effects of the recent war and trade embargo; the lure of western territories with far more productive soil (and far fewer rocks); and several years of cooler weather and poor harvests leading up to 1816.

They called it "Ohio fever," and the unparalleled coldness of the summer of 1816 followed by the calamitous harvest convinced many New Englanders that nature was sending them an indisputable message. "Something, it seemed, had gone permanently wrong with the weather," concluded Lewis Stilwell, "and when this cold season piled itself on top of all the preceding afflictions, a good many . . . were ready to quit." Generous terms for the sale of public land, cheap and easy credit from banks in the Western states, and the removal of Native American tribes from the Ohio Valley following the War of 1812 made the decision easier. Promoters and land agents set up offices in towns such as Portsmouth, Maine, and Cornish, New Hampshire, selling orders for land in Ohio, Indiana, Illinois, and even western Pennsylvania. They promised luxuriant lands with rich loam soil and a "mild and salubrious" climate, "an earthly Paradise, where every thing which is considered a luxury, might be had almost without care, labour or exertion," and boundless opportunities: Indiana had recently applied for statehood, but two-thirds of its land still lacked white settlers, as did nearly half of Ohio, and three-quarters of the Illinois territory.

Loading all their possessions—a bed, a few quilts, some dishes, the family Bible, kettles and pots, a churn, a blanket chest—into a covered wagon (or an oxcart for the less prosperous), hundreds and then thousands of New England farm families set out for the Western lands. Given the perilous state of American roads, the journey west required stamina and patience. (Rumor had it that roads were so rough that a pail of cream would churn into butter on the way west.) Some pilgrims traveled through the Mohawk Valley, then headed west to Buffalo; from there they could take a boat to Ohio or hug the eastern shore of Lake Erie into northern Ohio. Others chose to cross Pennsylvania, climbing the Alleghenies before descending into Pittsburgh and crossing the river into Ohio. Observers described the roads over the mountains as "rude, steep, and dangerous"; one physician who made the trip recalled that "some of the more precipitous slopes were consequently strewn with the carcases [sic] of wagons, carts, horses, oxen, which had made shipwreck in their perilous descent. The scenes on the road—of families gathered at night in miserable sheds, called taverns—mothers frying, children crying, fathers swearing—were a mingled comedy and tragedy of errors."

One route through western Pennsylvania ran over Laurel Hill, a mountain more than seventy miles long, where rains turned the track to soft clay mud more than a foot deep, obstructed by stones nearly as large as a barrel. A farmer from Stonington, Connecticut, who tried to navigate his wagon through the pass watched it nearly tip over four times as he descended a single slope, but the passage was so narrow and steep that the walls of the pass helped him push the wagon upright each time.

Not all the emigrants were young. In late September, a dozen wagons filled with passengers described as "consistently advanced in life" left Worcester, Massachusetts. And some left to avoid the prophesied apocalypse, including a band of religious zealots calling themselves "Christ-ians" who left Connecticut to find "a kind of Paradise on earth" in Ohio.

By the end of October, so many emigrants from New England were flooding into Ohio—to Columbus (recently named the new state capital), Steubenville, Chillicothe (the former state capital), and Circleville—that the Zanesville *Messenger* reported that "the number of emigrants from the eastward the present season, far exceeds what has ever before been heretofore witnessed." The *Messenger*'s editor estimated that at least several thousand refugees had passed through Zanesville in the past several weeks: "On some days, from forty to fifty wagons have passed the Muskingum at this place. The emigrants are from almost every state north and east of the Potomack, seeking a new home in the . . . territories of the west; traveling in various modes—some on foot, some on horses, and others in different kinds of vehicles, from the ponderous Pennsylvania wagon, to the light New England pleasure carriage."

Back east, fires continued to devastate woodlands. Smoke from a series of blazes in eastern New York State, from Ticonderoga to Plattsburgh, blinded sailors on Lake Champlain. One traveler reported that the smoke on the lake was so thick that "the steam boat moves very slow and cautious, continually sounding, not being able to discover either shore when near the middle of the Lake." A measure of relief finally arrived in the form of a snowstorm on October 17, weeks ahead of the first snow of autumn in a typical year. In Albany, snow fell for most of the evening. Chautauqua County, New York, received eight inches; St. Lawrence County reported slightly more. A correspondent in Haverhill, New Hampshire, reported a snowfall of "about 12 inches deep. . . . Sleighs have been going quite brisk today." Hanover, the home of Dartmouth University, also witnessed heavy snow, and travelers noted drifts several feet deep in the nearby White Mountains.

* * *

PRESIDENT Madison returned to Washington on October 9, after an absence of more than four months, only to find that workmen still had not finished repairing the Executive Mansion. Nor had much work been accomplished on the Capitol. Builders still awaited new stone for the House side, and renovations to the Senate were delayed when numerous legislators decided they wanted more extensive changes than originally planned. Cost overruns already plagued the project, but the architect in charge, Benjamin Latrobe, promised that the additional work would "render the building much more strong and durable than it was before the conflagration."

With only five months left in what Madison termed his "detention," tributes to the President filled the press. Unlike Washington, Adams, or Jefferson, Madison would leave office with the nation largely united behind the policies of his administration; as Henry Adams concluded, Madison "seemed to enjoy popularity never before granted to any President at the expiration of his term." John Adams agreed, in his own fashion. In a letter to Thomas Jefferson, Adams accused the Madison administration of "a thousand Faults and blunders," yet he acknowledged that Madison and his Cabinet had "acquired more glory, and established more Union than all his three Predecessors, Washington, Adams, Jefferson, put together." Indeed, Madison was so highly regarded by the American people at the end of his term that he still holds the record among presidents for having the most towns and counties named after him in the United States.

CONDITIONS in Ireland deteriorated rapidly in September and October. From all parts of the island, but especially from the west, came eyewitness reports of constant, drenching rain that ruined acre upon acre of crops. "Dreadful weather," Daniel O'Connell wrote to his wife on September 30. "There is nothing but rain and wretchedness." Accounts in *The Times* of London made clear the extent of the developing catastrophe:

Westport, County Mayo: There is not in this extended county 100 acres reaped—the heavy crops all floundered and rotted . . . no change of weather, at this advanced season, can render them productive—add to which, a complete failure in the potatoes.

Killarney, County Kerry: Wheat afflicted by blight. Well-ripened fields of oats flattened by rain. "I saw one field of flax not yet pulled; many spread, but no prospect of their drying. Very little of the turf [used for heating homes in winter] brought home."

Castlebar, County Mayo: Before today, we believe, there was not twenty acres of corn reaped throughout the whole of the county of Mayo, and scarcely an acre within six miles of this town, in any direction. . . . The potatoe [sic] crop is by no means as productive as usual, and a considerable part of it has been further injured by the late floods. . . . Every article of consumption, except flesh meat, is advancing in price."

Belfast, County Antrim and County Down: All the low grounds flooded—the people struggling to save whatever they can of the harvest, up to the knees, and many places to the middle, in water. The potatoes in the flooded ground are looked upon as lost, the season being so far advanced; the turf not saved.

Athlone, County Westmeath: I know not whether this letter will reach you, for the roads are quite inundated. I do not think we shall have an acre of wheat within ten miles round us. We are in the midst of a flood. The fields are covered, and I have not been able to discover, in an anxious walk, any vestige whatever of grain.

Mullingar, County Westmeath: The lakes around the town rose "to an height unprecedented in the memory of the oldest inhabitant." The road to Longford was nearly impassable. Lough Owel had completely inundated several acres of ground around its banks. "Yesterday morning it overflowed the supply cut (to the Royal Canal), the banks of which burst, and has inundated the country to an alarming extent."

Enniskillen, County Fermanagh: Lough Erne overflowed its banks. Meadows on low ground had been underwater for the past several months. By October 8, the water had risen to nearly four feet, and Lough Erne continued to rise. "There is no crop; we shall not have as much corn in this country as will support us. Potatoes are equally bad, which, you know, must be the case when we are under inundation."

A traveler who made the thirty-mile journey from Ballinasloe to Moate reported that nearly all the country he traversed was under water. "It was a miracle, he said, how the coachman made his way through." Along much of the route, slash walls—stone walls without mortar—were covered up to four feet high.

Skeptics in England suspected the Irish were exaggerating the extent of the destruction, but a recently returned traveler made it clear in the October 19 issue of *The Times* of London that was not the case. "Let no one impose upon you," he wrote, "the harvest is destroyed. . . . I see nothing before us but the prospect of the most grievous of all earthly calamities—*famine*." The only hope seemed to rest with heaven. "God is powerful, and can, by a miracle, save his creatures from destruction; but without such, we see nothing for it but the desolation of the land."

By the first week of October, Peel harbored no illusions about the state of the harvest in Ireland. In a series of letters to Lord Liverpool (October 9) and Lord Sidmouth (October 10), the chief secretary explained in detail the magnitude of the impending disaster. "Since the first of this month we have had almost an incessant storm—the Sun has scarcely made its appearance and the wind has done as much damage as the rain," Peel informed the prime minister. "I assure you nothing can be more melancholy than the Accounts which are received from every part of the Country . . . not one third of the average Crop of wheat will be saved." The recent rains had been especially destructive to the oat and barley crops, Peel continued, "and (what is of more consequence so far as this country is concerned) to the Crop of Potatoes. I fear the effect of the wet has been not only to reduce the size of the Potatoe [sic] but to make it soft and unwholesome." Moreover, the constant rain had rendered the turf—which Irish peasants depended upon as free and abundant fuel to compensate for shoddy housing and thin clothing—nearly unusable. "If there is a severe winter the want of fuel will be a greater source of misery than the want of food," Peel concluded. "I fear we have melancholy Prospects before us, and are threatened with calamities for which it is impossible to suggest a remedy."

Peel did not expect increased hardship to provoke widespread violence in Ireland. "Distress in this country has a different effect—almost a contrary effect—from what it has in England," he informed a colleague. "Sheer wickedness and depravity are the chief sources of our crimes and turbulence, and I am satisfied that severe distress would rather tend to diminish than to increase them." In any event, Peel believed the Irish peasantry would never challenge an open display of English armed force. "We burn people in their houses, and shoot at them from behind ditches, in this country in great abundance," he wrote, "but there is a most salutary terror of what is called 'the Army,' whether it consists of two regiments or of a couple of dragoons."

Perhaps Ireland could avoid violence in the aftermath of a disastrous harvest; it could not avoid disease. Typhus—known as "the contagious fever," or simply, "the fever"—already was spreading through parts of County Mayo by the end of September.

Presumably Peel did not know that lice and fleas carried the organism that caused the fever, but he did understand why Ireland in 1816 presented a fertile ground for an epidemic. As Peel subsequently explained to Parliament, "the causes of the disease are, I fear, want of employment, and the poverty it engenders, and the defective quality and quantity of food, from the wetness of the season and the want of fuel." Certainly Ireland qualified on all counts.

Hordes of itinerant beggars wandering across Ireland in the wake of the failed harvest exacerbated the situation, as did the Irish peasantry's custom of gathering for the wakes of their friends. "On such occasions," observed Peel, "the infectious disease of a few is communicated to the many, and the disorder becomes violent and general." Peel seemed genuinely moved by the irony of the situation: that the generosity and hospitality for which the Irish were justly renowned and praised also gave rise to epidemics of contagious disease. And the government could do nothing to stop it. "No persuasion can induce them to shut their door against the wandering beggar," he noted, "or refuse to pay the last sad tribute to the remains of their friends and kindred. . . . In Ireland, no fear of contagion—no fear of death—can operate to induce the people to forego the habits which they cherish."

On October 16, King Louis XVIII and the royal French court commemorated the twenty-third anniversary of the execution of Marie Antoinette. Every church in Paris held funeral services; every theater in the city closed. The king and his household were in mourning. Neither Louis nor his brothers appeared in public that day, but the late queen's eldest daughter, Marie Thérèse, the Duchess D'Angoulême, rode to St. Denis at eight o'clock in the morning to pray at the tomb of her mother. Several hours later, the room in the Conciergerie in which revolutionaries had imprisoned the doomed queen was dedicated as a chapel to her memory, hung with black cloth and illuminated with candles.

Final results from the elections for the Chamber of Deputies: 92 Ultra-Royalists (mostly from the south and west), and 146 supporters of the Moderate cabinet. The Ultras—who called themselves "pure royalists"—were well on their way to establishing a cohesive and disciplined political party, headed by the king's brother, the Count d'Artois, and backed by a majority of the French clergy. The new majority of deputies, on the other hand, were united primarily by their opposition to the Ultra-Royalist cause, and included both those who sincerely desired a constitutional monarchy, and smaller groups who favored a republic or the restoration of a Bonapartist regime, but felt it prudent to pose as constitutionalists for the time being.

All factions agreed on the need to rid France of the Allied army of occupation. The costs of feeding the Allied troops, added to the scheduled reparations payments, put a severe strain on the French budget, especially in light of the dismal harvest. Opposition to the Allied army united even King Louis XVIII and Madame de Staël. The doyenne of Coppet decided to return to France, but before she left Switzerland she married her longtime lover, the chevalier Albert Jean Michel de Rocca, a Swiss military officer who had served with the French army during the Peninsula War. Upon her arrival in Paris, Madame de Staël established a new salon in the rue Royale which quickly became the home of a group of French liberal intellectuals known as the Doctrinaires. Occasionally an Ultra stopped by to debate politics with the most famous woman in France. One "pure royalist" seeking respect for his party reminded her that "we also, Madame, we enter within the constitution," to which Madame de Staël replied, "Yes, as the Greeks did into the Trojan horse, to set fire to the city!"

Unlike Napoléon and the various revolutionary factions who had tried to silence Madame de Staël, Louis chose to simply ignore her. "We attach so little importance to anything you do, say, or write," the king informed her before she left Coppet, "that the government wants to know nothing about it; nor does it wish to give you any fear on this account, or even allow anyone to hinder you in any way in your projects and mysteries." Royal disdain notwithstanding, Madame de Staël retained substantial influence in Paris; the Doctrinaires who basked in her principles would play a vital role in ending the Bourbon dynasty in 1830. But in the autumn of 1816, she spent much of her energy—despite her chronic insomnia—attempting to persuade her old friend, the Duke of Wellington, to reduce the size of the army of occupation and remove it as soon as possible.

Wellington initially demurred. "All of you who have such short memories, and such a strong imagination, you forget everything that has brought France to the situation she finds herself in," the Iron Duke wrote to Madame de Staël. "You forget where she was last year, and the far worse situation she might have found herself in as a result . . . [and] national hatred now inspires you to cry that it is to England that we owe our misfortune, and that we are under English influence." The British government, he insisted, could not display weakness by backing down simply because the French people had turned against the Allied army. But Wellington also understood the parlous state of French finances. Without a loan from British bankers, he informed Lord Castlereagh from Paris, "France will be aground this year . . ."

Reports from the provinces confirmed Wellington's pessimism. The "general scarcity of the harvest," combined with widespread unemployment presaged a winter of hardship and discontent. In the fields around Le Havre, for instance, the harvest was reportedly "in a deplorable state." Cold weather throughout October added to the misery, since the necessity of maintaining fires forced up the price of fuel, and left the poor even less of their income to spend on food. The price of bread continued to rise, and shortages already had developed in Paris. In one quarter of the capital, bakers ran out of loaves by nine o'clock on a morning in late October, leaving long lines of angry citizens who continued to clamor for bread until a deputation of gendarmes dispersed them. "Nothing but the utmost vigour and wisdom can carry the Government through this trying season," predicted one resident.

Few contemporaries associated the words "utmost vigour and wisdom" with King Louis, but the monarch and his advisers recognized the crisis and responded with unwonted alacrity. At the end of September, the government issued a circular to the prefects in the provinces, urging them to ease the plight of the poor "during the rigorous season," specifically through a program of public works. "The repairing of highways and roads affording works of the greatest utility, his Majesty requests that they will promote them with all possible activity," the government announced. Not only should the prefects immediately spend their funds allocated for road repair, and ensure that they spent monies budgeted for charity throughout the coming winter, but if they had any funds left over from any other account, "they shall hasten to authorize the disposal thereof in useful works."

Wellington, meanwhile, ensured that the Allied army of occupation would have enough to eat during the winter by purchasing substantial quantities of grain from several northern German states that had escaped the ravages of the summer rains.

BYRON and John Hobhouse departed Geneva on October 5 for a tour of northern Italy—first Milan, and then Verona. Before departing, Byron sent detailed instructions to John Murray, his publisher in London, about the copyediting of several of his latest poems. In a moment of introspection, Byron mused that his compulsion to write poetry was, he feared, incurable. "God help me!" he confessed to Murray, "if I proceed in this scribbling, I shall have frittered away my mind before I am thirty; but it is at times a real relief to me."

As he entered Italy, Byron admitted that the autumn weather was "very fine, which is more than the Summer has been." He found Milan "striking—the cathedral superb," an opinion tempered

212 The Year Without Summer

by his admission that the city reminded him of a slightly inferior version of Seville. The inhabitants seemed "very intelligent and agreeable," although one suspects his opinion also reflected the fact that the region was "tolerably free from the English." Doubtless Byron's English contemporaries who were unaware of the Calvinistic side of his personality would have been surprised that he considered the state of morals in Italy "in some sort lax." During his stay in Milan, Byron attended the Teatro della Scala, where he met Stendhal, and visited the Ambrosian Library, where he purportedly managed to purloin part of a lock of Lucrezia Borgia's hair.

Byron resumed his friendship with Polidori in Milan—the doctor had arrived several weeks before Byron—but after quarreling with a police official, Polidori was asked to leave the city. The local authorities became suspicious of Byron, as well, accusing him of harboring liberal sympathies. So the poet and Hobhouse left Milan for Verona, but along the way the weather turned bad, and very heavy autumnal rains prevented them from visiting the country house of Catullus on Sirmione.

Northern Italy's harvest in 1816 mirrored those of its neighbors on the other side of the Alps. Late snowfalls in April delayed the planting of crops; cold temperatures persisted throughout the growing season; and frequent, pounding rains led rivers to overflow their banks. In many areas, desperate farmers—already impoverished from poor harvests the previous two years—cut their grain early to save what they could. A significant percentage of Italian crops never matured at all. Lombardy and Venetia, especially, suffered from flooding and frosts in late September and early October that rendered much of the wheat unsuitable for human consumption, or even as fodder. According to the American consul at Livorno, "the oil and wine crops had also failed" throughout northern Italy as a result of the frigid weather. Alarmed by the prospect of famine, the government of Naples offered a bounty for the importation of wheat and other grains.

Austrian officials decided to permit the importation of wheat, flour, oats, barley, and rice free of duty into their Italian provinces; by the first week of October, significant quantities of wheat from Odessa, Ukraine, and Alexandria, Egypt, had arrived at Trieste, and the government was negotiating contracts to purchase more grain for Dalmatia. Nevertheless, by the time Byron arrived in Milan, the price of bread was rising sharply.

In the Netherlands, where distress was "very great, owing to the failure of the harvest, and the incessant rains that have prevailed in that country," the government prohibited the export of potatoes and grain. Attempting to control the price of food, a number of German states followed suit; in Bremen, the storehouses of wheat had nearly disappeared. Rain continued to fall in Hanover, and the prices of most types of provisions rose "most uncommonly"; a scarcity of potatoes touched off a corresponding rise in the demand for and price of wheat. Baden suffered its worst harvest in 400 years. Facing a drastic shortfall in the harvest of rye, the King of Saxony, Frederick Augustus I, ordered the purchase of a large quantity of grain and potatoes to help feed the poor. From Switzerland came reports of rising food prices and philanthropic societies feeding hundreds of poor citizens daily, as cantonal authorities desperately sought supplies of foreign grain. In Liège, a full-scale food riot occurred following a dramatic surge in the price of grain.

To help alleviate the distress of the working class, petitions asked the German Diet at Frankfurt to prohibit the importation of English manufactured goods. German journals carried numerous articles outlining "the immense loss which the free trade of England occasions to German industry." A Brussels newspaper launched a campaign to urge Belgians to abstain from wearing any clothes made in England, to check the "inundation of British goods" that threatened to overwhelm native manufacturers.

At Salzburg, officials prohibited the distillation of grain-based liquor. Sadly for the wine-drinking population, the grape harvest failed across nearly the entire continent. Grapes ripened so late throughout France and Switzerland that the start of the harvest (the vendange) occurred later in 1816 in every single wine-producing region than in any other year from 1782 to 1879. One study of the area determined that the mean harvest date of October 29 was approximately four weeks past the average vendange, a highly unusual occurrence; as John D. Post has noted, "from 1601 to 1926 there were only six dates in the Paris region later than October 15." In Verdun the grapes never ripened at all that season. From Frankfurt came reports that "wines rise daily in price to an alarming extent," even though consumption seemed to decline every day: "The vintage is next to nothing." And if prices continued to rise, "we shall soon have nothing to quench our thirst but water or beer."

Württemberg, in southwestern Germany, faced far more severe problems. There, too, the frigid summer delayed the harvest for nearly six weeks. "Every storm of the past summer . . . was followed by the most severe cold, so that it regularly felt like November," a local almanac recalled years later, "and no month went by in which many houses were not heated." Whatever crops remained in the fields on October 17 perished from the one-two punch of a severe frost and a snowstorm several days later. "Fields in the highland districts could not be harvested at all," concluded one study, "and more than two-thirds of the oat fields rotted under snow and ice." Confronting this disaster, the King of Württemberg, the immensely corpulent Frederick William Charles (who recently had purchased a rhinoceros at great expense for the royal zoo), approved the release of a substantial quantity of wheat from the royal storehouses. The wheat was to be ground and made into bread sold at a discounted price and distributed every morning to needy residents of the capital, Stuttgart. Several days later, King Frederick—severely afflicted by gout—passed away.

After the frigid summer temperatures retarded the ripening of grapes in both Spain and Portugal, "immense rains" set in, beating down the grapes and causing them to rot on the vines. Early autumn brought snows to northeastern Spain that covered the peaks of Montserrat and Montseny, outside of Barcelona, and a cold wave froze the Llobregat River. According to José Manuel da Silva Tedim, "the vineyard harvest [in Spain] lasted until the 19th of November, due to the lack of heat necessary to mature grapes"; in Portugal, Franzini noted that "grapes have suffered for the same reason and never got ripe and as a consequence the wine was of inferior quality." Since the olive harvest also suffered, the price of olive oil on the Iberian peninsula commenced a yearlong rise that set a record for the years between 1750 and 1854. Wheat prices in Lisbon were not far behind. Although the abnormally low temperatures continued to reduce the frequency of the usual summer ailments—such as dysentery and bilious fevers—in the Iberian peninsula, they also produced more cases of scarlet fever and various inflammatory diseases that typically struck in the winter.

HARVEST time in Devon (on a good day): When wheat was ready to cut down, a farmer of a typical holding—say, ten to twenty acres—advertised in the neighborhood that he planned to begin reaping on a certain day. On that morning, a number of villagers (both men and women) gathered at the field and took breakfast (including ale and cider) before getting to work. (The turnout depended largely upon how highly the villagers regarded the farmer.) Additional workers often dropped by during the course of the morning, attracted by the shouts and jokes emanating from the fields.

Between noon and one o'clock, the farmer's wife brought a dinner of meat and vegetables (with more ale and cider) into the fields. Work recommenced around two o'clock, and the cutting and binding of the wheat continued for perhaps three hours. Then everyone retired to the shade to enjoy homemade cakes and buns, washed down with cider and ale. A few more hours in the fields brought the day's harvest to a close; occasionally the (somewhat inebriated) men finished with a competition to see who would be the first to knock down a target—usually a small sheaf of wheat—with a well-aimed toss of his reap-hook. (As they let fly with their hooks, the players emitted a cry which sounded to one observer like "We ha in! We ha in!")

As evening fell, all retired to the farmhouse for supper with ale and cider. Often no money changed hands; wages consisted of the day's food and drink, plus an invitation to enjoy the farmer's hospitality during the Christmas season, when "the house is kept open night and day to the guests, whose behaviour during the time may be assimilated to the frolics of a bear-garden."

And there were some good days in the first weeks of autumn, when some of the farmers in some parts of England harvested some of the crops that had survived the cold and the rains and the hailstorms. Newspapers printed advice columns on how to dry wheat that had been harvested while still wet. One suggestion included the construction of brick flues around the interior of barns; another imported an idea from Russia, whereby sheaves of grain were hung from ropes stretched high across the walls of a barn, and then dried by a fire of charred wood or cinders—but never an open flame—built on an earthen or brick floor. Nevertheless, much of the new grain offered for sale admittedly was "damp," "discoloured," and "materially injured by the late incessant rains," and prices varied widely depending on the quality. Generally, damp new grain—which threatened to glut the market—brought roughly the same price as stale old grain.

In early October the deluge resumed, with a week and a half of almost incessant rains, especially across northern Britain. "The unpropitious weather of the last ten days has, it is to be apprehended, given an unfortunate turn to the prospects of the farmer," reported *The Times* of London on October 15. "All harvest work has been again suspended by the return of rainy and uncertain weather." In Norwich, the editor of the local newspaper claimed that the flooding in the city "is as excessive as we ever recollect to have occurred, with one exception only." In nearby low-lying fields, bridges were washed out, and farmers reportedly navigated boats over their meadows.

In the East Riding of Yorkshire, the first two weeks of October brought "such heavy rains as nearly to put a stop to reaping of corn," most of which remained in the fields. The *Newcastle Mercury* reported that "the crops have sustained considerable injury, and that a very considerable portion of the grain, if got at all, will be completely unfit for human food." At Berwick, the northernmost town in England, the "immense quantity of rain which has fallen" rendered roads impassable and left meadows and lowlands under water. Without sufficient supplies of fodder, farmers brought their animals to market ahead of schedule, with predictably adverse effects on profits. At a fair in Wiltshire in early November, at least 70,000 sheep were offered for sale, "the largest quantity of sheep ever remembered." Most of them fetched prices considerably lower than usual, and about 10,000 found no buyers at all.

Southern Scotland suffered more severely from the same storms. Both the wheat and oat crops in Ayrshire were considerably damaged by the heavy and continued rains. Potatoes suffered nearly as much, and the cold weather retarded the growth of pasture grass. "The pastures were never good this season," noted one observer, "and now they look very ill." Lanarkshire reported similar difficulties, due to "the heavy and cold rains": "Seldom indeed has the ground at any season been so much drenched as at the present time." Livestock already felt the lack of fodder, and as farmers here, too, offered their animals for sale ahead of the usual market schedule, the price of cattle slid to less than half of its 1815 level. The price of human labor declined as well, and farmers who needed to hire workers found that they could be procured at an employer's pleasure.

Perhaps farmers took solace in the words of the renowned English cleric, Dr. William Paley, who argued in an essay published in the journal, *Natural Theology*, that the irregularity of the seasons—such as the abnormally cold and wet summer and autumn of 1816—was, in fact, a blessing, since it promoted the commendable qualities of vigilance and precaution in the rural population. Indeed, Dr. Paley went so far as to claim that "seasons of scarcity themselves are not without their advantages." They forced farmers to work harder; they encouraged ingenuity at work and thereby "give birth to improvements in agriculture and economy; [and] they promote the investigation and management of public resources."

10.

EMIGRATION

*"I must also say that the discontented are in great
force . . ."*

JANE AUSTEN'S HEALTH grew worse in the autumn. Her back
hurt nearly all the time, she tired easily, and she was too weak
to walk even a short distance outside. Austen insisted to her rela-
tives that she was not seriously ill, that she suffered from no more
than rheumatism or bile. But the cold, damp weather at Chawton
aggravated her illness. She spent much of her time collecting a
decidedly mixed set of reviews on *Emma*, including one in which
the reviewer admitted that he had read only the first and last
chapters of the novel "because he had heard it was not interesting."

Nearby in Bath, Percy Shelley and Mary Godwin spent much
of the autumn reading—he read *Don Quixote* aloud to Mary in the
evenings, and she claimed to see a resemblance between Shelley
and the knight—and writing. Apparently Mary's manuscript of
Frankenstein proceeded smoothly, except for a brief interruption
when her half-sister, Fanny, committed suicide. The child of Mary
Wollstonecraft and an American merchant (with whom Mary

lived as a common-law wife before she met William Godwin),
Fanny had been living with Godwin and his second wife in strait-
ened financial circumstances, growing increasingly lonely and de-
spondent, and bitter towards Mary, whom she felt had deserted
her. On October 9, Fanny checked into the Mackworth Arms Inn
in Swansea and drank half a bottle of laudanum. Perhaps she had
been in love with Shelley; perhaps she had recently discovered the
circumstances of her illegitimate birth. Since English law made
suicide a crime, Fanny's body was never officially identified, and
she was buried in an unmarked grave. A remorseful Shelley wrote:

> Her voice did quiver as we parted,
> 　Yet knew I not that heart was broken
> From whence it came; and I departed
> Heeding not the words then spoken,
> 　Misery—O Misery,
> 　This world is all too wide for thee.

FROM his vantage point in September and early October, Lord
Liverpool saw no reason to panic. More than a hundred years
before anyone heard the term *gross national product*, Liverpool and
his cabinet chose to measure the health of the British economy
by tracking tax returns, especially excise revenues, on a quarterly
basis. If revenues increased, consumers presumably were purchasing more goods and the economy was growing. If they decreased,
people either had less money, or were saving more and spending
less; in either case, the economy seemed to be headed for a downturn. It was not a particularly sophisticated or reliable indicator of
economic developments, but it provided Liverpool's ministry with
statistical support for its inaction.

Looking back over the summer months, Liverpool expressed
confidence that Britain's economic fundamentals were sound:
"The Revenue looks better. The Excise (which is the most mate-

rial Branch) good, the Customs still very low, but the great falling off is in the Port of London, which is a proof that it does not arise from Smuggling or diminished Consumption, but from want of Speculation growing out of Want of Confidence. We may trust therefore that this Evil will in a short Time be removed." The extensive gold reserves building up in the Bank of England in the postwar period—Britain seemed by far the safest place for European investors to park their money—further encouraged Liverpool. Low interest rates and easy access to credit, along with rising grain prices, made British landowners happy. And when the landed interest was happy, Liverpool's government was well content.

Liverpool and his ministers did not turn a blind eye to the distress wracking Britain in the autumn of 1816, but neither did they feel responsible for the hardship of the laboring classes. The lens through which they viewed "the condition of England" blended classical economic theory and the eighteenth-century tradition of limited government. Authorities firmly believed that they had neither the resources nor the duty to alter the course of the economic cycle; instead, they needed to allow market forces to work themselves out.

Whatever economic difficulties Britain faced in the autumn of 1816, Liverpool argued, stemmed primarily from the arduous transition from a lengthy war to peace, from a period of expansive government spending and frenetic production, to reductions in nearly every aspect of the economy. As an article (much admired by Liverpool) in the *Quarterly Review* of July 1816 explained, "a vacuum was inevitably produced by this sudden diminution, and the general dislocation which ensued may not unaptly be compared to the settling of the ice upon a wide sheet of water: explosions are made and convulsions are seen on all sides, in one place the ruptured ice is disloged and lifted up, in another it sinks . . . and thus the agitation continues for many hours till the whole has found its level, and nature resumes in silence its ordinary course."

There simply was no magic bullet in the government's limited arsenal of weapons to cure economic distress. "I see no immediate or adequate Remedy which Govt can apply," insisted William Huskisson, a member of Liverpool's ministry who subsequently earned a reputation as a fierce defender of free trade. "Their Game must be patience, temper and great discretion in all that is done or said." Such a policy enjoyed David Ricardo's wholehearted support. "I am sorry that the distresses still continue," Ricardo wrote to James Mill on November 17. "The short crop this year was most unfortunate, it aggravated all our former ills." Yet Ricardo insisted there was little the government could do to ameliorate the situation. "I am sorry to see a disposition to inflame the minds of the lower orders by persuading them that legislation can afford them any relief," he continued. "The country has a right to insist, and I hope will insist, on the most rigid economy in every branch of the public expenditure, but when this is yielded nothing further can be done for us."

Yet Liverpool and his ministers also recognized their responsibility to keep the British economy from falling off the cliff altogether. Clearly they could not permit widespread misery to accumulate until it exploded into a full-fledged revolution. So they issued reassuring statements to calm the public, and encouraged local communities to sponsor relief efforts through a limited program of public works and charitable contributions to feed the poor.

In an editorial on November 7, *The Times* of London explained this mind-set in detail. "In this country," *The Times* argued, "it generally happens that public difficulty and distress are relieved by the good sense of the nation itself; for the Government on such occasions is rather accustomed to follow, than to take the lead." Therefore "reliance must be placed on private liberality and wisdom to alleviate particular instances of hardship." But while the propertied classes had a duty to preserve peace and alleviate the misery of the poor, the means of providing assistance mattered greatly. There would be no relief without work. "The best way to assist the poor," *The Times* subsequently pointed out, "would be to maintain, together with their independent spirit, their industrious habits." There should be "an economy of relief" that provided the poor "with the means of labour, and they will then feel that they are assisting themselves." On another occasion, *The Times* charged, rather gratuitously, that workers who presently found themselves in desperate straits should have put more of their income into savings banks when they were employed, instead of spending it on "the gin-shop, the pawnbroker, and the lottery-offices."

Typically, communities took up a subscription among the middle and upper classes, and used the proceeds to fund various projects to benefit the community. In the northeastern port town of Scarborough, for instance, 150 local men were put to work in November clearing away a large quantity of accumulated rubbish from the harbor. The city of Salisbury raised enough money to pay 140 people to dig and screen gravel, and then to carry it to streets in need of repair. In Hampstead, a number of "labouring poor" found work "altering and improving the highways and footpaths of the parish, and in other works of general utility." The authorities at Frome, in Somerset, employed men to quarry stones and transport them to a depot; depending on how many loads they carried, the men earned from eight to ten shillings per week. A town meeting in Helston, Cornwall, elected to pay members of "the industrious poor" to enclose the Commons adjoining the town.

Seventy miles to the east, naval officials loaned shovels and wheelbarrows to Plymouth authorities so they could pay men to repair local roads. (The men were paid on a sliding scale—married men with families received the top pay of seven shillings and tuppence a week; "superannuated men"—i.e., the elderly—got only five shillings.) For counties in the London area, *The Times* suggested picking oakum (the laborious process of untwisting hemp rope) or making doormats. The most ambitious plan from the provinces came from Liverpool, where a meeting of "clergy, gentlemen, merchants" and other respectable citizens agreed to launch a fund-raising drive to employ up to 3,000 people during the winter on a project to expand and improve the docks.

Other communities, such as York, Newcastle, and Leeds, opened soup kitchens supported by private contributions. Rarely did they dispense any meals for free, except in extreme circumstances; most of these kitchens, such as the one in Limehouse, required the poor to pay a small fee for food—flour, potatoes, and beef—and for coals for fuel. Even so, the rapidly growing ranks of the needy threatened to overwhelm the limited charitable resources. A survey of Shropshire in early October revealed that one parish had "650 men, women, and children, totally destitute," while another neighborhood counted between 2,000 and 3,000 laborers either out of work or only partially employed. Shropshire itself totaled an estimated 12,000 people whom a local official described as "in a state of utmost privation."

Despite the reports of mediocre harvests, Liverpool's government convinced itself the country could survive the winter without a serious threat of famine, and that conviction never wavered. In a letter to Peel on October 18, Lord Liverpool predicted that Britain would have an adequate supply of grain; two months later, Castlereagh assured John Quincy Adams that even though the harvest "had been partially bad, there would turn out to be enough for the consumption of the people."

But reports of real and anticipated shortages drove grain prices higher in a very short time. In January 1816, wheat had sold for 52 shillings a quarter; by November, the price had nearly doubled, to 98s./9p. A few merchants initially supplemented domestic supplies with quantities of foreign grain illegally, in contravention of the Corn Laws. In October, smugglers along the Brittany coast sent shipments of French wheat clandestinely across the Channel, engaging in a brief skirmish with customs officials outside of Boulogne. In early November, however, the British government's complex calculations determined that wheat prices had reached the tipping point specified by the Corn Laws, and so it opened British ports to foreign grain.

Yet to only limited effect.

Britain's usual sources of supply on the Continent possessed little or no grain to sell except at exorbitant prices. Following the arrival of a few cargoes from the Netherlands—including grain that had been sent to England at considerably lower prices in 1815, only to be turned away when the Corn Laws went into effect—the Dutch government prohibited further shipments. British merchants who attempted to purchase wheat in Hamburg discovered that demand from other parts of Europe already had driven prices higher than their customers were willing to pay.

So the price of bread continued to rise in Britain, as did the price of milk—a direct result of the scarcity of fodder. A meeting of milkmen in Norwich declared that "through the Providence of God, the crops of corn and grain are almost all destroyed," hence it would cost them more to feed their cows. Accordingly, they raised their prices by 25 percent, from eight pence to ten pence a quart.

Liverpool fully expected the rising price of necessities—accompanied by higher unemployment and stagnant trade—to generate increased disorder in the coming months. He warned Sidmouth on October 21 that Britain faced "a Stormy Winter" stemming in large measure from the unusually cold and sodden summer: "The evil of a high Price of Bread coming upon us before we have got rid of our Commercial & Agricultural Distresses." Indeed the storm already had begun to break.

When the price of a quartern loaf (weighing about four pounds) of bread reached 1s. 2d. at the Surrey town of Guildford in the second week of October, an angry crowd of several hundred people gathered at the house of a baker whom they felt was charging excessive prices. Initially they expressed their outrage by banging on tin kettles and blowing horns; emboldened by reinforcements, the demonstrators soon graduated to violence, demolishing much

226 ° THE YEAR WITHOUT SUMMER

of the building before the local authorities arrived and read the Riot Act. Two days later, the mayor warned the local bakers to keep price increases to a minimum.

Two weeks later, a mob assaulted farmers at a market at Sunderland in northern England and grabbed all the grain they could carry, dividing the spoil among themselves. At Walsall, eight miles outside of Birmingham, rioters broke the windows of several bakers, then marched to a grain mill about a mile outside of town and demolished it, too. The panic-stricken magistrates summoned detachments of cavalry from Wolverhampton and Handsworth, but by the time they arrived, most of the rioters had fled with their plunder.

Birmingham itself enjoyed a long tradition of amicable relations between employers and laborers, but at the end of October a crowd attacked the house and shop of a printer who had published a circular advising the poor to "quietly and peaceably wait till Providence shall please to restore to you prosperity," adding that the penalty for violent riot would be death or exile. After demolishing the printer's house, the mob turned on the police and the local prison keeper; only the arrival of cavalry and the usual reading of the Riot Act quelled the disturbance around midnight, but not until several rioters were ridden down by horses, and one of them killed.

South Wales witnessed worse disorders. In Glamorgan, ironworkers struck on October 18 when their employers—facing a loss of government orders in peacetime—cut their wages to one shilling per day. Supported by local miners, the ironworkers forced the closure of furnaces in Merthyr Tydfil, the center of the Welsh iron industry. Claiming that the miners had assumed "a most alarming appearance," the high sheriff asked for troops from Swansea. Meanwhile, the strike spread to Monmouthshire and Newport. "I must also say that the discontented are in great force," reported one eyewitness, "and determined to oppose every thing sent against them." Several detachments of cavalry, including some troops who had fought at Waterloo a year earlier, eventually restored order. Thirty strikers were arrested and sent to Cardiff for trial. "I am much afraid," a bystander predicted, "distress will be severely felt this winter."

Spontaneous local disorders stemming from low wages and the high price of bread did not frighten Lord Liverpool and his cabinet unduly. What terrified them more than anything was the threat of mass action orchestrated by radical reformers whom the government believed were actually revolutionaries in disguise. With the French Terror less than twenty years behind them, Liverpool's ministry equated popular meetings with mob rule; hence their apprehension when approximately 8,000 people gathered at Spa Fields, just north of London, on Friday, November 15, to hear Henry Hunt urge them to petition the Prince Regent for relief from their distress.

The arrival of sharply colder weather deepened the misery of the poor. On the morning of November 8, residents of London arose to a severe frost, with temperatures falling to 27 degrees. In York, the mercury slid all the way to 21 degrees, "a circumstance not remembered by the oldest inhabitant at this early period of the winter." That evening the barometer dropped dramatically. On the morning of November 10, a powerful storm brought snow and sleet to the capital, followed by subfreezing temperatures that lasted until late the following day. This time, no one could blame sunspots for the frigid weather; as news reports pointed out, the spots had disappeared altogether from the face of the sun.

But Liverpool's stormy winter was already under way. As Hunt spoke to the massive crowd from the open window of a tavern at the edge of Spa Fields, he focused on the evils of corrupt government that burdened the people with a heavy load of taxes: "Everything that concerned their subsistence or comfort was taxed. Was not their loaf taxed, was not beer taxed, were not their coats taxed, were not their shirts taxed, was not everything that they ate, drank, wore, and even said taxed?" All of this was quite unexceptionable, but the government doubtless noticed that Hunt was accompanied by two men, one carrying a tricolor flag of green, white, and red ("the colours of the future British Republic," someone said recklessly) and the other a pike tipped with a cap of liberty. Nor did Liverpool and his colleagues welcome a reference to the nearby Coldbath Fields Prison as "the British Bastille, where so much tyranny had formerly been exercised." The meeting ended peaceably, but later that evening a mob looted several bakers' and butchers' shops in the area.

Instead of summoning Parliament at the end of the year, as previously planned, Liverpool decided to wait until February. By that time, he felt sure, the radicals would have thrown off their disguise, and the nation could see them for the insurrectionaries they really were.

On November 23, King George became the longest-reigning English monarch since the Norman Conquest: fifty-six years and twenty-nine days, surpassing the previous record-holder, Henry III. (Elizabeth I was in fourth place, just behind Edward III.) The occasion warranted few festivities; a month earlier, the royal family had celebrated the anniversary of the king's accession to the throne with a private dinner party. King George himself remained in seclusion. His physicians continued to issue reports on the state of his health; on November 2, for instance, they declared that "His Majesty was rather less composed than usual during the former part of the last month, but His Majesty has since resumed his tranquility, and is in good bodily health."

At two o'clock on the afternoon of November 4, King Louis entered the Chamber of Deputies to the accompaniment of artillery salvos outside the assembly. A larger crowd than usual had gathered to hear the monarch open the new session of the legislature:

Besides the diplomatic corps from other European nations, and the Peers of France (cloaked in their grand robes of state, bordered with ermine), there were numerous French and foreign dignitaries among the galleries, and two hundred ladies watching from the upper benches usually reserved for deputies.

"Tranquility reigns throughout the kingdom," Louis began, curtly dismissing a recently quashed insurrection in Lyon as "a senseless enterprise" that only proved the loyalty of the army to his throne. France was at peace with all its neighbors; his government had made its reparations payments on time; and it continued to meet its treaty obligations. Only one unfortunate development cast a cloud over France's tranquility. "The intemperance of the season has delayed the harvest," the king acknowledged. "My people suffer, and I suffer more than they do," he continued, with more ceremony than irony, "but I have the consolation of being able to inform you, that the evil is but temporary, and that the produce will be sufficient for the consumption." Perhaps, but Louis admitted that the dismal harvest would require the government to make substantial additional expenditures to assist the nation's poor. The king promised that the royal family would "make the same sacrifices this year as the last; and for the rest, I rely upon your attachment, and your zeal for the good of the State, and the honour of the French name."

Four days later, an angry crowd gathered at a marketplace in the southern French city of Toulouse to protest the high price of bread, and to prevent shipments of grain from leaving their region. The farms in the countryside around Toulouse, in the department of Haute-Garonne, had enjoyed a reasonably normal harvest, but the extremely heavy demand in areas such as Provence and Bas-Languedoc, which had suffered far worse from the cold and rain, enticed local merchants to ship their grains to the neediest regions to obtain the highest price. Even in Toulouse, the price of grain had risen to thirty-two francs per hectolitre (100 litres), an increase of approximately 33 percent over the past twelve months. Fearing that grain shipments out of Haute-Garonne would create shortages in their own region over the winter and drive up the price of bread even further, the protestors on November 8 demanded that the grain remain in the city and that local authorities lower the cost to a "just" price of twenty-four francs per hectolitre.

Police attempted to disperse the crowd, but the mob roughed them up. The arrival of the mayor, accompanied by a detachment of soldiers, finally broke up the protest as authorities arrested nearly a dozen demonstrators. But three days later the mob reassembled and repeated its demand for bread at twenty-four francs. This time it took a company of mounted troops to dislodge the protestors, who headed towards the town's granaries before the cavalry headed them off. The crowd responded by seizing three wagons loaded with grain and barricading themselves in the Faubourg Saint-Cyprien, relenting only when local officials summoned additional troops and a unit of the national guard from outside the city.

A similar incident occurred at the same time in the Vendée, on the west coast of France, where armed peasants stopped the shipment of wheat bound for Bayonne, and then stole what grain they could carry away. Peasants and townspeople in so many other departments followed suit, with merchants and soldiers battling mobs of men and women armed with pitchforks and sticks— sometimes aided by local authorities who wished to avoid shortages in their jurisdictions—that the minister of the interior issued instructions in mid-November to the nation's prefects "strictly prohibiting all such obstructions or restrictions, as preventing the abundance of one district from supplying the deficiencies of another." At the same time, the central government provided assurances that it would not allow French grain to be exported outside the nation's boundaries. Meanwhile, officials in Paris wondered if Ultra-Royalists, bitter over their losses in the recent elections, were encouraging the popular discontent to embarrass the government.

In the midst of the protests, a snowstorm dropped "a great quantity of snow" on the town of Niort, just north of the Vendée, on the evening of November 10. The phenomenon was "the more surprising," noted one newspaper, "as many years sometimes pass here without our seeing any snow; and when it does fall it falls in small quantities in the months of December and January." Five days later, Parisians were equally surprised by the combination of snow and thunder. "This day, at one, during a very cold temperature, and while the snow fell abundantly," reported the *Gazette de France*, "several claps of thunder were heard, preceded by lightning."

At noon on December 3, President Madison's secretary presented Congress with a copy of his eighth and final annual message. For the first time in any formal presidential communication to Congress, the weather took center stage. "In reviewing the present state of our country," Madison began, "our attention cannot be withheld from the effect produced by peculiar seasons which have very generally impaired the annual gifts of the earth and threatened scarcity in particular districts." The president comforted Congress, however, with an assurance that the frigid summer and prolonged drought had not created a national crisis. The United States, Madison pointed out, encompassed such a diversity of climates, soils, and agricultural products that it could provide enough food to fulfill its own needs despite the scanty harvests in the East. And if the scarcity of foodstuffs required the American people to practice "an economy of consumption, more than usual," they could still give thanks to Providence for "the remarkable health which has distinguished the present year."

Madison proceeded to list the positive developments of the past twelve months: The United States was at peace with every other nation; American exports continued to expand, though the president decried his fellow countrymen's tendency to purchase too many imported goods; and the frontier remained free of clashes with Indians, as the federal government continued its efforts to convert the natives into farmers and introduce them to "the arts and comforts of social life."

Actually, neither the United States's diplomatic affairs nor its relations with Native American tribes were quite as tranquil as Madison suggested. Two years after the Treaty of Ghent ended the War of 1812, relations between the United States and Britain were indeed improving rapidly. In London, negotiations between Lord Castlereagh and Ambassador Adams drew the two nations closer to agreements to demilitarize the Great Lakes—and effectively end American attempts to conquer southern Canada—and settle the boundary between the U.S. and Canada from the Great Lakes to the Rocky Mountains.

Relations with Spain, however, had begun to deteriorate. The Spanish government under the recently restored Don Carlos lacked the military resources to secure its possessions in the Western Hemisphere, and Americans seized the opportunity to enrich themselves at Spain's expense. During the War of 1812, Congress had snatched much of West Florida, and Jackson's victory at New Orleans in January 1815 solidified the American title to Louisiana—indeed, its presence all along the Gulf Coast. While the Spanish government embarked upon a quixotic attempt to regain West Florida and Louisiana, many Americans in the Southern states cast a covetous eye at Spanish-controlled East Florida, especially since local authorities proved unable to prevent bands of Seminole Indians from venturing occasionally into Georgia to raid American farms and kill American settlers. In less than a year, the First Seminole War would be well under way, with both sides committing horrific barbarities.

Spanish officials also objected when American seamen took advantage of the disorder in the Gulf of Mexico to plunder Spanish ships, or to convey supplies to rebels in Mexico and Latin America. A brief war scare erupted in the fall of 1816 when American newspapers reported that Spanish vessels had fired upon and seized the USS *Firebrand*, a naval schooner ostensibly assigned to suppress piracy in the gulf. Andrew Jackson, then the commander of U.S. Army forces south of the Ohio River, insisted that this example of "Spanish insolence" required a forceful American response. "If it was an unauthorised attack by Spain, it should have been repelled by another unauthorised act by us," Jackson wrote. "If authorised by the government of Spain, it was an act of war, and ought to be met as such." Cooler heads prevailed, but a British observer could see that Spanish possessions in North America were living on borrowed time. "So long as any part of the Floridas belong to the Spanish Crown," wrote a correspondent in *The Times* of London, "so long will there by no want of firebrands between that Monarchy and the United States."

Reviewing the state of government finances, Madison predicted that his administration would close the year with a surplus. Federal tax revenues for 1816 were estimated at $47 million, against total payments of $38 million for all of the national government's civil, military, and naval obligations. Madison suggested that the Treasury apply the $9 million surplus against the national debt of $110 million, largely the result of fighting the Revolution and the recently concluded war against Britain. Further, Madison predicted that the federal government would operate in the black again in 1817, thereby providing additional funds for "the effectual and early extinguishment of the public debt."

Looking ahead, Madison renewed his suggestion that Congress establish a national university in the District of Columbia, and called for states to build more roads and canals to facilitate domestic commerce. He closed by congratulating the American people on forty years of liberty and independence, and thanked them for their support. "If I have not served my country with greater ability," the president concluded, "I have served it with a sincere devotion."

One day later, the electoral college met to cast their votes for president. To no one's surprise, the Democratic-Republican ticket of James Monroe and Daniel Tompkins won an easy victory, carrying sixteen of nineteen states—only Massachusetts, Connecticut, and Delaware remained in the Federalist column. (There was some question as to whether the recently admitted state of Indiana was qualified to cast electoral votes in this election, but Congress ultimately decided that it could.) Undismayed by his defeat, but perhaps stung by its magnitude, Rufus King explained that he had lost because Monroe "had the zealous support of nobody, and he was exempt from the hostility of Everybody."

Most of the congressmen who arrived in Washington for the lame-duck session in December would not return when the fifteenth Congress convened in March. Popular outrage against the Compensation Act, exacerbated by anxieties about the distressing weather, poor harvests, and rising prices, cost 70 percent of incumbent congressmen their jobs—the highest rate of turnover in any congressional election in American history. Voters may not have blamed politicians directly for the frigid summer, but complaints about the "inauspicious season" and "precarious times" reflected a general mood of discontent that provoked a thorough purge of Congress. Not surprisingly, one of the first measures introduced in the December session was a resolution recommending repeal of the Compensation Act.

ON a pleasant morning in November, Ambassador John Quincy Adams went for a walk, leaving his house in West London and heading for Brentford. As he passed Gunnersbury, he saw a man lying facedown on the ground, apparently unconscious or dead. Enlisting the aid of a passerby, Adams revived the man and discovered that he was on his way to a hospital in Lambeth for treatment on his bad leg. "I asked him if he was in want," Adams noted in his diary. "He said he had eaten nothing for two days." Adams gave the stranger a shilling and suggested that he stop at a nearby pub for a hot meal. The encounter was not an isolated incident. "The number of these wretched objects that I meet in my daily walks is distressing," Adams acknowledged. "Not a day passes but we have beggars come to the house, each with a different hideous tale of misery. The extremes of opulence and want are more remarkable, and more constantly obvious, in this country than in any other that I ever saw."

Occasionally the British populace's patience wore thin despite Sir Francis Burdett's assessment that "no other country in the world could exhibit a population, suffering under such accumulated distresses, where so much forebearance and temper were manifested." On November 15, a crowd gathered at Lord Castlereagh's home in St. James's Square and threw stones at the windows, breaking a dozen panes of glass; the foreign secretary was not harmed. Several weeks later, radical leaders reconvened an assembly at Spa Fields. The previous gathering had dispatched Henry Hunt to present a petition for parliamentary reform to the Prince Regent. Twice Hunt attempted to meet with the prince; twice he was turned away.

As the crowd waited for Hunt to appear at Spa Fields, someone passed around a handbill that read, "A pot of beer for a penny and bread for two pence: HUNT REGENT and COBBETT KING: Go it, my boys!" Angered by the government's disdain for their cause, and encouraged by an agent provocateur, a portion of the mob broke away and headed for the Tower of London, which they fancied the English equivalent of the Bastille. Along the way, they broke into a gunshop and stole some weapons. When they arrived at the Tower, several shots were fired and one member of the mob brandished a cutlass and called upon the Tower to surrender. It did not. Instead, a delegation of three magistrates and five constables arrested three of the leaders, whereupon the rest of the crowd dispersed.

It was precisely the type of incident Liverpool's government had anticipated—"They sigh for a PLOT," wrote Cobbett, "They are sweating all over; they are absolutely pining and dying for a plot!"—and the Tories made the most of their good fortune. As Prince Klemens von Metternich, Austria's foreign minister, explained to the Duke of Wellington, "the effects of such violent crises always turn in favour of the good party." Lord Sidmouth and his colleagues chose to interpret the Spa Fields debacle as the opening shot in an organized conspiracy designed to end, as a secret parliamentary committee explained, in the "total overthrow of all existing establishments, and in a division of the landed, and extinction of the funded property of the country." By the time Parliament convened at the end of January, the government would have a full slate of repressive legislation primed for passage.

"THIS past summer and fall have been so cold and miserable that I have from despair kept no account of the weather," wrote Adino Brackett in his diary in December. "It could have been nothing but a repeatation [sic] of frost and drought." New England remained drier than normal throughout autumn, although a week of steady rain during the last week of October—the first prolonged period of precipitation since April—extinguished the forest fires across the region. A warm front arrived during the first week of November, sending temperatures briefly into the low 70s in Vermont and Massachusetts, followed by a storm that left a foot of snow in New Hampshire. The rest of November remained relatively warm, and December brought significantly milder weather than usual. "Warm month, very little frost," noted an observer in Plymouth, Massachusetts. "Quite warm and pleasant," agreed Reverend Samuel Robbins in East Windsor, Connecticut, on December 18. A sharp cold snap four days later persuaded Reverend Robbins that "the people appear to feel, in some measure, the frowns of heaven which lie upon them," but milder weather soon returned and remained through the middle of January.

So long as the weather cooperated, the stream of emigrants from New England continued westward. Sometimes a group of farmers from the same town organized an emigration company, purchased land in Ohio or Indiana, and then traveled together. One caravan from Durham, Maine, consisted of 16 wagons and 120 people (including their minister), bound for a township they planned to buy in Indiana.

Families who traveled by themselves found the journey wearisome. "I have seen some families of eight or 9 children on the road," wrote a young single farmer, "some with their horses tired others out of Money &c." Samuel Goodrich, a bookseller in Hartford, Connecticut, recalled seeing "families on foot—the father and boys taking turns in dragging along an improvised hand-wagon, loaded with the wreck of the household goods—occasionally giving the mother and baby a ride. Many of these persons were in a state of poverty, and begged their way as they went. Some died before they reached the expected Canaan . . ." A popular route from Maine to the west ran through Easton, Pennsylvania; in the course of a single month, 511 wagons carrying 3,066 travelers passed through the town. One family of eight bound for Indiana arrived in Easton in late December after walking all the way from their farm in Maine, pulling a cart loaded with their youngest children and a few possessions.

Many families left New England with very little money, hoping to find temporary employment on farms along the way. Those fortunate enough to find work typically received payment in food, such as oats or buckwheat; by December, however, the demand for labor had largely disappeared, and the emigrants were left to rely on the kindness of strangers. Thomas Baldwin, a farmer in his mid-forties from the Kennebunk River in Maine who intended to settle in Tennessee, arrived in New York City "somewhat depressed by fatigue," drawing behind him "a hand-cart containing all his effects, chattels and provisions, and two children of an age too feeble to travel; behind followed the elder children and the wife, bearing in her arms a robust infant seven months old." The Baldwins had already covered four hundred miles; their destination lay

another eight hundred miles ahead. As they labored past the corner of Pearl and Wall Streets, several bystanders took pity on the
family and handed them ten- and twenty-dollar banknotes.

Those who stayed behind suffered through a season of hardship, but not famine. Grain prices in the United States rose rapidly
in the last months of the year, especially as American merchants
shipped increasing amounts of wheat to Europe. (The rising volume of exports led several state legislatures to pass resolutions re-
questing a nationwide embargo on shipments of grain to other
countries. Congress demurred.) In New York and Boston, the price
of a bushel of wheat ranged between $1.50 to $2.00 from 1814
through the autumn of 1816; by late December 1816, it was nearing
$2.75. In the summer of 1816, corn had sold for $1.35 a bushel,
but it approached $1.75 by the end of the year.

Prices in inland towns were even higher, since the deplorable
roads hindered the movement of goods even in a mild winter. In
some isolated Maine towns, corn reached $3 a bushel, and flour
$16 per barrel. A band of Seneca Indians living in western New
York State who typically harvested 7,000 bushels of corn a year and
sold the surplus to importunate whites, lost more than 90 percent
of their crop and had to rely on assistance from private charities
and churches to survive the winter. The Massachusetts legislature
assumed responsibility for approximately 600 Native Americans
residing in Maine, and provided them with 300 bushels of corn.

Many farmers who had already sent their pigs to market lacked
their usual supply of pork over the winter. Starving wolves picked
off enough of the remaining sheep and chickens that several towns
in Maine posted bounties of forty dollars for each dead wolf, a
princely sum when a day laborer made only about three hundred
dollars a year. Long accustomed to improvisation, New England
farm families subsisted instead on the tops of potato plants, wild
pigeons, boiled leeks, and an occasional hedgehog. Oats, a hardier
grain which generally survived the frigid summer, replaced corn
on dinner tables. "Thousands of people subsisted on oatmeal who

had never tasted it before," wrote one observer. "Then it was that people blessed the Scotch for having invented oatmeal." Vermonters used maple syrup products as currency—it had been a good year for syrup—and traded them for fish caught along the Missisquoi River or shipped from the Atlantic, consuming so much seafood that 1817 became known in some parts of New England as the "mackerel year."

11.

RELIEF

"This year, 1817, was on the whole a melancholy one . . . "

AS 1816 DREW to a close, American and European writers continued to search for an explanation for the year's extraordinary weather. One thesis, advanced in the *National Register* and the *Petersburg Intelligencer*, attributed the frigid summer to two causes: a long-term cooling of the internal temperature of Earth, and a lack of circulation of the "electrical fluid" that was believed to move between the surface of Earth and the atmosphere. According to this theory, the internal heat of Earth—which the writer claimed had more influence upon the temperature of the air than any other factor—had been declining for the past thousand years. As evidence of a cooling trend, he cited the presence several centuries ago of human settlements in regions of Greenland and Iceland that were presently uninhabitable; alpine glaciers that were advancing across Switzerland and northern Italy; and significantly colder weather in Rome (snowstorms) and Lombardy (frozen lakes) than in the days of the Roman republic.

Nevertheless, the subnormal temperature of the summer of 1816 "appears to us to have been caused more by the absence of the usual circulation of the electrical fluid, than either a deficiency in the heat of the sun, or of that which we receive from the internal heat of the earth." According to this theory, "whenever the electrical fluid circulates, heat is produced. [And] whenever there is an equilibrium of the fluid for any length of time between the surface of the earth, and the atmosphere, the temperature of the air is much lower than in its usual state."

The electrical equilibrium allegedly existing in 1816 was attributed to a series of earthquakes that had occurred at various points around the world over the past three years—"more universal and terrible in their effects, than any which have been recorded for several centuries." Earthquakes, the theory maintained, were the result of a disequilibrium of electrical fluid between Earth's surface and the atmosphere, and "have been always preceded by a long tract of warm weather." Acting as a sort of electrical shock, the quakes restored the equilibrium and thereby ushered in a period of cold weather. The general absence of lightning and thunderstorms during the summer of 1816 seemed further proof of the insufficient circulation of electrical energy. "All nature seems to declare that electricity, the great agent of heat, when in a state of motion, is equally diffused at present through her system," the writer concluded, "and that no part either possesses a superfluity, or labours from a deficiency of this extraordinary & mysterious fluid. The earthquakes of the last years have produced this remarkable equilibrium; and we may calculate that several summers will yet pass away, before this equilibrium is destroyed, and the usual quantuum [sic] of heat necessary for vegetation will again be generated."

Others agreed that the normal circulation of electrical energy had gone awry, but blamed the disturbance on lightning rods instead of earthquakes. According to one theory, lightning rods prevented Earth from releasing heat into the atmosphere, keeping the air much cooler than normal. Or perhaps the rods actually absorbed heat from the air when they attracted lightning, thereby depriving the atmosphere of warmth.

For their part, several British writers focused on the movement of glaciers and icebergs to explain "the causes of this wet and cold season." Writing in the *Gentleman's Magazine*, one amateur meteorologist suggested that "the removal of a considerable number of icy mountains, by tempestuous winds, from the neighbourhood of the Arctic Pole into more Southerly latitudes in the Atlantic might occasion it." William Thomas Brande, a professor of chemistry at the Royal Institution of Great Britain and secretary to the Royal Society of London, suggested that the culprit was the slow buildup of Arctic ice over decades and centuries. For several hundred years, Brande argued, "the Climate of England has undergone a very material change for the worse." No one could doubt, he wrote, that "the Springs are now later and the Summers shorter; and that those seasons are colder and more humid than they were in the youthful days of many persons."

In fact, Brande claimed, the mean annual temperature across much of the Northern Hemisphere was declining, while the accumulation of ice and snow in the mountainous regions of Europe continued to expand. The trend seemed even more pronounced in the northern reaches of the hemisphere. As evidence, Brande cited the fate of eastern Greenland, where Norwegian and Icelandic traders had established outposts in medieval times. Since the fifteenth century, however, the east coast of Greenland, "which once was perfectly accessible, has become blockaded by an immense collection of ice." Brande blamed the "deterioration" of Britain's climate on this rapid buildup of ice—much of which, he argued, recently had begun to drift southward in the form of immense ice islands through the North Atlantic. The "extreme chilliness" of 1816, Brande concluded, "may in great measure be referred to these visitors from the north."

Other writers provided evidence to support this theory of an increasingly icebound hemisphere. One pointed out that in Norway, popular opinion held that "for fifty years past, the summers have been colder than they were before in that country." A French author cited the Scottish traveler Sir George Mackenzie's observation that the sea of ice between Iceland and Europe "has extended its empire over the vast space of sea between that island and the continent." Others pointed to the wrecks of two merchant ships in the Atlantic Ocean in the summer of 1803, lost when they reportedly collided with icebergs in the 40th degree of latitude—on the same line as Naples and Constantinople.

A more fanciful explanation for the frigid summer came from a resident of Albany, New York, who noticed a correlation between the advent of colder weather in the Northern United States and the Madison administration's failed attempt to invade Canada during the early stages of the recent war against Britain. "It seems very strange to me," he informed the editor of the *Columbian*, "that ever since our late 'just and necessary war,' these Canadian winds have all blown so cold upon us! Others have noticed this as well as myself and say, that our N. winds have, of late, been much colder than formerly. At this rate," he concluded, "it is very clear that Canada must be ours, or we must all migrate to the southward in a very few years."

Americans who still believed in malevolent magic ascribed the frigid summer to the machinations of witches, who were supposed to wield considerable power over the weather. More common were those who viewed the cold and drought as a warning from heaven: "That God has expressed His displeasure towards the inhabitants of the earth by withholding the ordinary rains and sunshine cannot be reasonably doubted," proclaimed one magazine editor.

Convictions of individual and collective sinfulness fueled the revival movement that was already well under way in New England, New York, and along the frontier. In late 1816, revivalism swept Vermont "from town to town in a manner very similar to an epidemic of disease," wrote Lewis Stillwell. "As many as fifty

244 ❧ THE YEAR WITHOUT SUMMER

persons succumbed to these onslaughts of emotionalism in a single town in a single day, and the total harvest of the churches ran into the thousands." Over the next several years, the revival movement produced numerous agencies dedicated to disseminating the gospel and setting sinners on the road to salvation: the Vermont Religious Tract Society, the Vermont Juvenile Missionary Society, the first New England convention of the Sunday School movement, the Vermont Colonization Society, and the northwestern branch of the American Society for Educating Pious Youth for the Gospel Ministry.

In the last week of January 1817, temperatures in the Northern United States suddenly plunged. Bitter cold gripped the region for the next month. On February 14, Dartmouth College recorded a low of 30 degrees below zero. "Fair, the coldest day has been for 40 years," claimed one New Hampshire farmer. At Alexandria, Virginia, the ice on the Potomac River reportedly was twenty-five inches thick. At Cincinnati, the Ohio River froze—"a circumstance rarely, if ever, known before."

Four days later, a storm brought both snow and rising temperatures that nearly reached the freezing point, but when the town of Salem, Massachusetts, attempted to put hundreds of men to work breaking up the ice that filled its harbor, they met with little success. On February 24, a minister in Salem noted in his diary that "the Barometer [was] as low as I ever observed it. I could make no fire in my study after repeated attempts so furiously was the smoak [sic] forced back into the chimney."

As the cold lingered into springtime and food remained scarce, prices continued to climb. In Maine, the price of oats tripled and the cost of potatoes doubled; in parts of New Hampshire, hay rose to $180 a ton, six times its normal price. Farmers whose corn crops had been devastated by the August frosts desperately sought seed for the new season. Occasionally neighbors would share supplies they had preserved from the 1815 harvest. Others sold their stocks at inflated prices; Samuel Goodrich recalled one New Hampshire farmer who walked forty miles for a half bushel of corn, paying two dollars when he finally found some. In Portland, Maine, residents at a town meeting authorized "the Overseers of the Poor to furnish seed of various descriptions to those individuals who are unable to procure the same from his own resources—the advances to be paid for either in labor on the highway, or in kind at the harvesting of crops."

Still the weather remained cold. On May 15, some towns in Vermont had five inches of snow on the ground. A report in the Hallowell (Maine) *American Advocate* confirmed that hundreds of families in the area were in severe distress. "Many charge it to the late cold seasons," the newspaper noted, "and are ready to sell their property for half what it cost, and migrate south." New Englanders who had stubbornly refused to give up finally surrendered to the elements and their fears. "New England seemed to many to be worn out and done for," wrote one historian of the exodus, "and the glacial age was returning to claim it again."

"We have had a great deal of moving this spring," reported Reverend Samuel Robbins from East Windsor, Connecticut. "Our number rather diminishes." June brought light snow and more frosts. By early summer, the river of emigrants swelled to a flood. "At last a kind of despair seized upon some of the people," wrote Samuel Goodrich, following a visit to New Hampshire. "In the pressure of adversity, many persons lost their judgment, and thousands feared or felt that New England was destined, henceforth, to become part of the frigid zone."

"Hardly a family seemed untouched by it," recounted historian Harlan Hatcher. "Younger sons determined to go west, daughters boldly marrying and setting out for the new land, neighbors loading their goods and youngest children into carts and wagons, fathers going along to prepare a place for their families—it was one of the largest and most homogeneous mass migrations in American history."

As the emigrants passed through western New York State, a correspondent for *Niles' Weekly Register* counted 260 wagons heading westward through the Genesee Valley in the space of nine days, plus scores of travelers on horseback or on foot. The editor of a local New York newspaper claimed that "he himself met on the road to Hamilton a cavalcade of upwards of twenty waggons, containing one company of one hundred and sixteen persons, on their way to Indiana, and all from one town in the district of Maine." In the town of Hamilton, New York, one writer estimated that "there are now in this village and its vicinity, three hundred families, besides single travellers, amounting in all to fifteen hundred souls, waiting for a rise of water to embark for 'the promised land.'" From St. Clairsville, Ohio—along the National Road—came word that "Old America seems to be breaking up, and moving westward. . . . Fourteen waggons yesterday, and thirteen today, have gone through this town. Myriads take their course down the Ohio. The waggons swarm with children."

One of the more conspicuous groups of emigrants was known as the Pilgrims, a band of religious zealots who left southern Canada in the spring of 1817 and came to rest at South Woodstock, Vermont, several months later. Numbering only about eight members when they arrived in Woodstock, the Pilgrims managed to attract thirty new adherents by the time they departed in late summer. They were led by Isaac Bullard, a red-bearded "prophet" known as "Elijah" to his followers and "Old Isaac" to others, who claimed to have received a revelation from God upon recovering from a lengthy illness. Bullard promised to lead his flock—who styled themselves after the lost tribe of Judah—to a Promised Land somewhere in the Western territories, where they would plant a new church of the Redeemer. Upon leaving Woodstock, the Pilgrims divided into two groups, one of which journeyed south through the Hudson River Valley and New Jersey before turning west, and the other walking westward across New York State and then south along the Ohio River. Along the way, they practiced a type of Christian communitarianism, under which they abjured material possessions and pooled all their resources—about $10,000—under Bullard's control. They also reportedly practiced free love, held frequent conversations with invisible spirits, and adamantly refused to bathe. Having discovered no Biblical admonition to wash oneself, Bullard decided that bathing was a sin, and boasted that he had not changed his clothes in seven years. His followers, garbed in bearskins and long knit caps, followed suit. They continued to enlist new converts along the route, and by the time they arrived at a spot subsequently named Pilgrim Island, about thirty miles south of New Madrid, Missouri, the sect numbered several hundred members. Shortly after their arrival, however, fevers killed dozens of the zealots, and Bullard's autocratic rule alienated so many others that the enterprise soon collapsed altogether.

More typical was the experience of Gershom Flagg, a young unmarried farmer who left his home in Richmond, Vermont, in the fall of 1816, spent the winter in Springfield, Ohio, and then moved on to the town of Harmony, alongside the National Road. Although the journey took him longer than expected ("we found some of the worst hills to travel up and down that I have ever seen where there was a Road"), and the price of supplies inflated in Ohio ("there are many things which are worth but little in Vermont that cost considerable here"), Flagg informed his brother back home that "I find the Country as fertile as I expected. Corn grows with once hoeing and some time with out hoeing at all to 14 feet high and is well filled. . . . Hogs & Cattle run in the woods in summers and in the winter are fed on Corn & prairie hay. In this vicinity are some as handsome Cattle as ever I have seen. . . . I am fully of the opinion that a man may live by farming with much less labour here than in the Eastern States." Moreover, "the weather is warm and pleasant now," Flagg reported in January. "We have had no snow."

Aided by similar testimonials from hundreds of other settlers, Ohio's population jumped from 230,760 in 1810 to slightly more than 400,000 in 1817. The increase in Indiana was even more spectacular, rising from 24,500 in 1810 to nearly 100,000 seven years later; in the year 1816 alone, Indiana gained 42,000 new settlers. And in the territory of Illinois, the population rose 160 percent between 1815 and 1818.

While no precise numbers exist for the number of emigrants from any particular location, the best estimates for Maine alone put the loss of residents between ten to fifteen thousand from 1810 to 1820, with most departing in 1816–20. Numerous towns in Maine—including Freeport, Eliot, Kittery, and Durham—suffered substantial declines in population, leading local officials to fear that the "ruinous emigration of their young men" might leave towns wholly unpopulated. In Vermont, more than sixty townships lost population from 1810–20, and another fifty or sixty barely managed to break even. (The state's population grew by only 8 percent between 1810 and 1820, compared to a 32 percent increase for the nation as a whole.) Hardest hit were the towns of northern Vermont. Worcester, just north of Montpelier, was reduced to one family; Granby, in Vermont's Northeast Kingdom, lost its legal existence altogether.

Newspaper editors attempted to stem the tide by vigorously promoting the alleged advantages of New England over Ohio or Indiana: easy coastal shipping to the markets of New York and Boston; better schools; greater proximity to Europe; a more industrious and more cultured population; and a healthier climate, with no "tropical" diseases such as malaria and other fevers that afflicted recent arrivals in the Western territories. The Massachusetts state legislature joined the campaign by approving an early version of a homestead act which opened up new townships in Maine (including some on land previously reserved for Native

Americans) and promised settlers one hundred acres for a payment of only five dollars (public land in Ohio was selling for approximately two dollars per acre), provided they built a house and barn on the land within a year and cleared ten acres for farmland within ten years.

Still the exodus continued, despite reports that the Western territories were considerably less hospitable than the advertisements claimed. Settlers discovered that they were going into "a great loneliness," a thinly settled region where farms were so isolated they might not see another family for several months at a time; where primitive cabins lacked furnishings or even chimneys; where cash was scarce, markets undeveloped, and prices for agricultural goods lower than in New England. "The bad things," recounted Gershom Flagg from Ohio, "are Want of Stone, Want of timber for building, Bad water, which will not Wash, overflowing of all the streams which makes it very bad building Bridges especially where the materials are scarce as they are here, Bad Roads, ignorant people . . . plenty of Ague near the large streams [and] Bad situation as to Trade. . . . Swarms of locusts have lately made their appearance." Material comforts remained few and far between. Household goods brought into the territories eventually broke or gave out—"glasses, cups, and hollow ware disappeared, iron pots were borrowed and broken"—and families had little money to purchase replacements, and few shops at which to buy them.

New Englanders also encountered recently arrived Southern farmers, particularly from Virginia and the eastern parts of North Carolina, defeated by their own poor harvests due to the cold summer and severe drought. The encounter produced something akin to culture shock for the Northerners. Their Southern brethren, observed one Vermonter, "are the most ignorant people I ever saw. . . . I have asked many people what township they lived in & they could not tell."

Some settlers gave up and headed back to New England, but

most decided that the benefits of life in the West outweighed the costs. After all, few prosperous farmers forsook their homes; most of the emigrants left behind farms that were only marginally profitable even in the best of times. Once they arrived in the new territories, "they spotted the mill sites, the town sites, and the best stands of timber," as one local historian pointed out, "and bought them up while they were still cheap." They chose the best land and cleared it and found the soil far more fertile than any in New England, and when the next wave of settlers arrived, they sold them the goods they needed. And as the population of the territories rose, so did the value of their lands.

But at last the price of grain stalled and then began to decline. After wheat reached a peak of $3.11 a bushel and corn nearly $1.75 a bushel in Eastern cities in May, the prospect of substantially improved harvests in the autumn of 1817 sent prices sharply lower.

ON January 28, 1817, a crowd of nearly 20,000 people gathered outside of Westminster Hall in London for the opening of Parliament. Many had come to support the presentation of petitions with hundreds of thousands of signatures—estimates ranged between 600,000 and 1,000,000—in favor of parliamentary reform. Others had gathered to gawk at the dignitaries who attended the ceremonies; and some were there to vent their anger and frustration with the government's failure to alleviate the growing distress among the poor throughout Britain.

By the time the Prince Regent—who had recently hosted a lavish dinner party at which thirty-six entrées were served—emerged after delivering his opening address, the mood of the crowd had turned quite dark; Sir Robert Peel noted that it was "amazingly increased both in numbers and violence." As the Prince Regent rode back to St. James's Palace, one or more bystanders threw large stones at his carriage, breaking at least one window. Perhaps someone in the crowd fired a couple of shots from an airgun; the government subsequently claimed that the left side of his carriage had been pierced by two small bullets, although John Quincy Adams reported that "no report was heard, no bullets [were] found in the carriage, and the opposite window, though up, was not broken." The Prince Regent was unharmed, but the incident persuaded Peel, among others, that "the general spirit of the country is worse, I apprehend, than we understood it to be."

Liverpool's government responded by submitting to Parliament a series of draconian measures to quash the revolution it had been expecting for months. Lacking any reliable information beyond the reports provided by the government (aided by a small army of spies and informants paid by the Home Office), Parliament had little choice but to approve the legislation. After establishing secret committees to investigate the state of the country, Parliament passed in less than two weeks a measure effectively suspending habeas corpus, a "gagging act" that allowed magistrates to silence any speech or publication they deemed "seditious or inflammatory," and a Seditious Meetings Act that required any assembly of fifty people or more to obtain prior permission from the government.

The government employed these new weapons enthusiastically. On March 10, a mass meeting in Manchester to publicize the plight of unemployed textile workers and protest the suspension of habeas corpus was broken up by a detachment of dragoons, and the leaders of the protest arrested. When a group of weavers decided to march from Manchester to London anyway, carrying blankets to indicate their profession (and keep them warm), they were attacked by cavalry before they reached the city; several demonstrators were wounded, and one killed.

Government informers also infiltrated a group of prospective revolutionaries centered in Pentrich, a village in Derbyshire, an area hard-pressed by the combination of rising food prices and growing unemployment in both the iron and hosiery industries. Throughout the spring of 1817, a veteran radical named Thomas

Bacon and Jeremiah Brandreth, an unemployed rib-stockinger from Nottingham, worked to recruit impoverished workers for a march on London to overthrow the government. While an order for 3,000 pike handles went out to a carpenter in Lincolnshire, a shipment of daggers arrived in neighboring Leicestershire. As Bacon and his lieutenants pondered the feasibility of appropriating a huge cannon from a local ironworks to accompany the rebels on their march, a government spy named William Richard, aka William Oliver, aka "Oliver the Spy," enthusiastically encouraged the plot. Oliver, as he was known to the conspirators, promised them that seventy-thousand sympathizers would join the marchers when they reached London.

On the evening of June 9, between 250–300 men—many of them reluctant converts pressed into service by Brandreth at gunpoint—left Pentrich in the pouring rain, armed with scythes, pikes, and a small number of guns. En route to Nottingham, where they expected sixteen thousand reinforcements to join them, they met a detachment of Light Dragoons, dispatched by the government in response to Oliver's reports. The marchers panicked and fled. Authorities tracked down and arrested more than eighty of them; in October, thirty-five were tried on charges of attempting "by force of arms to subvert and destroy the Government and Constitution." Twenty-three were found guilty: fourteen—including Bacon—were transported to Australia, six were imprisoned, and three (one of whom was Brandreth) were hanged and beheaded for treason. It was a pitiable end to a wretched enterprise that has been termed "England's last attempted revolution."

By that time, Parliament had begun to investigate alternatives to the traditional system of poor laws and parish relief. Alarmed by the rising cost of providing assistance to the poor in the early months of 1817, the House of Commons appointed a select committee to investigate the effects of the poor laws and recommend improvements. In July, the select committee delivered its conclusion that "unless some efficacious check be interposed, there is every reason to think that the amount of the [poor rate] will continue as it has done, to increase, till . . . it shall have absorbed the profits of the property on which the rate may have been assessed, producing thereby the neglect and ruin of the land."

In the meantime, Parliament approved the Poor Employment Act of 1817, which empowered the British government to make loans for up to three years to individuals or corporations who could demonstrate that the funds would be used to employ large numbers of workers. Initially, the total amount available for loans was capped at 1.75 million pounds sterling; within two months, the government had received applications for projects—generally for public works such as roads, canals, or draining marshlands—totalling more than a million pounds. The swift response proved the depth of the distress that still afflicted Britain in the summer of 1817. Although Parliament clearly intended the measure as a temporary expedient, it was renewed repeatedly. The act represented "a significant new departure," as M. W. Flinn has pointed out, since it "implicitly acknowledged the obligation of governments to do something more about depression than they had formerly considered adequate." Instead of limiting assistance solely to financial institutions or established commercial firms, it provided funds that would be used directly for the relief of unemployment and poverty, and in that sense provided critical momentum to the notion that the government bore a responsibility to improve the life of the ordinary British citizen.

JANE Austen's health deteriorated in the winter of 1816–17. She tired easily, and seldom left the house in Chawton; neighbors called her "the poor young lady." To her family, Austen pretended her illness was really nothing: "air and exercise are what I want," she insisted. She spent her days writing letters and the opening chapters of a new novel, *The Brothers*, even though her hand sometimes trembled badly. To her niece Fanny she admitted on March 23 that "I have had a good deal of fever at times & indifferent nights, but am considerably better now, & recovering my Looks a little. . . ."

But she was not. On May 24, Jane Austen rode in a carriage (it rained nearly all the way) to the hospital at Winchester. Although she rallied from time to time, her doctors knew of no cure for her illness, and she passed away on July 18. The precise nature of Austen's fatal illness remains a matter of controversy among biographers and physicians. Over the past fifty years, her death has been ascribed variously to Addison's disease, cancer, and, most recently, tuberculosis from the consumption of unpasteurized milk.

GRAIN prices in France rose throughout the winter and spring. By January 1817, the price of wheat nationwide was 180 percent higher than the average in 1815. In March, it was 190 percent higher; in May, 230 percent. But the national averages hid significant disparities among the various regions of France. Eastern provinces such as Alsace and Rhône-Alpes, where the summer's cold and rain had wreaked the most damage on the harvest, continued to face grain prices more than twice as high as those in most western regions.

For the most part, government officials held fast to the principles enunciated in the Interior Ministry's circular of November: They would brook no interference with the free movement of grain from one department to another, nor would they permit the mass intimidation of farmers or merchants to force the sale of grain at reduced prices. At the same time, Louis' government made substantial purchases of foreign wheat (largely from Baltic ports), which it intended to sell to the populace below cost; it also subsidized bakers directly, established soup kitchens, and advised the local prefects to provide assistance to the elderly and infirm.

Obsessed by fears of a popular uprising in Paris, Louis insisted that local authorities hold down the price of bread in the capital, preferably below the limit of ninety centimes for a two-kilogram

loaf established during Napoléon's reign. Nevertheless, Louis ada-
mantly refused to grant Parisian officials additional funds to help
them achieve that objective. As more and more peasants from the
surrounding countryside drifted into Paris in search of cheaper
bread in the late winter of 1817, the task grew even more daunting: one estimate classified nearly 200,000 Parisians as indigent
and therefore deserving of subsidized bread.

Although a loaf of bread in Paris—even with government
subsidies—nearly doubled in price between the spring of 1816 and
the spring of 1817, it still cost only about 60 percent of a similar
loaf in the Alsatian capital of Strasbourg. Meanwhile, prices rose
even higher in the French countryside, where bread often cost three
to four times as much as in the cities. And the quality of bread
suffered as well. The combination of prolonged cool weather during the summer (which kept the wheat kernels from ripening) and
rain during the harvest (which led to sprout-damaged wheat) produced grain that weighed only about 75 to 80 percent of top-quality
wheat. Consequently, the flour absorbed less water and frequently
resulted in bread that was sticky and gummy. "You could not eat
the bread," complained one disgusted peasant in central France.
"It stuck to the knife."

In February, riots broke out in northern France, particularly in
Haute-Normandie and the Somme, to prevent grain from leaving
the region. Throughout the country, authorities reported an increase in property crimes, particulary theft, and a rise in attacks by
armed bands of outlaws upon travelers. As a result, farmers often
refused to risk shipping their grain, at least until it was completely
paid for, and the dearth in eastern France deepened. In areas where
local authorities provided grain allowances for the poor—in the
larger cities, for the most part—they found it necessary to reduce
their allotments and substitute other food, such as potatoes, for
wheat or bread.

As grain from the Baltic and the United States began to arrive,
royal officials directed it first to Paris and then to the supply

routes in northern France through which grain shipments usually traveled, to reduce the likelihood of future disruptions. Between the cost of grain imports and the expense of bread subsidies—which together totalled nearly 70 million francs—the national budget slid quickly into the red. Only a hastily arranged loan from British and Dutch bankers in February kept the royal government afloat. Wellington, meanwhile, agreed to reduce the Allied occupation forces by 30,000 troops, particularly from the eastern departments, thereby alleviating pressure on both the French budget and local food supplies.

Despite the government's efforts, distress continued to grow throughout France during the spring of 1817. En route to Switzerland, Louis Simond—a native Frenchman who had achieved wealth as a merchant in New York City—noticed the rising number of indigent peasants as he traveled through eastern France. "Beggars, very numerous yesterday, have increased greatly," he noted in his journal. "At every stage, a crowd of women and children and of old men, gather round the carriage; their cries, the eloquence of all these pale and emaciated countenances, lifted up to us with imploring hands, are more than we can well bear." Numerous citizens already had died, Simond noted, "if not of hunger, at least of the insufficiency and bad quality of the food."

Sir Stamford Raffles, too, encountered hordes of beggars as he and his cousin, Thomas, passed through eastern France that spring. (The former lieutenant-governor of Java had recently dropped the "Thomas" from his name.) The beggars, wrote Thomas after leaving the town of Champagnole, "were chiefly children, and their numbers and their importunity was truly astonishing. From the very slow rate at which we traveled [ascending a hill], they were frequently enabled to follow us for a considerable distance, and this they did, entreating in the most piteous accents, and repeating the same words with a sort of measured intonation, *Monsieur, s'il vous plaît, donnez-moi charité.*" Thomas Raffles breathed a sigh of relief when the road leveled off and his carriage could pick up speed, leaving the unfortunate children behind.

Peasants and townspeople from the provinces surrounding Paris continued to flock into the capital; on the first of June, Simond noted one report that "one hundred thousand souls have been added to its destitute population within a few months!" Nevertheless, the government's policy of cheap bread in the city continued to avert any outbreak of disorder or famine. The rest of France was not so fortunate. In one department after another, food riots broke out in the spring and early summer. Much of the violence was perpetrated by bands of armed vagrants, usually peasants desperate for food, who migrated to areas where there was at least an adequate supply of grain. Sometimes they seized grain wherever they could find it; often, however, they offered to purchase it at a reduced price.

At the end of May, a series of large-scale disturbances shook one market town after another. On May 30, a mob of 3,000 peasants sacked the grain market in the Burgundy town of Sens; when local officials called in troops from a nearby garrison to quell the disorder, the rioters dispersed into the countryside, where they extorted grain from farmers by threatening to kill them and their families. The following day, an even larger crowd plundered a market town in the department of Aube, in northeastern France. Again, the authorities required regular army troops to crush the disturbance.

Five thousand rioters assaulted the town of Château-Thierry on June 3, pillaging the storehouses and seizing grain shipments on the Marne River. A pitched battle ensued between the peasants—armed with swords, bayonets, and sticks—and government soldiers, leaving several rioters dead. Once more, the trouble spread into the countryside, ending only when local officials essentially requisitioned grain from farmers to distribute among the protestors.

For the most part, these disturbances were remarkably free of any political content. From the government's perspective, however, the trouble that erupted at Lyon in the second week of June bore a far more ominous cast. Long a stronghold of Bonapartist sentiment, the town of Lyon was suffering acutely from the depression in the textile industry, and the surrounding countryside from the dearth of grain. Local officials prudently subsidized the cost of bread in Lyon, but could not afford to match that price in the rural areas. By June 1817 the price of bread in eastern France had increased to nearly four times its cost in the spring of 1816. Rumors of Napoléon's imminent return had swirled through the region for the past several months, and the royal government braced for a reprise of the Hundred Days. "The excessive price of bread and of all kinds of provisions," warned one local official, "has been the principal cause that has set off the ill-will likely to spur on the agitation in the country."

On the evening of June 8, several hundred demonstrators gathered in the suburbs of Lyon and raised the tricolor flag. Already on alert, government troops quickly quashed the rising, but the mayor and the commanding general in the department of the Rhône decided to treat the incident as if it had been a full-fledged insurrection. They convened military courts and swiftly tried more than a hundred suspected conspirators, convicting seventy-nine, including a dozen who were sentenced to death. Executions took place almost immediately.

During the following year, the Lyon conspiracy became a highly charged political issue. Moderate royalists and liberals, along with the merchants of Lyon, charged that the government exaggerated the danger of revolt, and blamed the uprising primarily on the desperate food situation. Ultra-Royalists insisted the demonstrators had posed a very real threat to the royal government, and that only severely repressive measures had thwarted an insurrection. Eventually even Decazes, the minister of police, concluded that the danger had been minimal.

Following the affair at Lyon, conditions gradually improved

across France. Most of the government's purchases of grain from abroad arrived during the summer, sparking a decline in the price of bread that began in July and continued through the remainder of the year, although in December grain still cost 166 percent of its base price in 1815. There were twice as many criminal prosecutions in French courts in 1817 as in 1815, but government officials were happy to attribute the increase to food shortages, rather than political discontent. Accordingly, the king issued a pardon on August 14 for all crimes committed as a result of the scarcity of grain. "The zeal and firmness which our courts and tribunals have brought to the maintenance of public order has merited our approval," Louis declared, "but our heart has groaned from the severities that justice and the law have commanded against a too large number of persons, who, in several parts of the kingdom, have been involved in criminal disorders through the scarcity and dearness of provisions. We feel the need not to confuse these unfortunates with the vicious men who would have tried, in some places, to push them into excesses whose most certain result was to aggravate their distress and to increase the ills of the state."

Louis spent the rest of 1817 trying to eradicate the memory of Napoléon from the consciousness of Parisians. The Austerlitz Bridge was renamed the Bridge of the King's Garden, and workers scratched the large letter "N" from the exterior of the Louvre. The first steamboat "smoked and clattered" its way up the Seine as a harbinger of a new era. And, as Victor Hugo pointed out, "all sensible people were agreed that the era of revolution had been closed forever by King Louis XVIII, surnamed 'the Immortal Author of the Charter.'"

But in the eastern provinces—particularly Alsace and Lorraine—an estimated 20,000 disillusioned farmers and laborers emigrated by the end of the year, lured by extravagant promises from agents for shipowners of the opportunities that awaited them in the promised lands of Russia and the United States. Nearly a fourth of the emigrants were Alsatians who chose to settle in the

United States. After making their way across France to the port of Le Havre, they found that passage across the Atlantic cost between 350 to 400 francs. Those who could not afford to pay were offered labor contracts which essentially turned the passengers into indentured servants; many ended up in Louisiana working in appalling conditions on cotton plantations. Treatment of these "redemptioners" was so brutal that the Louisiana legislature passed a measure in 1818 providing them with at least a modicum of protection by the state government.

By early 1817, the typhus epidemic in Ireland was spreading rapidly from the west. As cold, wet conditions persisted through the winter and spring, and food shortages mounted, the fever claimed more and more lives. Nearly all of those affected lived in impoverished rural areas; wealthy landowners, removed from physical contact with peasants and laborers, barely suffered at all.

Peel's hopes for continued peace in Ireland perished in the wake of the epidemic. The authorities attempted to redistribute what little grain remained in the country, taking supplies from those regions with even meager harvests to provide for those areas where the harvest had failed entirely. Not surprisingly, the residents of those towns forced to export food—many of whose residents were close to starvation themselves—rioted at the prospect of being left with even less. Merchants whose desire for profit outweighed their sense of charity began to buy grain, even at expensive prices, and hoarded it, believing that they could sell it for still more as the shortages worsened. Their actions provoked angry reactions from starving peasants, who demanded that the government set a maximum price for grain.

On the night of February 19, 1817, the residents of the western coastal town of Carrigaholt attacked the supply ship *Inverness*, which had been loaded at Limerick with butter, pork, and bacon to be shipped to London. When the ship landed briefly at Carrigaholt, a mob formed, apparently furious that Irish provisions were destined for the more affluent English. As the local police commander, Captain Miller, explained in a note to the shipment's owner, the crowd "boarded and rendered [the *Inverness*] not seaworthy, by scuttling her, and tearing away all her rigging." The rioters then proceeded to "rob the crew of all their clothes, tore their shirts, which they made bags of, to carry away the plunder, and then broached the tierces of pork and distributed the contents to people on shore, who waited to convey them to the country." The police intervened, recovered the goods, and arrested the rioters.

Trouble continued the following morning, however, when local residents "collected in some thousands, and went down to the beach, where they formed into three bodies . . . declaring that they defied the police, and would possess themselves again of what had been taken from them." This time the crowd succeeded in overcoming the police; again they boarded the ship and stripped it clean. "A more complete plunder," reported Captain Miller, "has seldom been witnessed." The mob even managed to steal the ship's anchors and bilge pump, while the women of the town supplied their husbands and brothers with whiskey. A detachment of twenty cavalry managed to disperse the crowd, but not before three men were killed and thirty-five arrested.

News of grain shortages in Ireland reached Parliament shortly thereafter. On March 7, the House of Lords debated whether to prohibit the distillation of grain alcohol in Ireland in order to make more grain available for food. Several days later, the Commons discussed a similar proposal brought in a petition from the people of Belfast, which sought to outlaw distillation in the whole of the United Kingdom. The measures elicited considerable debate. Lord Liverpool believed that suspending distillation would only shift production to the black market, resulting in no increase in grain supplies but a substantial rise in alcohol prices. Liverpool refused to acknowledge that the disorder in Ireland was widespread or warranted government intervention: as the *Morning*

Chronicle pointed out, "there was therefore no general measure wanted, the difficulties in Ireland were altogether local." In such situations, Liverpool believed government interference "frequently did more harm than good."

Faced with mounting public discontent and multiple riots, Peel did not have the luxury of Liverpool's caution. As grain stocks in Ireland reached precipitously low levels in March, Peel decided to import low-quality oats to be sold as seed at a fixed price of two shillings and six pence per stone (fourteen pounds). Farmers needed seed oats both to plant for the coming season—most had eaten their entire stocks over the winter, leaving no grain to plant in the spring—and to release for consumption the stocks of better-quality oats that remained. "Several cargoes of oats are on their way from abroad to the North of Ireland," reported the *Bury and Norwich Post*, "which will be a considerable help to the farmers, who are greatly in want of seed."

Peel's plan met with disaster. When the ships arrived in Ireland, the oats proved of even lower quality than seed oats: Some were already spoiled, and others were black-colored oats that farmers knew they would be unable to sell on the market. The government's price also proved far too high. Ultimately, Peel was forced to sell the unpalatable oats for a far lower price and admit that his scheme had done little to ease the country's grain shortage.

As the typhus epidemic continued to spread across Ireland, Peel turned to direct financial intervention. He established a seven-member committee, financed with £50,000, to distribute aid to the poor and starving. To avoid any accusations of religious prejudice, the committee included two Quakers and a Catholic. Peel instructed the committee to buy and sell grain, set up "soup shops," and provide handouts where necessary. This support paled in comparison to the contributions of private charitable concerns, however, which relied upon contributions from local landowners and other wealthy individuals. One estimate of these organizations' finances puts their combined budgets at £300,000, or six times that of the government relief fund. It was not until the passage of the Poor Employment Act in June 1817 that the British government provided substantial funds for alleviating Irish poverty. Of a total budget of £1.75 million across the United Kingdom, the act allowed the lord lieutenant to spend up to £250,000 to employ Irish workers, mostly on infrastructure projects such as building roads, bridges, churches, and schools.

Peel's response to the typhus epidemic followed the same strategy as his response to the food shortages. He set up a national relief committee that received and evaluated applications from local committees for funds, but by the time the epidemic subsided in 1819, the national committee had spent less than £20,000. The government again left the bulk of the charitable work to private committees, relying on the Irish national tradition of generosity.

An 1821 survey by Francis Barker and John Cheyne estimated that the typhus epidemic killed 65,000 Irish and rendered another 1.5 million—roughly one out of every four people on the island— seriously ill. Although the epidemic had ended, the disease never completely left Ireland. Periodic outbreaks occurred throughout the 1820s and 1830s, generally associated with poor harvests and famines in particular regions. With each period of "distress," London became steadily more involved in providing relief to the Irish. Although the food shortages in 1822 were not as severe as those in 1817, the government sent nearly £200,000 of assistance, four times Peel's original budget. Nevertheless, each round of famine and epidemic reduced the resilience of the Irish poor and depressed their standard of living still further. The events of 1816 and 1817 accelerated a vicious cycle of hunger, sickness, and poverty that would culminate in the disaster of the Great Famine in 1845.

No country on the European continent suffered more than Switzerland from the disastrous effects of the summer of 1816. The mountainous eastern cantons, including St. Gall, Glarus, and Appenzell, were particularly hard-hit. By April 1817, the price of wheat in that region had risen to 350 percent of the average level of 1815. Wages of weavers and cotton spinners, meanwhile, continued to fall, until many workers earned less for a full day's work than the price of a one-pound loaf of bread.

Widespread famine ensued. The misery was exacerbated by the political structure of the Swiss federation, as canton officials jealously guarded their own supplies and established barriers to the shipment of grain outside their boundaries. Most canton governments purchased grain abroad, typically from Russia or Egypt, but with no sea or ocean ports, the importation of food stocks proceeded even more slowly than in nations such as France or the Netherlands. In the meantime, authorities obtained whatever grain they could and provided it to their indigent citizens at prices below market, or else gave bakers subsidies to produce cheaper bread. Some cantons put a fraction of the unemployed to work on public works projects. Town governments also established soup kitchens to feed their poor, and private charities raised funds to care for local orphans and widows, but the task seemed overwhelming when more than 20 percent of the population of St. Gall and Appenzell were classified as paupers, and when "nearly one-quarter of the population of Glarus lacked means of subsistence."

Thousands of Swiss peasants took to wandering and begging, sometimes in vast throngs that stretched out along the highways. One writer noticed "the paleness of death in their cheeks"; another noted "a wild, benumbed look of desperation in their eyes." When Louis Simond reached the town of Herisau in Appenzell in June 1817, he discovered that "the number of beggars, mostly women and children, is perfectly shocking . . . Manufactures are without work, and it is impossible for them to procure food: they are supported by private and public charities, and distributions of economical soup (made with oatmeal and a little meat) in quantities scarcely sufficient to sustain life. We see nothing but meadows and pastures, not a patch of potatoes or grain, not even a garden." The following day, Simond arrived in the village of Wattwyl, where he found fewer beggars—but only because "many distressed people are dead, if not absolutely of hunger, yet of the consequences. After supporting for some time a miserable existence, on scarcely any thing but boiled nettles and other herbs, their organs became impaired . . . and they perished in a few days."

Few riots shook Switzerland, but crimes against property soared. Burglary, theft, embezzlement, arson—"crimes multiply with wants," noted one traveler, "the prisons are full, and executions frequent." In the spring of 1817, *The Times* of London published reports of "the perpetually increasing crowd of mendicants and vagabonds who menace the rights of property, and endanger the public health and safety." Still the price of bread continued to rise; by the summer of 1817, it peaked at four to five times the price in 1815. "The general impression," observed *The Times*, "is that the mass privation seems in no wise to diminish, and that hardships and sufferings may fairly be anticipated more grievous than have been experienced by the poor."

Local authorities responded with vicious punishments. Louis Simond reported that officials in the town of Appenzell had sentenced two convicted criminals to death by beheading—"one for setting fire to a barn, the other for repeated robberies." Eight others had recently been whipped. "There is," Simond concluded, "nothing Arcadian in all this." Yet even the harshest penalties appeared to have little effect. "Neither sentries nor bailiffs nor policemen nor begging-ordinances were any longer respected; not even severe penalties were feared—hunger and misery, instinct of self-preservation, and gross, often base temper engendered a far stronger command, which despised harsh measures as mere child's play."

Frequently canton officials encouraged emigration to reduce the poor rolls; nevertheless, the best estimates indicate that fewer than 20,000 Swiss left the country. Most either headed for southern Russia, or traveled down the Rhine to the Netherlands ports, where they took passage on ships bound for North America. A substantial number of Swiss settled in the Midwestern United States, including a community of Swiss Mennonites who bought land in the hill country of Ohio and Indiana, purportedly because it "reminded them of their former Swiss homeland." Others settled in Canada, where the Earl of Selkirk recruited Swiss mercenaries to defend his Red River Colony in Manitoba from native attacks. Meanwhile, negotiations commenced between the canton of Fribourg and the royal government of Portugal to establish the first Swiss colony in Latin America: the settlement of Nova Friburgo, in Brazil.

If sunspots and cataclysmic weather had seemed to presage the end of the world in the summer of 1816, the appalling spectacle of famine and misery in 1817 gave further evidence of an approaching apocalypse, and provided momentum to a revival movement that already was under way in Switzerland. The most notorious champion of divine reckoning was the Baroness de Krüdener, a Russian writer and mystic who had gained notoriety through her relationship with Tsar Alexander I in 1815. Convinced that corruption and evil governed Europe in the post-Napoleonic world, de Krüdener predicted that God would soon intervene and restore justice for the poor. "The Rhine rots with corpses; people, contrary to the law, are buying blood at butcher shops. Misery is rampant and menaces all our security," she wrote in January 1817. "The time is approaching when the Lord of Lords will reassume the reins. He himself will feed his flock. He will dry the eyes of the poor. He will lead his people, and nothing will remain of the powers of darkness save destruction, shame, and contempt."

Well-known for her benevolence, de Krüdener spent the spring of 1817 moving from one part of eastern Switzerland to another, dispensing food to the hordes of vagrants and beggars who followed her, and denouncing the wealthy and powerful who ignored the plight of the poor. "It is a disgraceful falsehood of the newspapers to talk of idle vagabonds at a time when no one has any work to do, and when thousands come and implore me to give them work; when all the factories are closed in consequence of the punishments inflicted on cupidity and selfishness," de Krüdener insisted. "Far from hearing of robberies as the papers declare, the only wonder is that the whole country is not given up to brigand-age." Alarmed by her gospel of social radicalism, and fearful of the crowds of starving paupers she attracted, police officials—enthusiastically supported by local residents—drove de Krüdener from village to village, dispersing and expelling her followers. By the end of the summer she had been driven out of Switzerland altogether, into Breisgau in southwestern Germany.

A fair harvest finally brought grain prices down in the autumn, but so many Swiss perished in the *Hungerjahre* of 1817 that the nation recorded more deaths than births for one of the few years in its history.

PRUSSIA escaped the worst of the devastation. The summer's weather wreaked slightly less damage upon its crops in 1816 than the states to the south, and a more efficient system of political administration, along with a strong tradition of active government intervention, limited the effects of the grain shortages that appeared in 1817. Officials moved aggressively to purchase foreign grain, even at inflated prices, and the leading citizens of numerous Prussian cities (including Coblenz, Düsseldorf, and Frankfurt) established *Kornvereine*—cooperatives funded by local businessmen and landowners that purchased grain abroad and then sold tokens that residents could redeem for bread at prices about twenty-five percent below the market price. (Some of these tokens subsequently became collectors' items for numismatists.)

Conditions in the southern German states and neighboring regions of the Austrian empire, however, rivaled those in Switzerland. Grain yields in Württemberg in 1816 were 15 percent lower than the previous year, but so much of the harvested grain was damaged that the effective yield was closer to 50 percent of a nor-mal year's harvest. Bavaria and Baden experienced similar prob-lems, and by the end of 1816, grain prices in Bavaria, Baden, and Württemberg had nearly doubled from their 1815 levels—then they rose by a similar amount over the following six months. Some towns witnessed even greater inflation in food prices; in Gerad-stetten, in Württemberg, the price of wheat more than doubled between November 1816 and July 1817, while the price of oats tripled, and the cost of potatoes quadrupled.

Governments in these areas moved more slowly and reluctantly than their counterparts in the north to respond to the crisis. The result was widespread starvation. Contemporaries' reports spoke of peasants eating rotting grain, or boiled weeds known as "pig's ears," or bread made from sawdust and straw, or the decaying flesh of dead animals. Some killed their own dogs and ate them. Travel-ing through Eifel (in the western Rhineland) in the spring of 1817, the noted Prussian military officer and theorist Carl von Clause-witz described "ruined figures, scarcely resembling men, prowling around the fields searching for food among the unharvested and already half rotten potatoes that never grew to maturity."

Local authorities attempted to purchase foreign grain, but the minimal amounts they imported fell far short of the public need. Bans on exports of grain failed to provide relief when the poor could not afford to purchase the wheat and oats that remained. When officials tried to set maximum prices for wheat, supplies often dried up as farmers and merchants withheld their grain from market. In the town of Laichingen, where nearly 80 percent of the population lacked the resources to purchase bread or grain, offi-cials refused to distribute wheat from the state granaries until the citizens threatened a violent hunger march. (Meanwhile, the wealthier citizens of Laichingen withheld donations to the fund for poor relief, and instead loaned money to the needy, and took advantage of the crisis to purchase property from their impover-ished neighbors.)

Towns that provided effective relief in the form of Rumford soup kitchens or subsidized bread found themselves overwhelmed with vagrants—"beggars appeared from all directions, as if they had crawled out of the ground." There were few organized food riots, but desperation bred contempt for law and order among individual beggars. A visitor to Württemberg saw "persons who looked like cadavers, and among them multitudes of children crying out for bread. Hunger and unnatural food produced wretched and chronic ill health among some, outbreaks of frenzy among others; those in the most desperate condition deemed themselves no longer bound by the laws that are adopted for the protection of private property."

In some German states, the death rate rose by more than 20 percent. In the region surrounding the Transvylvanian town of Arad, an estimated eighteen thousand people died of starvation. The famine in three counties in the mountains of eastern Hungary took another 26,000 lives. In Württemberg, deaths in 1817 outnumbered births by 3,000.

Northern Italy also suffered substantially from famine and disease. In the higher elevations of Lombardy, the wheat harvest failed almost completely in 1816. Tuscany and Bologna also experienced dearth conditions. Authorities imported significant amounts of grain, but primitive transportation systems prevented effective distribution. Here, too, beggars thronged the highways, often carrying disease with them. "A contagious malady, analogous to typhus fever, which at present afflicts a great part of Italy, has taken its source in crowded meetings of beggars and wretched persons, whose numbers are very great," reported *The Times* of London in April 1817. "It is attributed to famine and the use of bad aliment." Deaths mounted throughout the region; in Bologna, the official death rate rose by 80 percent.

Thousands of families escaped the devastation by leaving their homes and traveling down the Rhine to the ports of the Netherlands, or down the Danube to the Russian border. The band of religious extremists who had emigrated from Württemberg in September of 1816 and wintered in Grossliebental finally continued along the Black Sea coast to Rostov and Stavropol, crossing the Caucasus Mountains in the summer of 1817 and establishing the new village of Marienfeld, outside of Tiflis (Tbilisi). When word of their arrival reached their brethren in Württemberg, another 8,000 desperate people—not all of them members of the same separatist sect—gathered in Ulm to make the same journey. Nearly half of them died along the way; over a thousand reportedly perished from disease in a single day. Others simply gave up and settled wherever they stopped. About 5,000 survivors finally reached Bessarabia, recently ceded to Russia by its former Ottoman rulers, where they founded their own new villages.

Perhaps 15,000 Germans emigrated to Russia between the summer of 1816 and the end of 1817. Another 20,000—primarily from Baden and Württemberg—landed in the United States. They were the fortunate ones. An even greater number, perhaps as many as 30,000, reached Dutch seaports—especially Amsterdam—and discovered that they lacked sufficient funds to buy passage across the Atlantic, or that there was no room even on the vastly overcrowded ships. Forced to retrace their steps, they begged or stole their way back through the Rhineland, driven on at every turn by the local authorities.

ON December 10, London police removed the lifeless body of a young woman from the Serpentine River in the West End. They subsequently identified her as Harriet Shelley, the estranged wife of Percy Bysshe Shelley. Harriet had disappeared a month earlier; although an inquest declared only that she had been "found drowned," her death was presumed to be a suicide. Her husband blamed Harriet's death on "her abhorred and unnatural family," and particularly her sister, whom Shelley claimed had driven Harriet to kill herself.

Less than three weeks later, Shelley and Mary Godwin were married in London. The ceremony, Shelley informed Byron, was "simply with us a matter of convenience," performed primarily to please Mary's father. The couple soon returned to Bath, where Mary continued to work on the manuscript of her novel. In January, Claire Clairmont gave birth to a daughter, whom the Shelleys named (albeit temporarily) "Alba," a play on their nickname for Byron ("Albe," from his initials, "L.B.").

Byron spent the winter on the Continent. From Milan he traveled back to Geneva, and then to Venice. Although Shelley informed him of the birth of his daughter, and asked his intentions for the girl in several different letters, Byron refused to accept any responsibility for the care of the child at that time.

In March, the Shelleys moved into a house in Marlow. Shelley was spending an increasing amount of time with Leigh Hunt, a radical reformer and author who had become a vocal champion of Shelley's poetry. Their friendship encouraged Shelley in his own liberal political views. Beyond his own personal charitable donations to the unemployed laceworkers in and around Marlow—he purportedly once gave away his shoes and walked home barefoot—Shelley contributed a pamphlet entitled "A Proposal for Putting Reform to the Vote Throughout the Kingdom," and signed it "The Hermit of Marlow."

To no avail. As Liverpool's government shepherded its program of repressive legislation through Parliament, Shelley could only lament the nation's misfortune. "You will have heard that the ministers have gained a victory," Shelley informed Byron on April 23, "which has not been disturbed by a single murmur; if I except those of famine, which they have troops of hireling soldiers to repress."

Summer passed peacefully, although Shelley complained about the cold, wet weather in July. "At present we have little else than clouds and rain," he wrote to a friend in London. "We have a water chariot drawn by the oursers of Notus, but except some fine warm days . . . which lost their way in this abominable climate as they were crossing from Italy to Greece, it has been of little use to us. I hope you coming will be like that of Alcuone in storms, to this wintry season."

A month later, a London firm agreed to publish Mary Shelley's novel. The first printing of *Frankenstein*—a total of 500 copies—was scheduled for early 1818.

WHILE Tambora's stratospheric aerosol cloud had its greatest impact on the Atlantic climate during the year 1816, the thin veil of sulfuric acid droplets continued to affect weather patterns for at least another two years. The delayed effect of the aerosol on the North Atlantic Oscillation—due to tropical latitudes cooling more than the poles—continued during the winter of 1816–17. The positive phase of the Oscillation persisted throughout the season, with strong westerly winds bringing warm and moist air from the Atlantic to western and central Europe. This warm air was able to overcome the cooling from the aerosol cloud reflecting sunlight, such that the winter was one or two degrees Fahrenheit milder than normal throughout Europe. By this point, the amount of sulfuric acid in the stratosphere was beginning to decline. More than eighteen months after the eruption, gravity was beginning to take its toll on the tiny droplets. Chance collisions between the droplets caused them to coagulate into larger, heavier droplets that were more quickly extracted from the stratosphere. Occasionally, intense storm systems—such as those that produced colored snows across central Europe in the winter of 1815–16—were able to penetrate into the stratosphere and drag a fraction of the cloud into the troposphere and, from there, to the surface. Droplet by droplet, the aerosol cloud lost its coherence; by the end of 1817, very little of it remained.

Just as the land and ocean—through their reservoirs of heat—delayed the cooling effect of the aerosol cloud on global temperatures, they also opposed the climate's return towards its original, pre-Tambora balance of energies. Even though the aerosol cloud was dwindling by the summer of 1817, Europe experienced yet another abnormally cold season. The effect was not as dramatic as in 1816, though, due to the dissipating stratospheric veil: The summer of 1817 was only two or three degrees Fahrenheit cooler than normal, compared to the five- or six-degree cooling which Europe witnessed in 1816. Over the next year, as the aerosol cloud faded, the soil and oceans gradually absorbed and stored heat. After a final particularly cold winter across northern Europe and Scandinavia in 1817–18, the summer of 1818 saw temperatures on both sides of the Atlantic return to something approaching normal.

EPILOGUE

THE ERUPTION OF Mount Tambora disarranged weather patterns in Asia as well, although the scarcity of available contemporary records makes a detailed analysis difficult. In India, unusually low temperatures greatly reduced the summer monsoon rains, which typically arrive in June, last through September, and provide up to ninety percent of the annual rainfall. The monsoon winds that bring warm, moist air from the equatorial Indian Ocean to India arise from the temperature difference between the ocean and the subcontinent: The land warms more quickly than the ocean under the summer sun, when it shines directly overhead at India's latitude. The veil of stratospheric sulfuric acid from Tambora cooled land temperatures around the world much more than ocean temperatures, at least initially. This would have prevented the Indian landmass from heating up in the spring and summer of 1816, reducing the temperature contrast between the land and the ocean. While there are no accessible records of Indian land temperatures that summer, it is likely that the cooling from Tambora weakened the monsoon winds and led to much less precipitation than normal.

Much of the subcontinent remained parched until the end of the summer, although southern India—which is often wet when the rest of India is dry, and vice versa—experienced several torrential late-season downpours. As harvests failed, a combination of famine, internal migration, and densely crowded settlements produced the world's first cholera pandemic. Although a disease similar to cholera had long plagued India (and Indonesia), in the winter of 1816–17 the illness broke out of northeastern Bengal—where it killed 10,000 people in the course of several weeks—and spread rapidly across the peninsula. British troops carried the disease into Nepal, whence it spread into Thailand, the Philippines, Borneo, China, and Japan. By 1821 it had reached southern Iran; the following year it entered Syria. When the pandemic finally subsided, hundreds of thousands of people had died.

China also experienced unseasonably frigid weather in the summer of 1816. Summer snows struck southeastern China and Taiwan, and destroyed much of the rice crop in China's southern provinces. The East Asian monsoon, too, was disrupted, leading to floods in the Yangtze Valley in southern China but extreme drought in the north. Like its counterpart in India, the East Asian monsoon winds rely upon the land-ocean temperature contrast. Under normal conditions, the rains spread from south to north as the summer progresses, drawn across China and towards Japan and Korea by the warm Asian landmass. Substantially colder than normal land temperatures in 1816 might have led to the monsoon stagnating in southern China, which would explain the heavy rains there and the dearth of precipitation further north.

JAMES Madison spent his retirement at Montpelier, supervising the operations of his plantation while also serving as rector (succeeding Jefferson) and a member of the Board of Visitors of the University of Virginia. In 1819, he helped found the American Colonization Society, dedicated to the gradual abolition of slavery and the return of freed slaves to Africa. Ten years later, at the age of seventy-eight, Madison was elected a delegate to the Virginia Constitutional Convention. He died at Montpelier in June 1836.

From his home at Monticello, Thomas Jefferson completed his plans for the University of Virginia, chartered by the state legislature in 1819. Jefferson designed most of the university's buildings and supervised its construction, selected its faculty, and oversaw the acquisition of books for its library. Troubled by the growing rift between North and South over the issue of slavery, and fearful of the expanding power of the presidency, Jefferson sought solace in the visits of friends and family to Monticello. His generosity and lavish entertainments forced him to mortgage nearly everything he owned—including most of his remaining slaves—and he died deeply in debt on July 4, 1826.

JAMES Monroe ran for reelection in 1820. The Federalist Party, by now virtually extinct, did not bother to nominate anyone to run against him. The final electoral vote was 231 to 1. The only elector to vote against Monroe was Governor William Plumer of New Hampshire.

THE legal struggle between the trustees of Dartmouth College and the New Hampshire state legislature reached the United States Supreme Court in 1819. By a vote of 6 to 1, the court sided with the trustees. The majority decision, written by Chief Justice John Marshall, argued that the college's charter from the king remained a valid contract, and that the state could not impair the obligation of the contract without violating the United States Constitution. The decision proved a boon to the nation's business community by rendering corporations and institutions of higher learning less vulnerable to state interference.

* * *

Lᴏʀᴅ Byron remained in Italy, writing poetry (including "Don Juan" and the fourth canto of "Childe Harold's Pilgrimage") and several plays. In the summer of 1823 he traveled to Greece to help the Greeks in their fight to gain independence from the Ottoman Empire. He contracted a fever in February 1824 which worsened after Byron was caught in a cold, drenching rain in early April. He died at Missolonghi on April 19, at the age of thirty-six.

Percy Bysshe Shelley and his wife, Mary, left England in 1818—along with Claire Clairmont and Alba—and settled in Italy, where they renewed their acquaintance with Lord Byron. Over the following four years, Shelley composed most of his major works, including *Prometheus Unbound*. Nevertheless, Shelley sank into a gradually deepening state of depression, caused in part by the deaths of his son William and his youngest child, Clara. On July 8, 1822, Shelley drowned when a sudden storm struck as he was sailing in the schooner *Don Juan* from Leghorn to La Spezia. He was only twenty-nine years old.

Mary Shelley returned to England in the fall of 1823 with her only surviving child, Percy. She continued to write, publishing several more novels before turning to short stories, essays, biographies, reviews, and travel writing. She also oversaw the publication of several volumes of her late husband's poems and wrote extensive notes for some of them. She died of a brain tumor in February 1851.

Kɪɴɢ Louis XVIII of France remained in power until his death in 1824. Following the death of his brother, the Ultra-Royalist Duc de Berry, Louis' government became increasingly dominated by reactionaries as the king grew isolated from dissenting opinions. "History will state that Louis XVIII was a most liberal monarch reigning with great mildness and justice to his end," wrote King Leopold I of Belgium more than a decade later. But in reality, Leopold added, "Louis XVIII was a clever, hard-hearted man, shackled by no principle, very proud and false."

Madame de Staël continued to encourage opposition to the Bourbon dynasty until she suffered a stroke in the summer of 1817 and died in Paris on July 14—Bastille Day.

THE British economy gradually revived as harvests improved after the fall of 1817. Nevertheless, Lord Liverpool's government maintained its repressive policy against popular meetings in favor of parliamentary reform, although Parliament did repeal the suspension of habeas corpus in 1818. In August 1819, approximately 60,000 demonstrators gathered in St. Peter's Fields in Manchester to hear Henry Hunt speak in favor of reform. When local magistrates and the militia attempted to seize Hunt, the crowd resisted; the militia, aided by mounted troops, then attacked the protestors, killing eleven and wounding nearly 400 more. Several months later, Parliament passed another series of repressive measures known as the Six Acts. When discontent rose in Ireland in 1822, the British government reacted with similarly harsh legislation.

Meanwhile, a small group of extremists hatched a plot to assassinate the entire Cabinet—to behead them as they dined together—along with George IV (the former Prince Regent who had succeeded to the throne following George III's death on January 31, 1820) and then seize the Tower of London, with its storehouse of weapons, and establish a provisional government. The plan was betrayed to the authorities by one of Sidmouth's spies, who clearly had played a major role in organizing the plot in the first place. Five of the conspirators were hanged, and five more were transported.

Liverpool remained in office until he suffered a paralytic stroke in February 1827. He stepped down two months later, and died on December 4, 1828.

Sɪʀ Robert Peel resigned as Chief Secretary of Ireland in 1818 and spent the next four years out of office. In 1822, he accepted the post of home secretary, and spent much of the next six years reforming the British legal code—repealing over 250 laws he considered outdated, and reducing substantially the number of offenses that carried the death penalty. In 1829 he organized the Metropolitan Police Force for the city of London, who were thenceforth known familiarly (and not always in a complimentary sense) as "Bobbies" or "Peelers."

While the Whig Party held power for much of the 1830s, Peel served briefly as prime minister from December 1834–April 1835, and then returned to office in 1841. Determined to put a more humane face on the Tory Party, Peel sponsored legislation to establish minimum safety standards in dangerous industries, to prohibit the employment of women and children in underground mines, and to limit the working hours of women and children in factories. When the Great Famine struck Ireland in 1845, Peel initially failed to grasp the severity of the crisis; subsequently, however, he forced through Parliament—against the wishes of a majority of his own party—a bill to repeal the Corn Laws, in part to provide cheaper food to the starving Irish. The measure split the Conservative Party, and led to Peel's resignation in 1846. He continued to serve in Parliament for four more years, until he suffered fatal injuries when his horse stumbled and fell on top of him. He died on July 2, 1850.

Joseph Smith and his family continued to live and farm in the Palmyra area as religious enthusiasm steadily escalated throughout upstate New York. In 1820, fourteen-year-old Joseph Jr. claimed that God and Jesus had appeared to him while he was praying to warn him that none of the Christian churches that currently existed represented the true church. Three years later, Joseph purportedly received the first of numerous visitations from the angel Moroni, who told him of ancient records written on golden plates and buried in a hill several miles from the Smith farm. Those records, which Moroni said were the history of the peoples who had lived in North America two thousand years earlier, along with the "everlasting Gospel" delivered to those people, were subsequently translated by Joseph and published as *The Book of Mormon*. In 1830, Joseph Smith Jr. organized the Church of Jesus Christ of Latter-day Saints, popularly known as the Mormon Church.

Sɪʀ Thomas Stamford Raffles left England in November 1817 as the newly appointed lieutenant-governor of Sumatra. At the behest of the governor general of India, Lord Hastings, Raffles began searching for a suitable location for a fortified port somewhere east of the Straits of Malacca, to extend British influence in the region and protect the growing British trade with China. At the end of January, 1819, he landed on the island of Singapore, and negotiated a treaty with its rulers to establish a British trading mission on the sparsely settled island.

Over the next five years, Raffles' relations with the East India Company deteriorated once again, and he returned to England in declining health in February 1824. Much of his remaining years were spent organizing the Zoological Society of London and founding the London Zoo. He died of a brain tumor on July 5, 1826.

Iɴ the summer of 1883, volcanic ash again darkened the skies over Indonesia. The island of Krakatoa, essentially one large volcano, erupted periodically between May and August. The cataclysmic final explosion on August 27 was heard in Perth, southwestern Australia, more than 2,200 miles away, where—repeating Raffles' mistake of nearly 70 years prior—the residents assumed the sound to be cannonfire. Krakatoa produced less ash and sulfur dioxide than Tambora, but the plumes still penetrated into the stratosphere, cooling global temperatures by approximately two degrees until 1887.

As the temperatures fell, a wide range of scientific theories again emerged to account for the changing climate. In the decades since Tambora, however, the invention and proliferation of the telegraph had allowed news to travel much faster and farther. The destruction caused by Krakatoa's eruption—more than 35,000 died—made headlines around the world. Meteorologists took notice of the coincidence of the eruption and the cooling, but found themselves confronted by the same lack of data as their colleagues in 1816. Although the telegraph had made it possible for scientists to collect observations quickly, few weather stations reported data regularly for any length of time. And with only one eruption to study, scientists could not be certain that the volcanic ash and dust had caused the cooler temperatures.

Two more major eruptions followed Krakatoa relatively quickly: Santa Maria in Guatemala in 1902 and Novarupta in southern Alaska in 1912. The American meteorologist William Humphreys gathered temperature observations from immediately before and after each eruption, as well as data from after Krakatoa. He published a paper on his findings in 1913 that was one of the first to use observations and theories, instead of speculation, to demonstrate that volcanic dust and ash cooled the climate. Humphreys went further, however, arguing that large volcanic eruptions could initiate ice ages. Scientists now know that ice ages, which develop over millennia, are fundamentally the result of changes in Earth's orbit around the sun, but Humphreys' basic thesis linking rapid cooling to volcanic eruptions proved accurate.

Many climate scientists did not accept Humphreys' theory

immediately. While his temperature records were among the best available, they were patchy in many regions of the world and covered only three eruptions. A dearth of volcanic activity through the middle of the twentieth century provided few opportunities to collect supporting evidence; there were no eruptions to rival Krakatoa between 1912 (Novarupta) and 1991 (Pinatubo in Indonesia). Meteorologists tried to use industrial pollution as a surrogate for volcanic dust, but could not agree on whether pollution cooled the climate by reflecting sunlight or warmed it by trapping the heat radiating from cities. (The former outweighs the latter.) A lack of long-term, reliable observations again proved a stumbling block. Even as recently as 1977, a senior researcher in the field, Professor Sean Twomey, wrote that "the time and energy put into discussion perhaps outweigh the time and energy which have been put into measurements."

With no volcanoes to study and at a roadblock with industrial pollution, scientists turned to the only other source of energy powerful enough to force particles into the stratosphere: nuclear bombs. By monitoring changes in sunlight after the nuclear-weapons tests of the 1950s, meteorologists discovered that the fine dust driven into the stratosphere could remain there and reflect sunlight for years. Meanwhile, newly available computer simulations demonstrated that the volcanic sulfuric acid droplets were likely of a similar size to those dust particles. Armed with this information and a growing database of global temperature records, scientists closely monitored two relatively minor eruptions—Mount Agung (Indonesia) in 1963 and Mount St. Helens (Washington State) in 1980—and confirmed their hypotheses from the nuclear-weapons tests: Volcanic eruptions caused the climate to cool by several degrees for two or three years. As scientists worked through the history of volcanic eruptions, they were finally able to conclusively link the stratospheric aerosol veil from Mount Tambora to the Year Without a Summer.

*   *   *

MOUNT Tambora erupted again in 1819, albeit on a much smaller scale, registering only a 2 on the Volcanic Explosivity Index. Subsequently it has erupted twice more, once sometime between 1847 and 1913 (the exact date is uncertain, since this and the following eruption were confined to the caldera) and again in 1967. It is still active. A series of earthquakes on Sumbawa in 2011 led the government of Indonesia to warn that Mount Tambora may be preparing to erupt once more, although experts believe it very unlikely that any explosion would approach the magnitude of the volcano's eruption in April 1815.

ACKNOWLEDGMENTS

This book originated with a suggestion by our editor, Daniela Rapp, whose patient guidance and insights shepherded the manuscript to completion. Our agent and my longtime friend, Daniel Bial, provided essential support and his usual astute advice. I would also like to thank my research assistants, Anna Kearns, Miliana Budimirovic, and Julia Benjamin; Meg Grotti and the cheerfully helpful staff of the Morris Library at the University of Delaware; and Pat Garnett and the equally generous staff at the Albin O. Kuhn Library of the University of Maryland, Baltimore County. Any errors in the manuscript belong to Nick and myself alone.

My deepest gratitude, of course, goes to my family, without whom I could never have brought this book home.

—WILL KLINGAMAN

I would like to thank Dr. Bethan Harris of the Department of Meteorology, University of Reading, who pointed me in the direction of some very useful information on the eruption of Tambora and its effects on global climate. I should also thank Mrs. Catherine Turner, the Department of Meteorology librarian, who helped locate resources at the British Library. The staff at the British Library also provided assistance in locating the letters from Robert Peel to Lord Liverpool and Lord Sidmouth.

—NICK KLINGAMAN

NOTES

The first citation of a published source always includes an abbreviated title; subsequent citations employ only the author's last name, unless we have used more than one book by that author.

1. THE VOLCANO

1. "a firing of cannon": *Asiatic Journal*, August 1816, p. 165.
2. "several very distinct reports . . .": Raffles, *Memoirs*, vol. 1, p. 279.
2. "do as much good": Egerton, *Raffles*, p. 59.
3. "We had a most extensive . . .": ibid., pp. 127–8.
3. "the sound appeared . . .": Raffles, *History*, p. 30.
4. "seemed to forebode . . .": ibid.
4. "extremely irritable . . .": MacKenzie, *Escape*, p. 64.
4. "fatigue the senses . . .": ibid., p. 65.
5. "Taking towns at his liking . . .": Moore, *Letters*, p. 207.
5. "I want less . . .": Coote, *Napoleon*, p. 158.
5. "an enemy and disturber . . .": MacKenzie, p. 255.
5. "the sovereigns of Europe would be . . .": ibid., p. 254.
6. "We are really going on . . .": ibid., p. 198.
6. "a man fit only to cook . . .": *National Register*, May 18, 1816.
6. "the Parisians love for . . .": Coote, p. 84.
7. "the maintenance of an . . .": Thompson, *Letters*, p. 307.
7. "the need for rest . . .": Coote, p. 68.
7. "Our objective is to make sure . . .": MacKenzie, p. 10.

7. "a troubled confused . . .": Raffles, *Memoirs*, vol. 1, p. 283.
8. "to find it . . .": *Asiatic Journal*, August 1816, p. 161.
9. "a heavy mortar fired . . .": *Asiatic Journal*, August 1816, p. 166.
9. "Towards morning the reports . . .": ibid., p. 165.
9. "By this time . . .": ibid.
9. "By ten it was . . .": ibid.
10. "The ashes now began . . .": ibid., p. 166.
10. "perfect impalpable powder . . .": ibid.
10. "The darkness was so profound . . .": ibid.
10. "the atmosphere still continued . . .": ibid.
10. "utter darkness": Raffles, *Memoirs*, vol. I., p. 273.
10. "covered with ashes . . .": ibid., p. 274.
11. "Our chiefs here . . .": *Asiatic Journal*, August 1816, p. 164.
11. "supernatural artillery": Raffles, *Memoirs*, vol. I, p. 270.
11. "neither read nor write . . .": ibid.
11. "the trees also were . . .": ibid., p. 271.
11. "a tremulous motion . . .": Oppenheimer, "Consequences," p. 238.
11. "showers of ashes . . .": Raffles, *History*, p. 25.
12. "completely beaten down . . .": *Asiatic Journal*, August 1816, p. 166.
13. "The trees and herbage . . .": Raffles, *Memoirs*, vol. I., p. 284.
13. "the cattle and inhabitants . . .": *Asiatic Journal*, October 1816, p. 422.
14. "the whole of his country . . .": *Asiatic Journal*, August 1816, p. 167.
15. "the extreme misery to which . . .": Raffles, *History*, p. 27.

2. PORTENTS

17. "the heaviest snow ever . . .": *Niles' Weekly Register*, May 18, 1816.
17. "a greater quantity of snow . . .": *National Register*, May 11, 1816.
17. "was of a red and . . .": *Niles' Weekly Register*, May 18, 1816.
17. "something extraordinary has taken place . . .": *National Register*, May 11, 1816.
18. "the snow was not white . . .": Post, *Subsistence Crisis*, p. 22.
18. "It was brick red and . . .": Gibb, *Showers*, p. 33.
18. "the cause of this universal fog . . .": Franklin, "Meteorological Imaginations," pp. 373–77.
20. "the sky exhibited in places . . .": Symonds, *Eruption*, p. 394.
21. "The evening twilight . . .": ibid.
22. "We are, happily, at peace . . .": Cunningham, *Circular Letters*, p. 973.
23. "Go into the interior . . .": Wood, *Empire*, p. 705.
26. "Among the most auspicious . . .": Cunningham, p. 980.

27. "a spider, having parts . . .": *Maryland Gazette*, May 12, 1816.

27. "its general appearance . . .": *Niles' Weekly Register*, May 4, 1816.

27. "chasms in the [sun's] atmosphere . . .": *North American Review*, May 1816, p. 39.

27. "burning mountains of immense . . .": *Farmer's Cabinet*, May 11, 1816.

28. "a kind of excavation . . .": ibid.

28. "no less a miracle . . .": *Gentleman's Magazine*, February 1817, p. 110.

28. "the Sun has cast forth . . .": Chambersburg *Democratic Republican*, June 3, 1816.

29. "a very fine dust . . .": Skeen, *America Rising*, p. 10.

29. "It had nothing of the . . .": Bate, *Song*, p. 97.

29. "calamitous sign . . .": Vail, "Bright Sun," p. 186.

29. "the sun may, in time . . .": *Quarterly Journal of Science and the Arts*, vol. 2, 1817, p. 420.

29. "the observation . . . that the light . . .": *North American Review*, July 1816, p. 285.

30. "The winter was open . . .": Ludlum, *Vermont Weather*, pp. 88–9.

30. "most persons allowed their fires . . .": Schlegel, "The Year," p. 1.

30. "January was mild . . .": *Connecticut Courant*, October 19, 1850.

30. "shivering and shrinking . . .": Ford, *Writings, Jefferson to Charles Thomson*, January 9, 1816, p. 6.

30. "The first of March . . .": Ludlum, *Vermont Weather*, p. 89.

33. "Our own Winters are . . .": Laskin, *Braving*, p. 84.

33. "would be Turned into Ice . . .": ibid., p. 84.

33. "Both heats and colds . . .": Jefferson, *Notes*, p. 80.

34. "it is a common opinion . . .": Ludlum, *Early American Winters*, p. 214.

34. "in the cultivated part . . .": Laskin, p. 85.

34. "It is a popular opinion . . .": Webster, *Papers*, p. 119.

35. "I would enquire . . .": Fleming, *Meteorology*, p. 5.

35. "Few, if any, registers . . .": Laskin, p. 87.

36. "heathen wilderness . . .": ibid., p. 66.

37. "Of all the scenes . . .": Crevecoeur, *Sketches*, pp. 39–40.

38. "crops were destroyed by . . .": Ludlum, *Vermont Weather*, p. 87.

38. "The country has all the appearance . . .": *American Beacon*, May 9, 1816.

38. "the country in many places . . .": *National Register*, May 18, 1816.

39. "a temperature extraordinary . . .": *American Beacon*, May 9, 1816.

40. "We never experienced . . .": *Aberdeen Journal*, June 26, 1816.

40. "stormy in the extreme . . .": *Aberdeen Journal*, June 26, 1816.

40. "Even on the coast . . .": *Aberdeen Journal*, June 26, 1816.
40. "Throughout the whole of this month . . .": *Aberdeen Journal*, June 26, 1816.
41. "a considerable quantity of snow": *Gentleman's Magazine*, August 1816, p. 115.
41. "Never was there . . .": Spater, *Cobbett*, p. 346.
41. "The extreme changeableness . . .": *Royal Cornwall Gazette*, July 6, 1816.
42. "It is the opinion of the . . .": *Gentleman's Magazine*, January 1816.
43. "The nation was in the condition . . .": Reid, *Durham*, p. 97.
44. "The main root of the . . .": *Niles' Weekly Register*, May 18, 1816.
44. "Economy is more the order . . .": Hinde, *Castlereagh*, p. 235.
44. "Endless debates upon . . .": Reid, *Durham*, p. 92.
44. "one of the most . . .": ibid.
44. "With Napoléon safely locked away . . .": Hinde, p. 237.
45. "drain the people of England . . ." Hunt, *Memoirs*, III, p. 321.

3. COLD FRONTS

48. "large quantities of snow": *Charleston City Gazette*, June 5, 1816.
48. "the unusual long spell . . .": *New York Evening Post*, April 25, 1816.
48. "the ground was covered . . .": *Franklin Herald*, June 4, 1816.
49. "heavy black frost": Harrington, *Year Without*, p. 125.
49. "ploughing up and . . .": *National Register*, May 18, 1816.
49. "The season continues . . .": *New England Palladium*, June 4, 1816.
49. "The last spring and . . .": *New England Palladium*, June 14, 1816.
49. "the season has been . . .": Thomas, *Travels*, p. 1.
50. "the morning was rainy . . .": ibid., p. 10.
50. "so damp and chill . . .": ibid., p. 16.
50. "was so cold that we shivered . . .": ibid.
50. "wrapt in the drapery . . .": ibid., p. 29.
50. "This morning was very . . .": ibid., p. 32.
50. "a severe frost": ibid., p. 35.
50. "the clouds rolled on . . .": ibid., p. 39.
50. "When the last of May . . .": Schlegel, p. 1.
50. "The whole of the month . . .": Hoyt, "Cold Summer," p. 119.
50. "Everybody complains . . .": *Chambersburg Democratic Republican*, June 3, 1816.
51. "a crowned Jacobin . . .": Lucas-Dubreton, *Restoration*, p. 35.
52. "There are continual reports . . .": Frye, *After Waterloo*, p. 151.
53. "The uneasiness of the court . . .": *National Register*, July 13, 1816.

53. "There was a strange feeling . . .": *National Register*, July 13, 1816.

53. "The manners of the French . . .": Jones, *Letters of Mary Shelley*, p. 9.

55. "discontent and sullenness": Jones, *Letters of Percy Shelley*, p. 347.

55. "The spring, as the inhabitants . . .": ibid., p. 18.

55. "Never was scene more . . .": ibid.

55. "Unfortunately, an almost perpetual . . .": ibid., p. 19.

56. "hot and sultry . . .": *Albany Daily Advertiser*, June 19, 1816.

56. "the warmest day that . . .": *Vermont Mirror*, June 12, 1816.

56. "The mild influence of . . .": *National Aegis*, June 12, 1816.

56. "The night was so warm . . .": *Newburyport Herald*, June 14, 1816.

58. "the most distant apparently . . .": *Quebec Gazette*, June 13, 1816.

58. "and were to be met with . . .": *Quebec Gazette*, June 13, 1816.

58. "the roofs of the houses . . .": *Quebec Gazette*, June 13, 1816.

58. "the whole of the surrounding country . . .": *Quebec Gazette*, June 13, 1816.

59. "driving before it an immense . . .": *Quebec Gazette*, June 13, 1816.

59. "the frost was sharp . . .": *Albany Daily Advertiser*, June 19, 1816.

59. "Early this morning . . .": *Montreal Herald*, June 8, 1816.

59. "Probably no one living . . .": Danville *North Star*, June 15, 1816.

59. "a novel spectacle . . .": *Rutland Herald*, June 12, 1816.

60. "you could pick up . . .": Mussey, "Yankee Chills," p. 436.

60. "it had rained much . . .": Ludlum, *Early American Winters*, p. 190.

60. "in beautiful large flakes . . .": *Newburyport Herald*, June 14, 1816.

60. "a violent and heavy storm . . .": *Connecticut Courant*, June 25, 1816.

61. "The wind blew a gale . . .": Emery, *Reminiscences*, p. 289.

61. "our teeth fairly chattered . . .": ibid., p. 289.

61. "we shivered round . . .": ibid.

61. "as severe from half an hour . . .": *Albany Argus*, June 11, 1816.

61. "a considerable quantity of snow . . .": Ludlum, *Early American Winters*, p. 191.

61. "on the mountain to the west . . .": *North American Review*, May 1817, p. 154.

61. "The situation here . . .": *Albany Daily Advertiser*, June 7, 1816.

62. "The surface of the ground . . .": Ludlum, *Early American Winters*, p. 190.

62. "I well remember the . . .": Stommel, "The Year," p. 176.

62. "In the evening, the atmosphere . . .": *Connecticut Courant*, June 25, 1816.

62. "Moist earth was frozen . . .": *North American Review*, May 1817, p. 154.

63. "This morning, the 7th of June . . .": *Columbian*, June 7, 1816.

63. "The awful scene continued . . .": Ludlum, *Early American*, p. 190.

63. "Still uncomfortably cold . . .": *Danville North Star*, June 15, 1816.

63. "6th, snowed in considerable . . .": Ludlum, *Early American*, p. 192.

63. "large icicles pending . . .": *Salem Gazette*, June 11, 1816.

63. "snow fell in this town . . .": *Columbian Centinel*, June 12, 1816.

64. "I can find no person . . .": *Albany Daily Advertiser*, July 3, 1816.

64. "The weather was more severe . . .": *Danville North Star*, June 15, 1816.

64. "but still frost and ice . . .": *Connecticut Courant*, June 25, 1816.

64. "most severe frost . . .": *Connecticut Courant*, June 25, 1816.

64. "It has frozen very hard . . .": Ludlum, *Early American*, p. 190.

64. "severely cold and . . .": *Vermont Mirror*, June 12, 1816.

64. "the very face of . . .": *Vermont Mirror*, June 12, 1816.

65. "killed to the ground . . .": Stommel, *Volcano*, p. 37.

65. "Another frost, cold . . .": Ludlum, *Early American*, p. 190.

65. "Indian corn, beans . . .": *North American Review*, May 1817, p. 154.

65. "For three days we had . . .": Thomas, p. 53.

65. "but the fruit has been . . .": ibid., p. 82.

65. "We saw neither peaches . . .": ibid., p. 105.

66. "The trees on the sides of the hills . . .": *North American Review*, May 1817, p. 154.

66. "the crops of wheat . . .": *National Aegis*, June 12, 1816.

66. "great damage has been done . . .": *Albany Daily Advertiser*, June 11, 1816.

66. "totally destroyed . . .": *Niles' Weekly Register*, August 10, 1816, p. 385.

66. "a check is given . . .": *Eastern Argus*, June 12, 1816.

66. "In some instances the corn is . . .": *American Advocate*, June 15, 1816.

66. "What is to become . . .": *Connecticut Courant*, June 25, 1816.

67. "the most gloomy apprehensions . . .": *Brattleboro Reporter*, July 17, 1816.

67. "the weather, during the last week . . .": *Albany Argus*, June 11, 1816.

67. "the oldest inhabitants . . .": *Rutland Herald*, June 12, 1816.

67. "never before . . .": *Vermont Mirror*, June 12, 1816.

67. "we are very apt to misrecollect . . .": *Albany Daily Advertiser*, June 19, 1816.

68. "I began these experiments . . .": Fleming, *Meteorology*, p. 6.

69. "the chief object ought to be . . .": Wood, p. 726.

71. "so that we may know . . ." Quoted in Abbe, "History," p. 546.

4. THE HANDWRITING OF GOD

77. "This is an extraordinary spring . . .": *Columbian*, June 7, 1816.

77. "We do not recollect to have witnessed . . .": *American Beacon*, May 9, 1816.

77. "The sun is no doubt . . .": *Brattleboro Reporter*, July 7, 1816.

78. "The alarm from spots . . .": Mussey, p. 437.

78. "We think the alteration . . .": *Niles' Weekly Register*, August 10, 1816, p. 386.

79. "Very cold weather produced . . .": *Brattleboro Reporter*, July 17, 1816.

80. "The word had been given . . .": Latrobe, *Rambler*, p. 102.

80. "a very awful noise . . .": Dow, *Dealings*, p. 155.

80. "At the same time . . .": Johnston, "New Madrid," p. 346.

81. "the earth was horribly torn . . .": Dow, *Dealings*, p. 156.

81. "a feverish excitement": Sanford, *Quest*, p. 109.

81. "It is perfectly understood . . .": *Niles' Weekly Register*, August 10, 1816, p. 386.

82. "the extensive forests . . .": *Daily National Intelligencer*, September 5, 1812, p. 2.

82. "A few years ago . . .": Thomas, p. 58.

83. "a pernicious vapour . . .": ibid., p. 56.

83. "the very handwriting . . .": Laskin, pp. 56–7.

83. "When the Vapours rise . . .": ibid., p. 55.

84. "supplemented rather than replaced . . .": Murphy, "Prodigies," p. 399.

84. "the most general . . .": Saum, *Popular Mood*, p. 9.

84. "All things are known . . .": ibid., p. 3.

84. "The Wheel of Providence . . .": ibid.

84. "The King Providence . . .": ibid., p. 11.

84. "the Lord in his goodness . . .": ibid.

84. "I always consider the settlement . . .": Butterfield, *Diary*, p. 257.

85. "Perhaps we can assign . . .": *Brattleboro Reporter*, July 17, 1816.

85. "Great frost . . .": deBoer, *Volcanoes*, p. 153.

85. "By fasting, humiliation, & prayer . . .": Murphy, p. 403.

85. "The revivals in these years . . .": Hotchkin, *History*, p. 126.

86. "all classes were subjects . . .": ibid., pp. 127–8.

87. "the blaze being so brilliant . . .": Thomas, p. 46.

88. "full-blooded merinos . . .": Fletcher, *Pennsylvania Agriculture*, p. 195.

89. "Gather apples on the . . .": ibid., p. 341.

89. "dark of the moon": ibid.

89. "Hark! I heard the . . .": ibid.

90. "although I made the . . .": ibid., p. 355.

90. "Agriculture is at its . . .": Thomas, p. 48.

90. "truly indicative of . . .": ibid., p. 49.

91. "Often descending in . . .": ibid., p. 59.

91. "The peach, the plumb . . .": ibid.

91. "the character of the present . . .": *Ipswich Journal*, July 6, 1816.

91. "The atmosphere still seems . . .": *Lancaster Gazette*, June 8, 1816.

91. "considerable fall . . .": *Ipswich Journal*, July 6, 1816.

92. "the torrents of rain that have . . .": Paget, *Capel Letters*, p. 163.

92. "France is quite . . .": ibid., pp. 163–4.

92. "all scientists, writers or artists . . .": Lucas-Dubreton, p. 29.

92. "predictable forms of behaviour": Harrington, *Year Without*, p. 360.

93. "The only object visible . . .": *Times* (London), July 7, 1816.

93. "that can repay you for . . .": Jones, *Mary Shelley*, p. 19.

93. "Geneva is far from . . .": Jones, *Percy Shelley*, vol. I, p. 356.

95. "he asked me with an appearance . . .": Priestly, *Prince*, p. 180.

95. "never really knew what . . .": ibid., p. 183.

96. "exactly the kind of person . . .": Florescu, *In Search of*, p. 45.

96. "turned Geneva into an . . .": Edgcumbe, *Diary*, p. 236.

96. "The English in general are . . .": Gooden, *de Staël*, p. 277.

96. "Switzerland is a curst . . .": Florescu, p. 100.

97. "We watch them as . . .": ibid., p. 107.

97. "the nature of the principle . . .": Shelley, *Frankenstein* (1831), p. x.

97. "the component parts of . . .": ibid.

97. "The season was cold . . .": Shelley, *Frankenstein* (1818), p. 2.

98. "the story of a husband . . .": Florescu, p. 113.

98. "These tales excited in us . . .": Shelley, *Frankenstein* (1818), p. 2.

98. "suddenly thought of a woman . . .": Seymour, *Mary Shelley*, p. 157.

99. "manufactured, brought together . . .": Shelley, *Frankenstein* (1831), p. x.

5. DAY AFTER DAY

100. "Death is sweeping his scythe . . .": McCullough, A*dams*, p. 617.

100. "empire of superstition . . .": ibid., p. 619.

101. "still retains the appearance . . .": *Farmer's Cabinet*, July 13, 1816.

101. "Here a pivot . . .": McCullough, p. 618.

101. "my hearing is not quite . . .": Ford, *Writings*, vol. X, p. 6.

101. "In June, instead of . . .": ibid., p. 64.

101. "One could not be . . .": Brant, *Madison*, p. 411.

102. "Louis XVIII had just . . .": ibid., p. 408.

102. "an imbecile tyrant": *Niles' Weekly Register*, November 9, 1816, p. 169.

102. "hoped to hide the . . .": Brant, p. 409.

103. "A ruler more respected . . .": ibid., p. 407.

103. "He gave to this day . . .": *Richmond Enquirer*, July 13, 1816.

103. "With it, there is strength . . .": ibid.

103. "They have warred . . .": ibid.

103. "degraded and abject . . .": ibid.

103. "sinking back into . . .": *National Register*, July 6, 1816, p. 1.

103. "grinding her subjects . . .": ibid.

104. "sultry hot weather": Mussey, p. 437.

104. "a body could not feel . . .": ibid., p. 438.

104. "the wind was N. West . . .": *Middlesex Gazette*, August 15, 1816.

104. "so cold as to render . . .": ibid.

104. "Our climate is far from . . .": *Richmond Enquirer*, July 13, 1816.

104. "frozen down, about . . .": Mussey, p. 438.

104. "in consequence of the backwardness . . .": *Farmer's Cabinet*, July 27, 1816.

105. "the most gloomy apprehensions . . .": *Brattleboro Reporter*, July 17, 1816.

105. "Season very unpromising . . .": Hoyt, p. 121.

105. "fears of a general . . .": ibid., p. 122.

105. "the effects of an atmosphere . . .": *Richmond Enquirer*, July 13, 1816.

105. "and there was a considerable space . . .": *Stockbridge Star*, July 18, 1816.

106. "we have had several days . . .": *Farmer's Cabinet*, July 27, 1816.

106. "Think I never saw . . .": Mussey, p. 438.

106. "The possession of Java . . .": Egerton, p. 113.

106. "cannot longer be . . .": ibid., p. 126.

107. "Anxiety soon pulls a man . . .": ibid., p. 129.

108. "Although I am considerably . . .": ibid., p. 131.

108. "and for the remedy . . .": Adams, *Memoirs*, III, p. 382.

108. "the distresses of some classes . . .": ibid., p. 383.

108. "the miserable state of things . . .": *Daily National Intelligencer*, Sept. 13, 1816.

109. "Willing to work . . .": Martineau, *History*, p. 53.

109. "with the most perfect . . .": ibid.

109. "The season has been so unusually . . .": Adams, p. 405.

109. "I have not yet ventured . . .": ibid.

112. "The continuance of the present . . .": *Times* (London), July 20, 1816.

112. "Such an inclement summer . . .": ibid.

112. "the quantity of fine Wheat . . .": *Times* (London), July 27, 1816.

112. "Melancholy accounts have been . . .": *Norfolk Chronicle*, July 20, 1816.

112. "An indescribable misery . . .": *Times* (London), August 2, 1816.

113. "to the almost . . .": *Times* (London), July 13, 1816.

113. "In every part . . .": ibid.

113. "Our rich grass lands . . .": ibid.

113. "the grass which was cut . . .": ibid.

113. "Even if the weather were . . .": ibid.

113. "We continue to receive . . .": *Times* (London), July 24, 1816.

114. "continual rains, torrents . . .": *Times* (London), July 22, 1816.

114. "The hopes of a very fine harvest . . .": ibid.

114. "the country was flooded . . .": Edgcumbe, p. 215.

114. "the whole country . . .": ibid., p. 222.

114. "the severity of the present season . . .": *Times* (London), July 24, 1816.

115. "the harvest, which has been . . .": *Times* (London), July 27, 1816.

115. "an unexampled dearth": *National Register*, July 13, 1816.

115. "does not give any . . .": *Times* (London), July 27, 1816.

115. "All the fine plain . . .": *Times* (London), July 24, 1816.

115. "completely destroyed the hopes . . .": *Times* (London), July 22, 1816.

115. "the churches and . . .": Adams, p. 405.

115. "offered up in the churches . . .": *Times* (London), July 20, 1816.

116. "a mad Italian prophet": *Times* (London), July 22, 1816.

116. "and those who escaped . . .": ibid.

116. "Old women have taken . . .": *Times* (London), July 13, 1816.

116. "to prepare themselves . . .": ibid.

116. "the weather was gloomy . . .": *Times* (London), July 23, 1816.

116. "Suddenly cries, groans . . .": *Times* (London), July 23, 1816.

117. "an enormous mass of clouds . . .": *Gentleman's Magazine*, July 1816, p. 72.

117. "In France as well . . .": *Times* (London), July 23, 1816.

117. "added to the severe distress . . .": *Times* (London), July 20, 1816.

117. "fairly frightened some of our . . .": *The Atheneum*, I, 1817, p. 37.

117. "outrageous fooleries . . .": Vail, "Bright Sun," p. 185.

117. "the multitude are . . .": ibid., p. 186.

117. "the Italian mountebanks": *Times* (London), July 29, 1816.

117. "not unconnected with . . .": Vail, p. 186.

117. "the end of the world . . .": *Times* (London), July 13, 1816.

118. "this end of the World Weather . . .": Vail, p. 188.

118. "in a fit of . . .": Adams, p. 405.

118. "Another wet morning . . .": Vail, p. 188.

118. "a dense whitish cloud . . .": *Gentleman's Magazine*, September 16, 1816, p. 173.

119. "The next year . . .": Huntington, "Eighteen Hundred," p. 94.

119. "This was enough . . .": ibid.

120. "unusual excitement on the . . .": Backman, "Awakenings," p. 302.

6. THE LOST SUMMER

121. "The month was, without, perhaps . . .": Harington, *The Year*, p. 369.

123. "a single room . . .": Donnelly, *The Land and the People*, p. 24.

123. "rough stones . . .": ibid.

125. "particularly suitable to . . .": Smith, *Wealth of Nations*, p. 185.

127. "had neither the will . . .": Ó Tuathaigh, *Ireland Before*, p. 94.

128. "generated universal amazement": Brynn, *Crown and Castle*, p. 28.

128. "cool and sure intellect . . .": ibid., p. 32.

129. "the country is in a . . .": Gash, p. 176.

129. "intermittent social warfare": ibid., p. 174.

129. "The enormous and overgrown . . .": Parker, *Peel Correspondence*, p. 233.

130. "You can have no idea . . .": ibid., p. 207.

130. "In truth, Ireland is . . .": ibid.

131. "The people see that there is . . .": Crossman, *Politics*, p. 24.

131. "Eight weeks of rain . . .": Harington, p. 369.

132. "We were held prisoners . . .": Sraffa, *Ricardo*, p. 48.

132. "a taste for other objects . . .": ibid.

132. "rouse the Irish . . .": ibid., pp. 48–9.

133. "could not find . . .": *Daily National Intelligencer*, September 12, 1816.

133. "I hear old England . . .": Paget, p. 161.

133. "I should think England . . .": ibid., p. 166.

133. "too small for . . .": ibid., p. 165.

134. "been violent & incessant . . .": ibid., p. 170.

134. "It is being . . .": ibid., pp. 168–9.

134. "the divine beauty": Jones, *Percy Bysshe Shelley*, vol. 1, p. 352.

134. "In my mind . . .": ibid., p. 357.

134. "I never saw a monument . . .": ibid., p. 485.

135. "a town more beautiful . . .": ibid., p. 487.

135. "What a thing it would be . . .": Vail, p. 189.

135. "Really we have had lately . . .": ibid., p. 185.

136. "the general headquarters of . . .": Goodden, *Dangerous Exile*, p. 284.

136. "as at some outlandish beast . . .": ibid., p. 278.

137. "I believe Madame . . .": ibid.

137. "She has made Coppet . . .": Fairweather, *Madame de Staël*, p. 456.

137. "ventured to protect me . . .": Goodden, p. 283.

137. "the cornfields on each side . . .": Feldman, *Journals*, p. 113.

137. "The rain continued . . .": ibid., p. 118.

138. "This is the most desolate . . .": ibid., p. 119.

138. "a Hurricane of Thunder . . .": Paget, pp. 170–1.

138. "but felt the wind . . .": ibid., p. 171.

138. "seasons the most adverse . . .": Ford, p. 51.

138. "On account of the extreme . . .": *Albany Argus*, July 19, 1816.

139. "It is acknowledged on all hands . . .": *Brattleboro Reporter*, July 17, 1816.

139. "rye is said to be . . .": Hoyt, p. 122.

140. "It would astonish the plain . . .": *Maryland Gazette*, May 2, 1816.

140. "commerce is languishing . . .": *Maryland Gazette*, July 4, 1816.

140. "There has never been an instance . . .": Wood, p. 719.

141. "the alien or sedition laws . . .": ibid.

142. "A mind neither rapid . . .": Wilentz, *Rise of American Democracy*, p. 202.

142. "Madison is quick . . .": Skeen, *1816*, p. 212.

142. "stupid and illiterate . . .": ibid., p. 213.

142. "this ridiculous man of straw . . .": *Maryland Gazette*, August 1, 1816.

142. "A belief begins to . . .": Vail, p. 184.

143. "are the conceived cause . . .": Vail, p. 185.

143. "a kind of cone . . .": *Gentleman's Magazine*, February 1817, pp. 109–110.

143. "has occasion'd this change . . .": quoted in Vail, p. 187.

143. "the wheat crop has suffered . . .": *Times* (London), August 6, 1816.

144. "The rain descended . . .": ibid.

144. "I thought I was to leave . . .": ibid.

144. "in such a state . . .": *Gentleman's Magazine*, September 1816, p. 170.

146. "grain, meal of . . .": *Times* (London), August 14, 1816.

147. "And the necessary consequence . . .": *Times* (London), August 12, 1816.

148. "Instead of crowding our ports . . .": Spater, *Cobbett*, vol. II, p. 343.

148. "a circumstance without parallel . . .": Ashton, *Social England*, p. 279.

148. "Scarcely a day passes . . .": Spater, p. 343.

148. "When no other sufficient cause . . .": *Times* (London), August 15, 1816.

149. "the present distressed . . .": *Gentleman's Magazine*, July 1816, p. 149.

149. "No newspaper can describe . . .": Halévy, *Liberal Awakening*, p. 13.

150. "it be impossible for any . . .": *Gentleman's Magazine*, August 1816, p. 174.

150. "It is impossible . . .": *Gentleman's Magazine*, July 1816, p. 76.

7. POVERTY AND MISERY

152. "the crops of wheat and rye . . .": *Niles' Weekly Register*, August 10, 1816, p. 386.

152. "It has been observed . . .": ibid., p. 385.

154. "a very violent storm . . .": *Farmers' Cabinet*, August 24, 1816.

154. "all of a sudden . . .": *Daily National Intelligencer*, September 3, 1816.

155. "Indeed we have the air . . .": ibid.

155. "a temperature, such as is . . .": *Daily National Intelligencer*, August 30, 1816.

155. "frost so severe . . .": Skeen, p. 6.

155. "a hard frost . . .": Stommel, *Volcano Weather*, p. 41.

156. "had perverted the college . . .": Turner, *Ninth State*, p. 295.

158. "August proved to be . . .": Schlegel, p. 1.

159. "August was more cheerless . . .": *Connecticut Courant*, October 19, 1850.

159. "was white with frost . . .": *Connecticut Courant*, October 1, 1816.

159. "The crops will be . . .": ibid.

159. "a circumstance unparalleled . . .": *Daily National Intelligencer*, September 3, 1816.

160. "the oldest inhabitants . . .": Skeen, p. 7.

160. "killed much corn . . .": Ford, *Writings*, p. 64.

160. "Oh! It rains again . . .": Austen, "Jane Austen's Letters," Letter 130, July 9, 1816.

161. "Whoever is fond . . .": Nokes, *Austen*, p. 480.

161. "so much nature . . .": ibid., p. 478.

161. "I could no more . . .": Austen, Letter 126, April 1, 1816.

162. "We were obliged . . .": Austen, Letter 130, July 9, 1816.

162. "it's being bad weather . . .": ibid.

162. "I have often observed . . .": ibid.

162. "She speaks of France . . .": Austen, Letter 133, September 8, 1816.

163. "Weather miserably wet . . .": Bailey, *Standing*, p. 211.

163. "a summary of all that . . .": Wilton, *Turner*, p. 27.

163. "reflect the form and essence . . .": Hamilton, *Turner's Britain*, p. 114.

164. "flat and tame": Edgcumbe, p. 226.

164. "was violently lashing . . .": ibid., p. 224.

165. "It is a country to be in . . .": Fairweather, p. 454.

165. "Lord Byron looked in . . .": Edgcumbe, p. 236.

165. "had washed away . . .": ibid., p. 241.

165. "Alas! All our . . .": ibid., pp. 241–2.

166. "The inundations . . .": ibid., p. 251.

166. "was not only a believer . . .": Feldman, p. 126.

167. "A foolish girl . . .": Marchand, *Byron*, p. 125.

167. "at Geneva, where there was . . .": Vail, p. 184.

8. THE PRICE OF BREAD

169. "The waters are . . .": *Times* (London), August 13, 1816.

169. "Thunderstorms brought forth . . . ": Lederer, "Report of the Famine," p. 1.

170. "The weather continues . . .": *Times* (London), August 8, 1816.

170. "burst its dikes . . . and in consequence . . .": *Times* (London), August 12, 1816.

170. "The increase of waters . . .": *Times* (London), August 17, 1816.

170. "the harvest is completely . . .": *Times* (London), August 14, 1816.

170. "with an immense concourse . . .": *Times* (London), August 9, 1816.
170. "the first crop of hay . . .": *Times* (London), August 13, 1816.
171. "laid on with a . . .": *Times* (London), August 9, 1816.
171. "inflammation of . . .": Adams, p. 434.
171. "a girdle of . . .": ibid.
172. "He said that he hoped . . .": ibid., p. 422.
172. "The wheats everywhere . . .": *Times* (London), August 10, 1816.
172. "The late rains have . . .": ibid.
172. "The weather continues fine . . .": *Times* (London), August 20, 1816.
173. "notwithstanding the lateness . . .": Adams, p. 430.
173. "It is strange that . . .": ibid.
173. "So certain is the result . . .": Skeen, p. 229.
173. "There was no election . . .": ibid.
174. "it may be crossed on foot . . .": *Farmer's Cabinet*, September 7, 1816.
174. "never has there been . . .": *Daily National Intelligencer*, September 7, 1816.
175. "every part of the . . .": *Connecticut Courant*, October 8, 1816.
175. "A failure of the crops . . .": *American Advocate*, September 28, 1816.
175. "corn froze to . . .": Worthen, *Sutton*, p. 222.
175. "It is believed . . ." *Farmer's Cabinet*, September 7, 1816.
176. "the corn is said to be . . .": *Daily National Intelligencer*, September 13, 1816.
176. "July of 1816 . . .": Trigo, "Iberia," p. 102.
177. "in many ways the basest king . . .": Payne, *A History of Spain*, p. 428.
178. "July had only . . .": Trigo, p. 102.
179. "the unusual cool weather . . .": ibid.
179. "I note here as something . . .": ibid., p. 103.
179. "A cold and humid temperature . . .": *Times* (London), September 9, 1816.
180. "The state of the weather . . .": *Times* (London), September 5, 1816.
180. "Such a set of venal . . .": Frye, *After Waterloo*, p. 151.
181. "pure but moderate . . .": de Sauvigny, *Bourbon*, p. 111.
181. "who do not believe . . .": ibid.
181. "They are more considerable . . .": *Times* (London), September 20, 1816.
181. "with its cheeks . . .": *Times* (London), September 20, 1816.
181. "There has not been . . .": Adams, p. 438.
182. "one of the most . . .": *Times* (London), September 5, 1816.

182. "In the orchards and . . .": *Times* (London), September 5, 1816.

182. "Snow in harvest . . .": quoted in *Times* (London), September 3, 1816.

182. "a considerable fall . . .": *Times* (London), September 7, 1816.

182. "somewhat extraordinary . . .": ibid.

182. "the weather here . . .": *Times* (London), September 11, 1816.

182. "Indeed, the whole . . .": *Times* (London), September 5, 1816.

182. "and still the weather . . .": *Times* (London), September 7, 1816.

183. "The gale has abated . . .": Adams, pp. 440–1.

183. "extraordinary visitation . . .": *Times* (London), September 7, 1816.

183. "the hops have been . . .": *Times* (London), September 11, 1816.

183. "the present harvest . . .": ibid.

183. "as large as . . .": *Times* (London), September 16, 1816.

183. "Snow fell once or twice . . .": ibid.

183. "the late and wet . . .": ibid.

184. "the continuance of the cold . . .": Sraffa, pp. 66–7.

184. "has begun about us . . .": ibid., p. 68.

185. "Secrecy is looked upon . . .": *Times* (London), September 23, 1816.

185. "the friends of the Government . . .": Adams, p. 440.

186. "the distresses of the country . . .": *Daily National Intelligencer*, October 29, 1816.

186. "Of distresses, such as now . . .": *Quarterly Review*, October 1816, p. 276.

186. "Every expedient should be used . . .": *Times* (London), September 4, 1816.

186. "the season has been even . . .": *Daily National Intelligencer*, September 10, 1816.

186. "the corn here is . . .": Sraffa, pp. 61–2.

187. "The Swiss are very slow . . .": Feldman, p. 132.

187. "In all that essentially belongs . . .": ibid., pp. 132–3.

187. "Our passage from . . .": Jones, *Percy Shelley*, p. 504.

188. "The harvest is not yet . . .": ibid., pp. 505–6.

188. "Even now we have . . .": Paget, p. 172.

189. "does not answer to . . .": Cochran, "Hobhouse," p. 191.

189. "Grapes appeared many . . .": ibid., p. 194.

189. "the most inclement . . .": *Times* (London), October 3, 1816.

189. "thousands of fathers . . .": ibid.

189. "How cold and triste . . .": Edgcumbe, p. 280.

189. "the weather is dreadfully cold . . .": ibid., p. 283.

190. "incalculable": Post, *Subsistence Crisis*, p. 18.

190. "of the lower class": *Times* (London), September 2, 1816.

190. "This looked as dismal . . .": Edgcumbe, p. 288.
190. "The peasants must . . .": ibid., pp. 291–2.
191. "rendered the seasons . . .": *Daily National Intelligencer*, September 3, 1816.
191. "I recollect no period . . .": Parker, p. 228.
192. "There never was such distress . . .": O'Connell, *Correspondence*, p. 112.
192. "I have had an immense . . .": ibid., p. 116.
192. "Between the fall of prices . . .": ibid., p. 121.
193. "I think it still more . . .": Parker, pp. 233–4.

9. HARVEST

194. "The whole summer has also . . .": *Connecticut Courant*, October 15, 1816.
194. "No prospect of crops . . .": Hoyt, p. 123.
194. "The four greatest frosts known . . .": Mussey, p. 444.
195. "These frosts have destroyed . . .": Ludlum, *Vermont Weather*, p. 98.
195. "Frost killed almost . . .": Hoyt, p. 123.
195. "The ice on the ponds . . .": *Connecticut Courant*, October 29, 1816.
195. "The oldest inhabitants . . .": *Connecticut Courant*, October 15, 1816.
195. "The woods are every where . . .": ibid.
196. "We have seen a gentleman . . .": quoted in *Connecticut Courant*, October 15, 1816.
196. "I fear that the smoke . . .": *Connecticut Courant*, October 15, 1816.
196. "Europeans can have little idea . . .": *Gentleman's Magazine*, November 1816, p. 454.
197. "Never before in this vicinity . . .": Ludlum, *Vermont Weather*, p. 99.
197. "Many parishes in Quebec . . .": *Albany Advertiser*, October 19, 1816.
197. "A fall of snow . . .": *Daily National Intelligencer*, October 29, 1816.
197. "self-sufficiency and survival . . .": Schlegel, p. 1.
198. "people were in . . .": Warren, *Waterford*, p. 128.
198. "It is not probable . . .": *Vermont Journal*, October 7, 1816.
198. "Indian corn on which . . .": Hoyt, p. 123.
199. "of excellent quality": *Connecticut Courant*, October 15, 1816.
199. "there will not be . . .": Stommel, *Volcano Weather*, pp. 74–5.

199. "It would be well . . .": *National Register*, September 14, 1816.

199. "The uncommon failure . . .": Galusha, "Executive Speech," pp. 3–4.

200. "coldness and dryness . . .": Skeen, p. 11.

200. "poison" and "intended by the bounty": Stellhorn, "Governors," p. 95.

200. "cause such restrictions . . .": Skeen, p. 12.

201. "Something, it seemed . . .": Stilwell, *Migration*, pp. 229–230.

201. "an earthly Paradise . . .": Hatcher, *Western Reserve*, p. 71.

202. "rude, steep, and . . .": Mussey, p. 449.

202. "some of the more . . .": Hatcher, p. 73.

202. "consistently advanced . . .": Mussey, p. 449.

203. "a kind of Paradise . . .": ibid.

203. "the number of emigrants . . .": Stommel, *Volcano*, pp. 96–97.

203. "On some days . . .": ibid.

203. "the steam boat moves . . .": *Niles' Weekly Register*, November 16, 1816, p. 191.

203. "about 12 inches deep . . .": *Connecticut Courant*, November 5, 1816.

204. "render the building . . .": Skeen, p. 36.

204. "seemed to enjoy . . .": Rutland, *Madison*, p. 237.

204. "a thousand Faults . . .": Wood, p. 699.

204. "Dreadful weather . . .": O'Connell, *Correspondence*, p. 121.

205. "There is not . . .": *Times* (London), October 19, 1816.

205. "I saw one field . . .": ibid.

205. "Before today . . .": ibid.

205. "All the low grounds . . .": ibid.

205. "I know not whether this . . .": ibid.

205. "to an height unprecedented . . .": ibid.

206. "Yesterday morning it overflowed . . .": ibid.

206. "There is no crop . . .": ibid.

206. "It was a miracle, he said . . .": ibid.

206. "Let no one impose upon you . . .": ibid.

206. "Since the first of this month . . .": Peel to Liverpool, October 9, 1816, Peel Papers, British Library Additional Manuscript 40291.

207. "Distress in this country . . .": Parker, p. 235.

207. "the causes of the disease . . .": ibid., p. 261.

208. "On such occasions . . .": ibid.

208. "No persuasion . . .": ibid.

209. "we also, Madame . . .": *Times* (London), November 11, 1816.

209. "We attach so little . . .": Lewis, "Madame de Staël." Also see Lewis, "Madame de Staël," *Hudson Review*, pp. 416–426.

210. "All of you who . . .": Fairweather, p. 458.

210. "France will be aground . . .": Longford, *Wellington*, p. 36.

210. "general scarcity of . . .": *Times* (London), October 14, 1816.

210. "in a deplorable state": *Times* (London), October 26, 1816.

210. "Nothing but the utmost . . .": *Times* (London), October 25, 1816.

211. "during the rigorous season . . .": *Times* (London), October 17, 1816.

211. "God help me! . . .": Moore, *Byron* (1838), p. 324.

211. "very fine, which is more . . .": Moore, Byron (1830), p. 373.

211. "very intelligent and . . .": ibid., p. 377.

211. "tolerably free from . . .": ibid., p. 383.

212. "in some sort lax . . .": ibid., p. 385.

212. "the oil and wine . . .": Post, *Subsistence Crisis*, p. 24.

213. "most uncommonly": *Times* (London), October 16, 1816.

213. "the immense loss . . .": *Times* (London), November 3, 1816.

213. "inundation of . . .": *Times* (London), November 9, 1816.

214. "from 1601 to 1926 . . .": Post, *Subsistence Crisis*, p. 17.

214. "wines rise daily . . .": *Times* (London), October 11, 1816.

214. "The vintage is next to . . .": *Times* (London), October 16, 1816.

214. "we shall soon have . . .": *Times* (London), October 11, 1816.

214. "Every storm of the past . . ." Post, *Subsistence Crisis*, p. 18.

214. "Fields in the highland . . .": ibid.

214. "immense rains": *Gentleman's Magazine*, November 1816, p. 452.

214. "the vineyard harvest . . .": Trigo, p. 102.

215. "grapes have suffered . . .": ibid.

216. "the house is kept . . .": *Gentleman's Magazine*, November 1816, p. 409.

216. "damp," "discoloured," and "materially injured": *Times* (London), October 23, 1816.

216. "The unpropitious weather . . .": *Times* (London), October 15, 1816.

216. "is as excessive as . . .": ibid.

217. "such heavy rains as . . .": *Times* (London), October 14, 1816.

217. "the crops have sustained . . .": ibid.

217. "immense quantity of rain . . .": ibid.

217. "the largest quantity of sheep . . .": *Times* (London), November 12, 1816.

217. "The pastures were never . . .": *Times* (London), October 17, 1816.

217. "the heavy and . . .": ibid.

218. "seasons of scarcity . . .": *Times* (London), October 14, 1816.

10. EMIGRATION

219. "because he had heard . . .": Nokes, *Austen*, p. 498.

220. "The Revenue looks . . .": Cookson, *Administration*, p. 91. Cookson also provides an excellent insight into the mind-set of the Liverpool administration in pp. 90–129, passim.

221. "a vacuum was . . .": *Quarterly Review*, July 1816, p. 566.

222. "I see no immediate . . .": Cookson, p. 96.

222. "I am sorry that . . .": Sraffa, p. 90.

222. "In this country, it generally happens . . .": *Times* (London), November 7, 1816.

222. "The best way to . . .": *Times* (London), November 27, 1816.

223. "the gin-shop . . .": *Times* (London), October 22, 1816.

223. "labouring poor" and "altering and . . .": *Times* (London), November 27, 1816.

223. "the industrious poor": ibid.

224. "650 men, women . . .": *Times* (London), October 12, 1816.

224. "in a state of . . .": ibid.

224. "had been partially bad . . .": Adams, p. 453.

225. "through the Providence . . .": *Times* (London), October 18, 1816.

225. "a Stormy Winter": Cookson, p. 102.

226. "quietly and peaceably . . .": *Times* (London), November 1, 1816.

226. "a most alarming . . .": *Times* (London), October 22, 1816.

226. "I must also say . . .": ibid.

227. "I am much afraid . . .": ibid.

227. "a circumstance not . . .": *Times* (London), November 16, 1816.

227. "Everything that concerned . . .": Halévy, p. 16.

228. "the colours of the future . . .": ibid.

228. "the British Bastille . . .": *Times* (London), November 16, 1816.

228. "His Majesty was rather . . .": *Times* (London), November 3, 1816.

229. "Tranquility reigns . . .": *Gentleman's Magazine*, November 1816, p. 450.

230. "strictly prohibiting . . .": *Times* (London), November 20, 1816.

231. "a great quantity . . .": *Times* (London), November 25, 1816.

231. "the more surprising as many . . .": ibid.

231. "This day, at one . . .": quoted in *Times* (London), November 21, 1816.

231. "In reviewing the present state . . .": Madison, "Eighth Annual Message," December 3, 1816.

233. "Spanish insolence" and "If it was an . . .": Moser, *Papers of Andrew Jackson* (Jackson to Edward Livingston, October 24, 1816), p. 71.

233. "So long as any part . . .": *Times* (London), November 21, 1816.

233. "the effectual and early . . .": Madison, "Eighth Annual Message."

233. "If I have not . . .": ibid.

234. "had the zealous support . . .": Skeen, p. 230.

234. "inauspicious season" and "precarious times": ibid., p. 89.

234. "I asked him if . . .": Adams, p. 448.

235. "no other country . . .": Cookson, pp. 104–5.

235. "A pot of beer . . .": Spater, *Cobbett*, vol. II, p. 350.

235. "They sigh for a PLOT . . .": ibid.

236. "the effects of such . . .": Longford, p. 42.

236. "This past summer . . .": Hoyt, p. 123.

236. "Warm month . . .": Mussey, p. 446.

236. "Quite warm and pleasant": ibid.

236. "the people appear to feel . . .": ibid.

237. "I have seen some families . . .": Lawrence, *Flagg*, p. 5.

237. "families on foot . . .": Hatcher, p. 73.

237. "somewhat depressed by fatigue . . .": Mussey, p. 451.

238. "Thousands of people . . .": Mussey, p. 442.

11. RELIEF

241. "appears to us to have been . . .": *National Register*, September 28, 1816, p. 70.

241. "whenever the electrical fluid . . .": ibid.

241. "more universal and terrible . . .": ibid., p. 71.

241. "All nature seems to declare . . .": ibid.

242. "the causes of this . . .": *Gentleman's Magazine*, February 1817, p. 111.

242. "the removal of a . . .": ibid.

242. "the Climate of England . . .": *Gentleman's Magazine*, February 18, 1818, p. 135.

243. "for fifty years past . . .": *American Atheneum*, I, 1817, p. 43.

243. "has extended its empire . . .": ibid.

243. "It seems very strange . . .": *Daily National Intelligencer*, September 3, 1816.

243. "That God has expressed His displeasure . . .": Mussey, p. 442.

243. "from town to town . . .": Stilwell, p. 136.

244. "Fair, the coldest day . . .": Mussey, p. 446.

244. "a circumstance rarely . . .": ibid.

244. "the Barometer [was] as low . . .": ibid., p. 447.

245. "the Overseers of the Poor . . .": *Eastern Argus*, May 18, 1817.

245. "Many charge it . . .": Day, *Maine Agriculture*, p. 111.

245. "New England seemed to many . . .": Hatcher, p. 70.

245. "We have had a great deal . . .": Mussey, p. 447.

245. "At last a kind of despair . . .": Goodrich, vol. II, p. 79.

245. "Hardly a family . . .": Hatcher, p. 72.

246. "he himself met on the road . . .": Boggess, *Illinois*, p. 119.

246. "there are now in this village . . .": ibid., p. 119.

246. "Old America seems to be . . .": ibid., p. 119.

247. "we found some of the . . .": Lawrence, p. 6.

247. "there are many things . . .": ibid., p. 5.

247. "I find the Country . . .": ibid., p. 3.

247. "the weather is warm . . .": ibid., p. 6.

248. "ruinous emigration of . . .": Mussey, p. 449.

249. "a great loneliness": Hatcher, p. 73.

249. "The bad things . . .": Lawrence, pp. 7–8.

249. "glasses, cups and hollow ware . . .": Hatcher, p. 85.

249. "are the most ignorant . . .": Lawrence, p. 3.

250. "they spotted the . . .": Stilwell, pp. 141–2.

250. "amazingly increased . . .": Priestly, *Prince*, p. 187.

251. "no report was heard . . .": Adams, p. 465.

251. "the general spirit . . .": Priestly, p. 187.

252. "unless some efficacious check . . .": Boyer, *Poor Law*, p. 196.

253. "a significant new departure . . .": Flinn, "Poor Employment Act," p. 92.

253. "air and exercise . . .": Honan, p. 393.

254. "I have had a . . .": Austen, Jane to Caroline, March 23, 1817.

255. "You could not eat . . .": Post, *Subsistence Crisis*, p. 41.

256. "Beggars, very numerous . . .": Simond, *Switzerland*, p. 9.

256. "were chiefly children . . .": Raffles, *Letters*, p. 156.

257. "one hundred thousand souls . . .": Simond, p. 10.

258. "The excessive price of bread . . .": Post, *Subsistence Crisis*, p. 82.

259. "The zeal and firmness . . .": ibid., p. 95.

259. "all sensible people . . .": Hugo, *Les Misérables*, p. 121.

261. "boarded and rendered . . .": *Liverpool Mercury*, April 4, 1817.

261. "rob the crew of . . .": ibid.

261. "collected in some thousands . . .": ibid.

261. "A more complete plunder . . .": ibid.

262. "there was therefore no . . .": *Morning Chronicle*, March 8, 1817.

262. "frequently did more harm . . .": ibid.

262. "Several cargoes of oats . . .": *Bury and Norwich Post*, March 26, 1817.

264. "nearly one-quarter of the . . .": Post, *Subsistence Crisis*, p. 64.

264. "the paleness of . . .": ibid., p. 91.
264. "a wild, benumbed . . .": ibid.
264. "the number of beggars . . .": Simond, pp. 91–2.
265. "many distressed people . . .": ibid., p. 93.
265. "crimes multiply . . .": ibid., p. 77.
265. "the perpetually increasing crowd . . .": *Times* (London), May 9, 1817.
265. "The general impression . . .": ibid.
265. "one for setting fire . . .": Simond, p. 92.
265. "There is nothing Arcadian . . .": ibid.
265. "Neither sentries nor bailiffs . . .": Post, *Subsistence Crisis*, p. 92.
266. "reminded them of their . . .": Schelbert, *Swiss Migration*, p. 230.
266. "The Rhine rots with . . .": Knapton, *The Lady*, p. 178.
266. "It is a disgraceful . . .": Ford, *Life and Letters*, p. 263.
268. "ruined figures, scarcely . . .": Post, *Subsistence Crisis*, p. 44.
269. "beggars appeared from . . .": ibid., p. 89.
269. "persons who looked like . . .": ibid., pp. 89–90.
269. "A contagious malady . . .": *Times* (London), April 23, 1817.
270. "her abhorred and . . .": Jones, *Percy Shelley*, p. 521.
271. "simply with us . . .": ibid., p. 540.
271. "You will have heard . . .": ibid.
271. "At present we have little else . . .": ibid., p. 545.

EPILOGUE
277. "History will state . . .": Benson, *Letters*, pp. 66–7.
282. "the time and energy . . .": Twomey, *Atmospheric*, p. 290.

BIBLIOGRAPHY

NEWSPAPERS AND PERIODICALS

UNITED KINGDOM:
Aberdeen Journal
Asiatic Journal
Bury and Norwich Post
Caledonian Mercury
The Gentlemen's Magazine
Ipswich Journal
Lancaster Gazette
Liverpool Mercury
Morning Chronicle (London)
The Quarterly Journal of Science and the Arts
Quarterly Review
Royal Cornwall Gazette
The Times (London)

UNITED STATES AND CANADA:
Albany Advertiser
Albany Argus
American Advocate (Hallowell, Maine)
The Atheneum (Boston)
Camden Gazette (South Carolina)
Chambersburg Democratic Republican (Pennsylvania)
Charleston City Gazette (South Carolina)
Columbia Centinel (Boston, Massachusetts)
The Columbian (New York)
Connecticut Courant
Daily National Intelligencer (Washington, D.C.)
Danville North Star (Vermont)
Eastern Argus (Portland, Maine)
Farmer's Cabinet (Amherst, New Hampshire)
Franklin Herald (Greenfield, Massachusetts)
Halifax Weekly Chronicle
The Literary and Philosophical Repertory (Middlebury, Vermont)

Maryland Gazette

Middlesex Gazette (Middletown, Connecticut)

Nantucket Gazette

National Aegis (Worcester, Massachusetts)

The National Register

New Bedford Mercury

New England Palladium (Boston)

New Hampshire Patriot

New Hampshire Sentinel

New York Gazette

New York Post

Newburyport Herald

The North American Review

Niles' Weekly Register

Norfolk Beacon (Virginia)

North American Review

Quebec Gazette

Richmond Enquirer

Rutland Herald

Salem Gazette

Stockbridge Star (Massachusetts)

Vermont Intelligencer

Vermont Journal

Vermont Mirror

Virginia Patriot

WEB SITES

Austen, Jane, "Jane Austen's Letters to Her Sister Cassandra and Others," etext.lib.virginia.edu/toc/modeng/public/AusLett.html

Cochran, Peter, "The Diary of John Cam Hobhouse: Switzerland, August 26–October 11, 1816," petercochran.files.wordpress.com/2009/12/22-switzerland.pdf

Galusha, Jonas, "Executive Speech of Jonas Galusha as It Appears in the Records of the Governor and Council of the State of Vermont," vol. VI, 1816. vermont-archives.org/govhistory/gov/govinaug/inaugurals/pdf/Galusha1816.pdf

Huntington, Ray L., and David M. Whitchurch, "'Eighteen Hundred and Froze to Death': Mount Tambora, New England Weather, and the Joseph Smith Family in 1816," rsc.byu.edu/sites/default/files/pubs/pdf/new-england-05-huntington.pdf

Lederer, David Friedrich, "Report of the Famine and Hyperinflation of 1816 and 1817," www.physics.ohio-state.edu/~palmer/Geradstetten/Report of the Famine and The hyperinflation of 1816 and 1817.pdf

Lewis, Tess, "Madame de Staël: The Inveterate Idealist," www.hudsonreview.com/lewisAu01.html

Madison, James, "Eighth Annual Message: December 3, 1816," millercenter.org/president/speeches/detail/3629

Payne, Stanley G., "Chapter 19: The War of Independence and Liberalism," A History of Spain and Portugal, vol. 2, libro.uca.edu/payne2/payne19.htm

Schlegel, Lee-Lee, "The Year Without a Summer: 1816, In Maine," Milbridge Historical Society, www.milbridgehistorical society.org

Stellhorn, Paul A., and Michael J. Birkner, eds., "The Governors of New Jersey 1664–1974: Biographical Essays: Mahlon Dickerson." Slic.njstatelib.org/slic_files/imported/NJ_Information/Digital_ Collections/Governors_of_New_Jersey/GDICM.pdf

ARTICLES

Abbe, Cleveland. "History of the Barometer," *Monthly Weather Review*, 27:12 (1899).

Angell, J. K., and J. Korshover. "Surface Temperature Changes Following the Six Major Volcanic Episodes Between 1780 and 1980," *Journal of Climate and Applied Meteorology* 24 (September 1985).

Auchmann, R., et al. "Extreme Climate, Not Extreme Weather: The Summer of 1816 in Geneva, Switzerland," *Climate of the Past Discussions* 7 (November 2011).

Backman, Milton V., Jr. "Awakenings in the Burned-Over District: New Light on the Historical Setting of the First Vision," *BYU Studies* 9:3 (1969).

Briffa, K. R., et al. "Influence of Volcanic Eruptions on Northern Hemisphere Summer Temperature over the Past 600 Years," *Nature* 393 (June 4 1998).

Chenoweth, Michael. "Two Major Volcanic Cooling Episodes Derived from Global Marine Air Temperature, AD 1807–1827," *Geophysical Research Letters* 28 (2001).

———, "Ships' Logbooks and 'The Year Without a Summer,'" *Bulletin of the American Meteorological Society* 77 (1996).

Clubbe, John. "The Tempest-toss'd Summer of 1816: Mary Shelley's *Frankenstein*," *The Byron Journal* 19 (1991).

Earle, C. J., et al. "Summer Temperature Since 1600 for the Upper Kolyma Region, Northeastern Russia, Reconstructed from Tree Rings," *Arctic and Alpine Research* 26 (February 1994).

Evans, Robert. "Blast from the Past," *Smithsonian* (July 2002).

Flinn, M. W. "The Poor Employment Act of 1817," *The Economic History Review* 14:1 (1961).

Franklin, Benjamin. "Meteorological Imaginations and Conjectures (Paper read 1784)," *Memoirs of the Literary and Philosophical Society of Manchester*, 2nd ed., 1789. [*Weatherwise*, 35 (1982).]

Goulding, Christopher. "A Volcano's Voice at Eton: Percy Shelley, James Lind MD, and Global Climatology," *Keats-Shelley Review* 17 (2003).

Gray, Lesley J., et al. "Solar Influences on Climate," *Reviews of Geophysics* 48 (2010).

Hamilton, K. "Early Canadian Weather Observers and the 'Year Without a Summer,'" *Bulletin of the American Meteorological Society* 67 (1986).

Hoyt, Joseph B. "The Cold Summer of 1816," *Annals of the Association of American Geographers* 48:2 (1958).

Johnston, Arch C., and Eugene S. Schweig. "The Enigma of the New Madrid Earthquakes of 1811–1812," *Annual Review of Earth and Planetary Sciences* 24 (1996).

Lewis, Tess. "Madame de Staël: The Inveterate Idealist," *Hudson Review* 43:3 (2001).

MacAlpine, Ida, and Richard Hunter. "The 'Insanity' of King George III: A Classic Case of Porphyria," *British Medical Journal* 1 (1966).

Murphy, Kathleen S. "Prodigies and Portents: Providentialism in the Eighteenth-Century Chesapeake," *Maryland Historical Magazine* 97:4 (2002).

Mussey, Barrows. "Yankee Chills, Ohio Fever," *New England Quarterly* 22 (December 1949).

O'Neill, Timothy P. "Clare and Irish Poverty, 1815–1851," *Studia Hibernica* 14 (1974).

Oppenheimer, Clive. "Climatic, Environmental and Human Consequences of the Largest Known Historic Eruption: Tambora Volcano (Indonesia) 1815." *Progress in Physical Geography*, 27:2 (2003).

Post, John D. "The Economic Crisis of 1816–1817 and Its Social and Political Consequences," *Journal of Economic History* 30:1 (1970).

Shindell, Drew T., et al. "Dynamic Winter Climate Reponse to Large Tropical Volcanic Eruptions Since 1600," *Journal of Geophysical Research* 109 (2004).

———, "Volcanic and Solar Forcing of Climate Change During the Pre-industrial Era," *Journal of Climate* 16 (2003).

Stenchikov, Georgiy L., et al. "Arctic Oscillation Response to Volcanic Eruptions in the IPCC AR4 Climate Models," *Journal of Geophysical Research* 111 (2006).

Stommel, Henry, and Elizabeth Stommel. "The Year Without a Summer," *Scientific American* 240:6 (1979).

Stothers, Richard B. "The Great Tambora Eruption in 1815 and Its Aftermath," *Science* 224:4654 (June 15, 1984).

Tilly, Louise A. "The Food Riot as a Form of Political Conflict in France," *The Journal of Interdisciplinary History* 2:1 (1971).

Trigo, Ricardo M., et al. "Iberia in 1816, the Year Without a Summer," *International Journal of Climatology* 29 (2009).

Vail, Jeffrey. " 'The Bright Sun Was Extinguish'd': The Bologna Prophecy and Byron's 'Darkness.' " *Wordsworth Circle* 28:3 (1997).

Vaquero, José M. "Historical Sunspot Observations: A Review," *Advances in Space Research* 40 (2007).

Webb, Patrick. "Emergency Relief During Europe's Famine of 1817 Anticipated Crisis-Response Mechanisms of Today," *Journal of Nutrition* 132 (2002).

Wood, J. David. "The Complicity of Climate in the 1816 Depression in Dumfriesshire," *Scottish Geographical Magazine* 81:1 (1965).

Zerefos, C. S., et al. "Atmospheric Effects of Volcanic Eruptions as Seen by Famous Artists and Depicted in Their Paintings," *Atmospheric Chemistry and Physics* 7 (2007).

BOOKS

[REPRINTS ARE IN BRACKETS.]

Adams, Charles Francis, ed. *Memoirs of John Quincy Adams*, vol. III. Philadelphia: J.B. Lippincott & Company, 1874. [Freeport: Books For Libraries, 1969.]

Alexander, Robert S. *Re-Writing the French Revolutionary Tradition.* Cambridge: Cambridge University Press, 2004.

Ammon, Harry. *James Monroe: The Quest for National Identity.* Charlottesville: University of Virginia Press, 1990.

Arnold, David. *Colonizing the Body: State Medicine and Epidemic Disease in Nineteenth-Century India.* Berkeley: University of California Press, 1993.

Ashton, John. *Social England Under the Regency*, vol. II. London: Ward and Downey, 1890.

Aspinall, A., ed. *The Letters of King George IV*, vol. II. Cambridge: Cambridge University Press, 1938.

Bailey, Anthony. *Standing in the Sun.* New York: Harper Collins, 1998.

Barker, Juliet. *The Brontës.* London: Weidenfeld and Nicolson, 2005.

Bastin, John. *The Native Policies of Sir Stamford Raffles in Java and Sumatra.* Oxford: The Clarendon Press, 1957.

Bate, Jonathan. *The Song of the Earth.* Cambridge: Harvard University Press, 2000.

Beckley, Hosea. *The History of Vermont.* Brattleboro: George H. Salisbury, 1846.

Benson, Arthur C. *The Letters of Queen Victoria*, vol. 1. London: Echo Library, 2009.

Bernard, J. F. *Talleyrand: A Biography.* New York: G.P. Putnam's Sons, 1973.

Betts, Edwin Morris, annot. *Thomas Jefferson's Garden Book, 1766–1824.* Philadelphia: The American Philosophical Society, 1944.

Boggess, Arthur C. *The Settlement of Illinois, 1778–1830.* Chicago: Chicago Historical Society, 1908. [Freeport, N.Y.: Books For Libraries Press, 1970.]

Boyer, George R. *An Economic History of the English Poor Law, 1750–1850.* Cambridge: Cambridge University Press, 1990.

Brant, Irving. *James Madison: Commander in Chief, 1812–1836.* Indianapolis: The Bobbs-Merrill Company, Inc., 1961.

Brewer, William D. *The Shelley-Byron Conversation.* Gainesville: University Press of Florida, 1994.

Brown, Judith. *Modern India: The Origins of an Asian Democracy.* Oxford: Oxford University Press, 1994.

Brynn, Edward. *Crown and Castle: British Rule in Ireland, 1800–1830.* Toronto: Macmillan of Canada, 1978.

Burstein, Andrew, and Nancy Isenberg. *Madison and Jefferson.* New York: Random House, 2010.

Burt, Christopher C., and Mark Stroud. *Extreme Weather.* New York: W. W. Norton and Co., 2007.

Butterfield, Lyman H. *The Diary and Autobiography of John Adams,* vol. 1. New York: Atheneum, 1964.

Chester, David. *Volcanoes and Society.* London: Edward Arnold, 1993.

Clark, Allen C. *Life and Letters of Dolley Madison.* Washington, D.C.: W. F. Roberts Co., 1914.

Cobb, R. C. *The Police and the People.* London: Oxford University Press, 1970.

Collins, Irene, ed. *Government and Society in France, 1814–1848.* London: Edward Arnold, 1970.

Cookson, J. E. *Lord Liverpool's Administration.* Hamden, Connecticut: Archon Books, 1975.

Coote, Stephen. *Napoleon and the Hundred Days.* Cambridge: Da Capo Press, 2005.

Crevecoeur, J. Hector-St. John de, *Sketches of Eighteenth-Century America.* New Haven: Yale University Press, 1925.

Cross, Whitney R. *The Burned-Over District.* Ithaca: Cornell University Press, 1950.

Crossman, Virginia. *Politics, Law and Order in Nineteenth-Century Ireland.* New York: St. Martin's Press, 1996.

Cunningham, Noble E., ed. *Circular Letters of Congressmen to Their Constituents, 1789–1829,* vol. II. Chapel Hill: University of North Carolina Press, 1978.

Davis, James E. *Frontier Illinois*. Bloomington: Indiana University Press, 1998.

Davis, W.W.H. *The History of Bucks County, Pennsylvania*. Doylestown: Democrat Book and Job Office Print, 1876.

Day, Clarence Albert. *A History of Maine Agriculture, 1604–1860*. Orono: University of Maine Press, 1954.

De Suvigny, Guillaume Berthier. (Lynn M. Case, trans.) *The Bourbon Restoration*. Philadelphia: University of Pennsylvania Press, 1966.

DeBoer, Jelle Zelinga, and Donald T. Sanders. *Volcanoes in Human History: The Far-Reaching Effects of Major Eruptions*. Princeton: Princeton University Press, 2002.

Donnelly, James S., Jr. *The Land and the People of Nineteenth-Century Cork*. London: Routledge & Kegan Paul, 1975.

Dorchester, Charlotte Hobhouse Carleton, Baroness. *Recollections of a Long Life, by Lord Broughton (John Cam Hobhouse)*, vols. I and II. London: John Murray, 1910. [New York: AMS Press, 1968.]

Dow, Lorenzo, and Peggy Dow. *The Dealings of God, Man and the Devil*. New York: Nafis & Cornish, 1850.

Dupigny-Giroux, L.-A., and C. J. Mock, eds. *Historical Climate Variability and Impacts in North America*. Dordrecht: Springer, 2009.

Edgcumbe, Richard, ed. *The Diary of Frances Lady Shelley (1787–1817)*. New York: Charles Scribner's Sons, 1912.

Edwards, J. R. *British History, 1815–1939*. New York: Humanities Press, 1970.

Egerton, Hugh E. *Sir Stamford Raffles: Builders of Great Britain*. New York: Longmans, Green & Company, 1897. [Whitefish, Mont.: Kessinger, 2008.]

Elwin, Malcolm. *Lord Byron's Family*. London: John Murray, 1975.

Emery, Sarah Smith. *Reminiscences of a Nonagenarian*. Newburyport, Massachusetts: W. H. Huse & Co., 1879.

Fagan, Brian. *The Little Ice Age*. New York: Basic Books, 2000.

Fairweather, Maria. *Madame de Staël*. New York: Carroll & Graf, 2005.

Feldman, Jay. *When the Mississippi Ran Backwards*. New York: Free Press, 2005.

Feldman, Paula R., and Diana Scott-Kilvert, eds. *The Journals of Mary Shelley, 1814–1844*. Oxford: The Clarendon Press, 1987.

Field, David Dudley, and Chester Dewey. *A History of the County of Berkshire, Massachusetts*. Pittsfield, Massachusetts: Samuel W. Bush, 1829.

Fleming, James Rodger. *Meteorology in America, 1800–1870*. Baltimore: The Johns Hopkins University Press, 1990.

Fletcher, Stevenson Whitcomb. *Pennsylvania Agriculture and Country Life, 1640–1840*. Harrisburg, Pennsylvania: Pennsylvania Historical and Museum Commission, 1971.

Florescu, Radu. *In Search of Frankenstein*. London: Robson Books, 1975.

Ford, Clarence. *The Life and Letters of Madame de Krudener*. London: Adam and Charles Black, 1893.

Ford, Paul Leicester, ed. *The Writings of Thomas Jefferson, vol. X, 1816–1826*. New York: G. P. Putnam's Sons, 1899.

Fraser, John Lloyd. *John Constable: 1776–1837*. London: Hutchinson, 1976.

Frye, W. E. *After Waterloo: Reminiscences of European Travel, 1815–1819*. London: William Heinemann, 1908.

Gash, Norman. *Lord Liverpool*. London: Weidenfeld and Nicolson, 1984.

———. *Mr. Secretary Peel: The Life of Sir Robert Peel to 1830*. Cambridge: Harvard University Press, 1961.

Gibb, George Duncan, Sir. *Odd Showers*. London: Kerby & Son, 1870.

Goodden, Angelica. *Madame De Staël: The Dangerous Exile*. Oxford: Oxford University Press, 2008.

Goodrich, Samuel G. *Recollections of a Lifetime*. New York: Miller, Orton, and Mulligan, 1856.

Green, Daniel. *Great Cobbett*. London: Hodder and Stoughton, 1983.

Gronow, Rees Howell. *The Reminiscences and Recollections of Captain Gronow*. London: John C. Nimmo, 1892.

Halévy, Elie. *The Liberal Awakening: 1815–1830*. New York: Barnes and Noble Inc., 1961.

Hall, John R. *The Bourbon Restoration*. London: Alston Rivers, Ltd., 1909.

Haly, W. T. *The Opinions of Sir Robert Peel, Expressed in Parliament and in Public*. London: Whittaker & Co., 1843.

Hamilton, James. *Turner's Britain*. London: Merrell, 2003.

Harington, C. R., ed. *The Year Without a Summer? World Climate in 1816*. Ottawa: Canadian Museum of Nature, 1992.

Harrison, Mark. *Crowds and History: Mass Phenomena in English Towns, 1750–1835*. Cambridge: Cambridge University Press, 1988.

Hatch, Nathan O. *The Democratization of American Christianity*. New Haven: Yale University Press, 1989.

Hatcher, Harlan. *The Western Reserve*. Indianapolis: Bobbs-Merrill Company, 1949.

Havighurst, Walter. *Men of Old Miami, 1809–1873*. New York: Putnam, 1974.

Hempel, Sandra. *The Medical Detective: John Snow and the Mystery of Cholera*. London: Granta Books, 2006.

Hinde, Wendy. *Castlereagh*. London: Collins, 1981.

Hobhouse, John Cam (Lord Broughton). *Recollections of a Long Life*, vols. I and II. London: John Murray, 1910. [New York: AMS Press, 1968.]

Honan, Park. *Jane Austen: Her Life*. New York: St. Martin's Press, 1987.

Hotchkin, James H. *A History of the Purchase and Settlement of Western New York, and of the Presbyterian Church in That Section*. New York: M.W. Dodd, 1848.

Hugo, Victor. *Les Misérables*. New York: Penguin, 1982.

Hunt, Henry. *Memoirs of Henry Hunt, Esq.*, vol. 3. London: T. Dolby, 1822. [New York: Augustus M. Kelley, 1970.]

Jardin, Andre, and Andre-Jean Tudesq. *Restoration and Reaction, 1815–1848*. Cambridge: Cambridge University Press, 1983.

Jefferson, Thomas. *Notes on the State of Virginia*. New York: W. W. Norton & Co., 1972.

Jones, Frederick L., ed. *The Letters of Mary W. Shelley*, vol. 1. Norman: University of Oklahoma Press, 1944.

———, ed. *The Letters of Percy Bysshe Shelley*, vol. 1. Oxford: The Clarendon Press, 1964.

Klein, Philip S., and Ari Hoogenboom. *A History of Pennsylvania*. New York: McGraw-Hill, 1973.

Knapton, Ernest John. *The Lady of the Holy Alliance: The Life of Julie de Krudener*. New York: Columbia University Press, 1939.

Lamb, H. H. *Climate, History and the Modern World*. London: Routledge, 1995.

Laskin, David. *Braving the Elements: The Stormy History of American Weather*. New York: Doubleday, 1996.

Latrobe, Charles Joseph. *The Rambler in North America, 1832–1833*. London: R. B. Seeley, 1835.

Lawrence, Barbara, and Nedra Branz, eds. *The Flagg Correspondence: Selected Letters, 1816–1854*. Carbondale: Southern Illinois University Press, 1986.

Leslie, Edmund N. *Skaneateles: History of Its Earliest Settlement, and Reminiscences of Later Times*. New York: A. H. Kellogg, 1902.

Leslie, R. A. *Memoirs of the Life of John Constable*. Ithaca: Cornell University Press, 1951.

Longford, Elizabeth. *Wellington: Pillar of State*. New York: Harper & Row, 1972.

Lucas-Dubreton, J. *The Restoration and the July Monarchy*. London: William Heinemann Ltd., 1929.

Ludlum, David M. *Early American Winters, 1604–1820*. Boston: American Meteorological Society, 1966.

———. *Social Ferment in Vermont, 1791–1850*. Montpelier: Vermont Historical Society, 1948.

———. *Vermont Weather Book*. Montpelier: Vermont Historical Society, 1985.

MacArtney, Carlile. *The Hapsburg Empire: 1790–1918*. New York: Macmillan, 1969.

MacKenzie, Norman. *The Escape from Elba: The Fall and Flight of Napoleon, 1814–15*. New York: Oxford University Press, 1982.

Marchand, Leslie A. *Lord Byron: Selected Letters and Journals*. Cambridge, Massachusetts: Harvard University Press, 1982.

Martineau, Harriet. *The History of England from the Commencement of the XIXth Century to the Crimean War*, vol. II. Philadelphia: Porter & Coates, 1864.

Mattern, David B., and Holly C. Shulman, eds. *The Selected Letters of Dolley Payne Madison*. Charlottesville: University of Virginia Press, 2003.

McCaffrey, Lawrence J. *The Irish Question: Two Centuries of Conflict*. Lexington: University Press of Kentucky, 1995.

McClellan, James E. *Science Reorganized: Scientific Societies in the Eighteenth Century*. New York: Columbia University Press, 1985.

Mergen, Bernard. *Snow in America*. Washington, D.C.: Smithsonian Institution Press, 1997.

Metcalf, Henry H. *New Hampshire Agriculture: Personal and Farm Sketches*. Concord, New Hampshire: Republican Press Association, 1897.

Moore, Thomas, ed. *Letters and Journals of Lord Byron: With Notes of His Life*. Paris: A. & W. Galignani, 1830.

———, ed. *Life, Letters, & Journals of Lord Byron*. London: J. Murray, 1838.

Morgan, George. *The Life of James Monroe*. Boston: Small, Maynard and Company, 1921.

Moser, Harold D., et al., eds. *The Papers of Andrew Jackson: 1816–1820*. Knoxville: University of Tennessee Press, 1994.

McCullough, David. *John Adams*. New York: Simon and Schuster, 2001.

Murphy, James H. *Ireland: A Social, Cultural and Literary History, 1791–1891*. Dublin: Four Courts Press, 2003.

Nattrass, Leonora. *William Cobbett: Selected Writings*, vol. III. London: Pickering & Chatto, 1998.

Nokes, David. *Jane Austen: A Life*. New York: Farrar, Straus and Giroux, 1997.

Nolt, Steven M. *Foreigners in Their Own Land: Pennsylvania Germans in the Early Republic*. University Park: Pennsylvania State University Press, 2002.

Ó Tuathaigh, Gearóid. *Ireland Before the Famine, 1798–1848*. Dublin: Gill and Macmillan, 1972.

O'Connell, Maurice R., ed. *The Correspondence of Daniel O'Connell*, vol. II. Shannon: Irish University Press, 1972.

Oppenheimer, Clive. *Eruptions That Shook the World*. Cambridge: Cambridge University Press, 2011.

Paget, George Charles Henry Victor Anglesey (Marquess of), ed. *The Capel Letters, 1814–1817*. London: Jonathan Cape, 1955.

Parker, Charles Stuart. *Sir Robert Peel . . . From His Private Correspondence*, vol. I. London: John Murray, 1891.

Patterson, M. W. *Sir Francis Burdett and His Times (1770–1844)*, vol. II. London: Macmillan and Co., Ltd., 1931.

Peterson, Merrill D. *Thomas Jefferson and the New Nation: A Biography*. London: Oxford University Press, 1970.

Post, John D. *The Last Great Subsistence Crisis in the Western World*. Baltimore: Johns Hopkins University Press, 1977.

Potash, P. Jeffrey. *Vermont's Burned-Over District: Patterns of Community Development and Religious Activity, 1761–1850*. Brooklyn, New York: Carlson Publishing, Inc., 1991.

Price, Roger. *A Social History of Nineteenth-Century France*. London: Hutchinson, 1987.

Priestly, J. B. *The Prince of Pleasure and His Regency, 1811–20*. New York: Harper & Row, 1969.

Raffles, Sophia, Lady. *Memoirs of the Life and Public Services of Sir Thomas Stamford Raffles*. London: J. Duncan, 1835.

Raffles, Thomas. *Letters, During a Tour Through Some Parts of France, Savoy, Switzerland, Germany, and the Netherlands, in the Summer of 1817*. New York: Kirk and Mercein, 1818.

Raffles, Thomas Stamford. *The History of Java*, vol. I. London: Black, Parbury, and Allen, 1817.

Reid, Stuart J. *Life and Letters of the First Earl of Dunham, 1792–1840*. London: Longmans, Green, and Co., 1906.

Remini, Robert V. *Andrew Jackson and the Course of American Empire, 1767–1821*. New York: Harper & Row, 1977.

Ross, Ian Campbell. *Umbria: A Cultural History*. New York: Viking, 1966.

Rotberg, Robert I. *Social Mobility and Modernization*. Cambridge, Massachusetts: MIT Press, 2000.

Rubinstein, W. D. *Britain's Century*. London: Arnold, 1998.

Rudé, George. *The Crowd in History*. London: Lawrence and Wishart, 1964.

Rutland, Robert A. *James Madison: The Founding Father*. New York: Atheneum, 1987.

Sanborn, Edwin. *History of New Hampshire*. Manchester, New Hampshire: J. B. Clarke, 1875.

Sanford, Charles L. *Quest for America: 1810–1824*. New York: New York University Press, 1964.

Saum, Lewis O. *The Popular Mood of Pre–Civil War America*. Westport: Greenwood Press, 1980.

Schelbert, Leo. *Swiss Migration to America: The Swiss Mennonites*. New York: Arno Press, 1980.

Seymour, Miranda. *Mary Shelley*. New York: Grove Press, 2000.

Shalhope, Robert E. *A Tale of New England: The Diaries of Hiram Harwood, Vermont Farmer, 1810–1837*. Baltimore: The Johns Hopkins Press, 2003.

Shelley, Mary W. *Frankenstein, or, The Modern Prometheus*. London: Lackington, Hughes, Harding, Mavor, and Jones, 1818.

———. *Frankenstein, or, The Modern Prometheus*. London: H. Colburn and R. Bentley, 1831.

Shelley, Mary W., and P. B. Shelley. *History of a Six Weeks' Tour*. London: T. Hookum, 1817. (Oxford: Woodstock Books, 1989.)

Simond, Louis. *Switzerland; or, A Journal of a Tour and Residence in That Country, in the Years 1817, 1818, and 1819*, vol. I. Boston: Wells and Lilly, 1822.

Skeen, C. Edward. *1816: America Rising*. Lexington: University Press of Kentucky, 2003.

Smith, Adam. *The Wealth of Nations*. New York: Modern Library, 1994.

Spater, George. *William Cobbett: The Poor Man's Friend*, vol. 2. Cambridge: Cambridge University Press, 1982.

Sraffa, Piero, ed. *The Works and Correspondence of David Ricardo*, vol. 7. Cambridge: Cambridge University Press, 1952.

Stevenson, John. *Popular Disturbances in England, 1700–1832*. New York: Longman, 1979.

Stilwell, Lewis D. *Migration from Vermont*. Montpelier: Vermont Historical Society, and Rutland: Academy Books, 1948.

Stommel, Henry, and Elizabeth Stommel. *Volcano Weather*. Newport, Rhode Island: Seven Seas Press, 1983.

Symons, George James, ed., for Royal Society of Great Britain, Krakatoa Committee. *The Eruption of Krakatoa: And Subsequent Phenomena*. London: Trübner & Co., 1888.

Thomas, David. *Travels Through the Western Country in the Summer of 1816*. Auburn, New York: David Rumsey, 1819. (Darien, Connecticut: Hafner Publishing Company, 1970.)

Thompson, J. M., ed. *Napoleon's Letters*. London: J. M. Dent & Sons, 1954.

Tomalin, Claire. *Jane Austen: A Life*. New York: Alfred A. Knopf, 1997.

Tucker, Pomeroy. *Origins, Rise and Progress of Mormonism*. New York: D. Appleton & Co., 1867.

Turner, Lynn W. *The Ninth State*. Chapel Hill: University of North Carolina Press, 1983.

Twomey, Sean A. *Atmospheric Aerosols*. Amsterdam: Elsevier, 1977.

Walker, Mack. *Germany and the Emigration, 1816–1885*. Cambridge: Harvard University Press, 1964.

Warren, Henry P. *The History of Waterford, Oxford County, Maine*. Portland: Hoyt, Fogg, & Donham, 1879.

Webster, Noah. *A Collection of Papers on Political, Literary, and Moral Subjects*. New York: Webster and Clark, 1843.

Wigley, T.M.L., et al., eds. *Climate and History*. Cambridge: Cambridge University Press, 1981.

Wilentz, Sean. *The Rise of American Democracy: Jefferson to Lincoln*. New York: W.W. Norton & Company, 2005.

Williams, James Thaxter. *The History of Weather*. Commack, New York: Nova Science Publishers, 1999.

Wilson, Ben. *Decency and Disorder: The Age of Cant, 1789–1837*. London: Faber and Faber, 2007.

Wilton, Andrew. *Turner in His Time*. New York: Thames and Hudson, 2006.

Woolf, Stuart. *A History of Italy, 1700–1860*. London: Methuen & Company, Ltd., 1979.

Wood, Gordon S. *Empire of Liberty*. New York: Oxford University Press, 2009.

Workers of the Federal Writers' Project of the WPA. *New Hampshire: A Guide to the Granite State*. Boston: Houghton Mifflin, 1938.

Worthen, Augusta H. *The History of Sutton, New Hampshire*, vol. I. Concord, New Hampshire: The Republican Press Association, 1890.

Wurtzburg, C. E. *Raffles of the Eastern Isles*. London: Hodder and Stoughton, 1954.

INDEX